MAKING CONVERSATION IN MODERNIST FICTION

THEORY AND INTERPRETATION OF NARRATIVE
James Phelan, Peter J. Rabinowitz, and Katra Byram, Series Editors

# MAKING CONVERSATION IN MODERNIST FICTION

Elizabeth Alsop

THE OHIO STATE UNIVERSITY PRESS
COLUMBUS

Copyright © 2019 by The Ohio State University.
All rights reserved.

Library of Congress Cataloging-in-Publication Data
Names: Alsop, Elizabeth, author.
Title: Making conversation in modernist fiction / Elizabeth Alsop.
Other titles: Theory and interpretation of narrative series.
Description: Columbus : The Ohio State University Press, [2019] | Series: Theory and interpretation of narrative | Includes bibliographical references and index.
Identifiers: LCCN 2019015274 | ISBN 9780814214077 (cloth) | ISBN 081421407X (cloth) ISBN 9780814255490
Subjects: LCSH: American fiction—20th century—History and criticism. | English fiction—20th century—History and criticism. | Dialogue in literature. | Conversation in literature. | Modernism (Literature)
Classification: LCC PS374.D43 A47 2019 | DDC 823/.90926—dc23
LC record available at https://lccn.loc.gov/2019015274

Cover design by Andrew Brozyna
Text design by Juliet Williams
Type set in Adobe Minion Pro

# CONTENTS

| | | |
|---|---|---|
| *Acknowledgments* | | vii |
| INTRODUCTION | Modernism and the Poetics of Talk | 1 |
| CHAPTER 1 | Dialogue and Its Discontents | 9 |
| CHAPTER 2 | The Consensual Voice: Fantasies of Reciprocity in James and Hemingway | 39 |
| CHAPTER 3 | The Exceptional Voice: Joyce, Faulkner, and the Dream of Autonomy | 69 |
| CHAPTER 4 | The Paradoxical Voice: Faulkner's and Woolf's Implausible Speech | 98 |
| CHAPTER 5 | The Choral Voice: Woolf's and Stein's Democratized Talk | 128 |
| CONCLUSION | What Is the Dialogue Doing Now? | 160 |
| *Works Cited* | | 169 |
| *Index* | | 181 |

## ACKNOWLEDGMENTS

In *The Making of Americans,* Gertrude Stein describes the feeling of laboring over a writing project, and then "someone says yes to it, to something you are liking, or doing or making." I am indebted to countless people who have said yes to this book in one way or another over the years I've been working on it.

In the course of my career, I've been fortunate to meet several scholars who have proved to be lifelong mentors. André Aciman has been an unwavering advocate, someone whose writing spurs me to think more carefully about my own. Giancarlo Lombardi has offered boundless support, both moral and professional. John Brenkman was an early and important reader of this book; his shrewd advice, critical insights, and editorial guidance have been invaluable to the manuscript's development.

I am similarly grateful to my former colleagues in the English department at Western Kentucky University for their encouragement and advice as I pursued this project as a junior faculty member. The Potter College of Arts and Letters provided valuable financial support in the form of grants to fund research travel and reassigned time. Finally, I am thankful to Elizabeth Gish, Ingrid Lilly, Lauren McClain, and Nahed Zehr—members of our short-lived but lovingly remembered writers' group.

More recently, my CUNY colleagues at both the Graduate Center and the School of Professional Studies offered their backing during the crucial, final stages of the project. Luke Waltzer arranged for me to have the time I needed to finish the manuscript; Katina Rogers and Kitana Ananda provided solidarity and accountability; and George Otte and John Mogulescu granted me the space necessary to complete revisions. An award from CUNY's Professional Staff Congress supplied me with subvention funds and defrayed indexing costs. I am also grateful to many others at CUNY whose curiosity and enthusiasm about the project helped motivate its completion. Thanks especially to Elizabeth Decker, Jenny Furlong, Amy Herzog, David Gerstner, and Joseph McElhaney.

I am also grateful to the network of friends and fellow travelers whose knowledge and generosity I continue to rely on. Tahneer Oksman and Laurel Harris shared their feedback and expertise at the proposal stage. Anne Langendorfer and Sarah Copland brought me into the "narrative" fold, introducing me to a group of scholars who have become a vital intellectual community. That community also includes members of the 2015 Project Narrative Summer Institute, where I workshopped portions of the book. Many thanks to PNSI alums Greta Matzner-Gore, Jacqueline Whitt, Malcah Effron, Pedro Ponce, Liz Walker, Aili Pettersson Peeker, Anneleen Masschelein, Rae Muhlstock, Sandra Beals, and Nathan Leaman; to the workshop's coordinator, Yonina Hoffman; and especially to faculty members, Angus Fletcher and James Phelan, whose rigorous engagement with the theoretical concerns of this project was instrumental to its revision.

I can't overstate how much the book has benefited from the efforts and expertise of the editorial team at The Ohio State University Press. I am lucky to have had the chance to work with not one but two wonderful editors: Lindsay Martin, who first acquired the project and shepherded it through the proposal and review process; and Ana Jimenez-Moreno, whose editorial guidance and insights have undoubtedly strengthened the book. I am also deeply obliged to the manuscript readers, whose reports on both the initial submission package and the final manuscript were unfailingly thoughtful, generous, and constructive—what everyone hopes for in peer review. Laura Green and William Cohen provided valuable editorial feedback on an article derived from chapter 2 of this work, "The Question of James's Speech: Consensual Talk in *The Ambassadors*," published in the May 2019 volume of *Narrative*.

I owe an especially large debt to Jim Phelan, who first invited me to submit a proposal to the Theory and Interpretation of Narrative series and whose own work on the subject of character dialogue served as an impetus and continual inspiration for my own. I am thankful for the encouragement and honest input he offered at every step of the way. As series editors, Jim, Peter Rabinowitz, and Katra Byram furnished me with substantive, generative, and rigorous feedback on the manuscript, along with thoughtful line edits, which immeasurably improved the book's arguments and its prose. Any errors or infelicities that remain are my own.

Sincere thanks to my parents, Reid and Annette, and my sister Cate, who have been steadfast in their support. Thanks, too, go out to the Plunketts, the family I was fortunate to marry into. Then there are friends who are like family: Elyse, Kathryn, Liz—I'm lucky to have you to lean on.

Finally, I cannot offer enough thank-you's to my husband, Tony, who for years has done more than his fair share to ensure I had time to write and edit this book. Thank you for never doubting, always encouraging, and, frequently, copy-editing. This book is dedicated to him and my daughter, Lucinda—who wants to be a "different kind of doctor" when she grows up.

INTRODUCTION

# Modernism and the Poetics of Talk

FEW CHARACTERS in Western literature are as closely associated with a line of dialogue as Herman Melville's Bartleby the scrivener, whose implacable response to his employer's demands—"I would prefer not to"—remains one of fiction's most famous retorts. What is often overlooked, however, is the fact that Bartleby's signature phrase is not entirely *his*, in the sense that it is uttered at least once, and in some iteration, by nearly all of the characters in Melville's short story. In this way, the line Bartleby repeats with such stunning recalcitrance becomes attached not just to him but to his fellow employees, Turkey and Nippers, as well to the character narrator himself—to his great dismay. Deeply unnerved by his "involuntary" use of "this word, 'prefer,'" the lawyer "tremble[d]" to imagine the consequences: "I thought to myself, surely I must get rid of a demented man, who already has in some degree turned the tongues, if not the heads of myself and my clerks" (21). What concerns the narrator, then, is the possibility that another's language might unknowingly, even unwillingly, become one's own. For such an event stands to disrupt what his comments imply is a deeply held belief: that words, or "tongues," must be linked to discrete bodies; that speech must reflect, in some profound and immutable way, only the subject doing the speaking.

I begin with Melville's narrator because his belief in the indexical power of speech is one that has historically been shared by many readers of the novel, trained as we have been to assume that fictional utterances exist primarily (if not exclusively) to express the characters doing the uttering. The problem with this assumption is not only that it rests on another, perhaps even more deep-seated conviction: that the novel is at heart a mimetic enterprise, one in which dialogue needs only to play its verisimilar part. It also entails the suppression of an obvious yet troublesome truth about fictional speech: that even at its most true-to-life and putatively transparent, dialogue is always the product of at least *two* speakers—always an emanation of the author, by way of the character. On the one hand, Mikhail Bakhtin's theoretical work on the novel has rendered commonplace the notion that "double-voicing" is a ubiquitous feature of narrative discourse. Yet somehow *character* discourse—what Bakhtin calls "represented or objectified discourse," and Gérard Genette, "reported speech"—has continued to be treated as a special case: regarded, however tacitly, as beyond the reach of authorial meddling, and thus one site in the novel "free" from the kinds of discursive doubling that so disturbs Melville's lawyer (Bakhtin, *Problems* 189; Genette 174). The result is not only a surprising paucity of critical work on the subject of character speech but, more practically speaking, a certain disinclination to consider the ways dialogue might "point" to the author, or to anyone other than the fictional subject uttering the lines.

The goal of this book is not simply to rebut such received ideas about novelistic speech by demonstrating the extent to which, as James Phelan has argued, conversation is always a form of narration, albeit a more "indirect" or "mediated" one ("Conversational Disclosure" 4; "Rhetoric, Ethics" 66).[1] Indeed, the book takes as its theoretical and methodological point of departure the notion that, as Genette put it more than fifty years ago, "'showing' can be only a *way of telling*" (166). Instead, this study aims both to develop and ultimately to complicate such claims by documenting the startlingly heterogeneous ways in which dialogue can be seen to "tell" and by making the case for its status as a rhetorical mode at once continuous with but also distinct from narration. At the same time, it also offers a historically grounded account of dialogue's function in the twentieth-century novel by assessing its role within the specific context of Anglo-American modernist fiction: a literary tradition in which, I will argue, dialogue's expressive potential came radically to the fore. To this end, the following chapters survey some of the surprising ways in which canonically modernist authors such as Henry James, Ernest Hemingway, James Joyce, Virginia Woolf, William Faulkner, Gertrude Stein, and Jean Toomer deployed character speech in their writing, and suggest that such deployments, considered cumulatively, reflect the significantly expanded

---

1. See Phelan's "Conversational," "Imagining," and "Rhetoric, Ethics," for more on dialogue as narration and the way "scenes of dialogue function not just as showing but also as telling" ("Imagining" 248).

and rhetorically diversified role that talk came to assume within early twentieth-century British and American fiction. If dialogue has historically been treated as a subordinate element in the novel—a tool for developing character, or advancing plot[2]—this book demonstrates a divergent tendency among Anglo-American modernist writers, who frequently emphasize it as a poetic structure in its own right. In so doing, I argue, these authors can be seen to "make" conversation in substantively new ways, and for a previously unacknowledged range of expressive ends. If the rich communicative potentialities of character speech had always been latent in the English-language novel, it was not until the twentieth century that they were fully realized and exploited.

A central contention of this study, then, is that dialogue—long considered one of the most prosaic of literary conventions—became in the hands of certain British and American modernist writers one of the most intensely poetic. Equally central, however, is the theoretical claim implied by and adjacent to this historical one: that fictional dialogue must be reconceived as a work of *poiesis* rather than *mimesis* and should be treated, even in instances where it is less conspicuously wrought, as something not just "imitated" but truly *made*. Both of these claims are driven by empirical findings about dialogue's behavior in modernist fiction: in particular, its detachment from individual subjects and its tendency to manifest in both more intersubjective and authorially orchestrated configurations (an apparent contradiction, which in fact reflects the diverse presentations of character discourse these texts catalyze or permit). For example, it is not unusual to come across instances of dialogue in modernist prose which, on the basis of idiolect and tone, might feasibly "belong" to more than one speaker—or, conversely, to none. Interestingly, direct discourse's potential *distance* from character exists in tension with what some theorists see as indirect discourse's more proximate relationship to character during this period. Genette, for one, argues that interior monologue—one of the discursive modes most closed associated with modernist fiction—is distinguished precisely by the fact that it is "emancipated . . . from all narrative patronage . . . from the word go," so that it might be identified, immediately and unambiguously, with a diegetic speaker (174).[3] Similarly, Hugh Kenner, in his well-known study of voice in Joyce's work, *Joyce's Voices*, formulates the "Uncle Charles Principle" precisely to describe Joyce's

---

2. The *Routledge Encyclopedia of Narrative Theory* summarizes the position of many critics when it notes that "dialogue fulfils the important narrative functions of characterisation and advancing the plot" (105).

3. For an alternate account of the operation of interior and, specifically, free indirect discourse, which departs significantly from Genette's, see Daniel P. Gunn, "Free Indirect Discourse and Narrative Authority in *Emma*."

formidable capacity for making narration more subtly characterological. Even as forms of indirect discourse in modernist fiction draw closer to character, then, direct discourse—the discursive mode typically understood *in terms of character*—appears newly able to detach from it.

The chapters that follow seek not only to substantiate these claims by examining textual manifestations of such dialogic decoupling but to consider its implications for readers and theorists of the novel. What does it mean, after all, when dialogue becomes liberated from the demands of fictional subjectivity and aligned more closely with an author's own? I begin in my first chapter by identifying and redressing some of the prevailing assumptions that have shaped (and frequently distorted) our understanding of fictional talk. Subsequent chapters offer evidentiary support for my own proposed approach in the form of case studies: analyses of distinct conversational dynamics, which I trace through a pair of texts and which demonstrate the utility, and often the necessity, of treating fictional talk as an authorially as well as a characterologically driven phenomenon. In particular, I draw attention to the capacity for the very *structures* of talk to bear meaning, both individually and cumulatively, and the potential for characters' utterances to communicate ideas in excess of their semantic content. The second chapter, for instance, examines the trend toward consensual speaking that emerges in Henry James's *The Ambassadors* and Ernest Hemingway's *The Sun Also Rises*. In particular, I suggest that such "consensual" arrangements are used to express a fantasy of reciprocity that is at once broadly attributable to the novels' speakers and to the authors themselves. The third chapter considers the countervailing concern with preserving individuation that manifests in the monologic speech habits of two characters, Gabriel Conroy in Joyce's "The Dead" and Quentin Compson in Faulkner's *The Sound and the Fury*, and suggests this ambition is one to which the narratives are at once opposed and residually sympathetic. My fourth chapter shifts the focus from what Phelan calls the "thematic" dimension of dialogue—its capacity to express salient themes within the narrative—and toward its "synthetic" aspect: its ability to call attention to its own construction and that of the narration.[4] Specifically, this chapter explores the movement toward undifferentiated speech that occurs in Faulkner's *Absalom, Absalom!* and Woolf's *The Waves*, novels which, despite their apparent investment in disambiguating voices, emphasize the high degree of similarity among them. By so distorting the conventions used to render novelistic talk, I argue, Woolf and Faulkner offer a powerful critique of them and of certain of the ideological assump-

---

4. For more on Phelan's definition of the "mimetic," "synthetic," and "thematic" dimensions of character (and, by extension, character narration and dialogue) see his concise summary in *Living to Tell about It* (20) or his extended discussion in *Reading People, Reading Plots*.

tions they have served to perpetuate and endorse. My fifth and final chapter considers the further vitiation of speech as a mechanism for the expression of discrete characters, by exploring the "choral" configurations of voice in Woolf's *Between the Acts* and Stein's "Melanctha," texts that gesture toward a fundamentally decentered and democratized way of distributing fictional talk. In so doing, I suggest, they offer an implicitly feminist challenge to the representational systems characteristic of the nineteenth-century European novel, which, as Alex Woloch demonstrates in *The One vs. the Many*, tended to be organized hierarchically, around principles of competition rather than collaboration.

Cumulatively, these analyses serve to illustrate a somewhat paradoxical truth: that even the most idiosyncratic of dialogic phenomena should, in the context of early twentieth-century British and American fiction, also be understood as exemplary—representative, in their very distinctness, of the *kinds* of innovative talk on display in modernist prose. At the same time, the close readings of individual texts are also meant to model a new methodological approach: a way of reading fictional conversation that takes into account the signifying capabilities of its form as well as its content. Moreover, they consider the distinct role such conversational structures might play in texts that aspire to something beyond mimesis, as many modernist and postmodernist texts do. Indeed, the decision to embed the word "poetics" in the title of this introduction, and throughout the book, was intended to highlight its focus on dialogue's *extra*mimetic functions, the very ones that Phelan and Peter Rabinowitz suggest remain comparatively overlooked.[5]

A primary impetus behind framing dialogue as poiesis, then, is to position it as an expressive affordance of the author, or "maker"—a move intended to correct for its default association with character. In this sense, I follow Phelan in treating dialogue as a form of authorial as well as conversational "disclosure" and in seeing it more generally as a "neglected channel of narrative communication."[6] At the same time, this perspectival shift also makes possible several more concrete insights into the dynamics of modernist narrative. On the one hand, a less character-dependent approach to dialogue reveals the modernist capacity to "outsource" to direct discourse the kinds of rhe-

---

5. In their chapter on character in *Core Concepts*, Phelan and Rabinowitz argue that compared to dialogue's "mimetic" function, its "thematic" and "synthetic" dimensions remain underexplored. As they note, "Character-character dialogue, which typically heightens our interest in the mimetic component, can simultaneously be used . . . to report, interpret, or evaluate"—a possibility that "deserves more attention than it has received so far" (115).

6. The phrase comes from Phelan's conference presentation, "Dialogue, Voice, and Tone," subsequently published as an article under the revised title, "Voice, Tone, and the Rhetoric of Narrative Communication."

torical functions typically carried out by more "indirect" discursive means. If literary modernism witnessed what Fredric Jameson called the "laundering of authorial intervention"—at least, intervention of the "omniscient" variety—it may also have witnessed the reassertion of authorial presence, albeit through more covert narrative channels (*Political* 221). Thus, for instance, Faulkner will repackage as dialogue lines originally intended as indirect narration,[7] while James has the characters in his later fiction speak in a way that bears more resemblance to his own writerly voice than any "actual" one. Just as important, however, is the conspicuousness of these rhetorical gestures *as* gestures, so that the lack of dialogic variety presents as a deliberate authorial choice rather than as an accident or oversight.

Notably, such moves are in keeping with Phelan's own observation about modernism's narratological praxis, namely, that it would increasingly license and privilege forms of authorial indirection ("Rhetoric, Ethics"). In this sense, modernist authors' cooption of a historically characterological avenue of expression might reflect not only *writers'* increased appetite for and "reliance on indirect communication" (67) but *readers'* willingness to accept what Phelan describes as a new "ethics of the telling" which modernism helped to inaugurate (67). According to this unspoken pact, "the audience assumes that if they give the author their attention, they will be repaid with a worthwhile experience"—while "the author assumes that the audience can be trusted to connect the dots, fill in the gaps, follow the art of mediated communication" (67). In short, this newly poetic dialogue may represent both a catalyst and a confirmation of reconfigured author-reader relations.

Additionally, the reframing of dialogue as authorial rather than exclusively or even primarily characterological produces a further insight: that modernist texts are markedly less concerned (or less centrally concerned) with using speech to maintain the illusion of character autonomy. To varying extents, all of the texts considered here reveal a marked propensity to conflate rather than individuate characters' idioms, some to the extent of troubling the conventional relationship between voices and bodies, as it has historically been instantiated in the novel. By challenging the default logics of attribution traditionally used to make sense of character speech, these texts present not only interpretive difficulties—or even, as Melville's narrator discovers, philosophical ones. They also exert a more "positive" influence, prompting readers (how-

---

7. See Gerald Langford's account of *Absalom, Absalom!*'s composition and revision, especially p. 21.

ever subtly) to shift their focus from discrete utterances and toward the larger "network" of utterances within a given text.[8]

Finally, I'd like to conclude by offering some additional clarifications—and caveats—regarding terminology. First, I am aware of both the semantic distinctness and varied resonance of terms such as *talk, speech, dialogue,* and *voice,* which I have used more or less interchangeably throughout this introduction. This choice was intended in part to counter the excessive scrupulousness with which some narrative theory seems to superintend the usage of its terms. My goal, then, is not to imply that these terms are theoretically equivalent but rather to highlight their functional equivalence in the mind of many readers. (An additional, practical benefit of this approach was to permit stylistic variation and prevent excessive repetition.) That said, it is important to clarify what I intend these terms to signify. For the purposes of this study, I will be using *talk, speech,* and *dialogue* to designate instances of what is commonly known as *direct discourse,* which purports to represent or report characters' utterances "directly," by means of conventions such as quotation marks and speech tags. Additionally, while I most commonly use "dialogue" or "character dialogue" to denote conversation in its conventional, dyadic form—as a verbal exchange between two or more subjects—it's important to note that I will *also* use it to refer to instances of talk that are monologic or nonreciprocal. By contrast, I use the term *voice* more sparingly throughout the study, both in recognition of its greater theoretical valence and because it applies to authorial as well as characterological discourse and thus is more open to ambiguity. In this way, I aim to embrace a pragmatic approach to the study of narratological phenomena without sacrificing clarity and rigor.

At this point, it also seems important to address those critical terms the book does *not* use, or does not use with as much frequency, including some (such as *free indirect discourse* [FID], *character narration,* and *stream of consciousness*) that readers might reasonably expect me to invoke in discussions, say, of the Benjy and Quentin sections of *The Sound and the Fury.* In the interest of providing a fuller accounting of character speech—which manifests primarily in the form of quoted dialogue but which I also trace through various, less direct discursive channels—this study will occasionally appear to transgress established categories and theoretical boundaries. In part, I intend this as a heuristic strategy to surface expressions of figural voice where preexisting categories might have discouraged readers to look for them. At stake, in a sense, is the possibility of a continuum of talk in the novel, one that

---

8. I'm indebted to Franco Moretti's use of the term *network* in *Distant Reading,* discussed in greater detail in chapter 1.

stretches from the subvocal monologues of *The Sound and the Fury,* to the fully externalized speech of "Melanctha" or *Absalom, Absalom!*; from the inaudible or unacknowledged asides in *Between the Acts,* to the richly reciprocated exchanges of *The Ambassadors*—a spectrum whose complete theorization lies beyond the bounds of this study, but to which it nonetheless hopes to contribute. In short, character talk generally appears within quotation marks, but, as the following analyses suggest, it can also occur outside them: as in "The Dead," offset by punctuation one moment, then submerged in FID the next. The goal of this study, then, is not to discredit any of the foundational categories of narrative theory or to overstep the lines it has usefully drawn between, say, the direct and the indirect, the spoken and thought, the authorial and the characterological. But it does suggest the regularity with which modernist texts may encroach upon those lines. To this end, it also seeks to highlight the ways in which excessive deference to established discursive categories might function to occlude as well as clarify the operation of at least certain types of narrative—if not because of the canonical force of such categories, which may shape critical inquiry a priori, then because their theoretical appeal might outstrip their interpretive utility. Categories, in other words, are useful only to the point to which they are overridden by praxis.

As should be evident from even this brief overview, this book grants dialogue a greater capacity for signification than it has typically been afforded in the scholarly literature. Though it is understandable that many theorists of narrative and the novel have focused primarily on what characters say rather than *how* they say—or on the more overt manifestations of authorial "saying"—one inadvertent by-product of such reading practices has been to create the impression that dialogue, however admired or beloved, remains a largely instrumental feature of fiction. By contrast, a primary goal of my approach, which treats dialogue as a rhetorical mode as flexible and nuanced as narration proper, is to elucidate the insufficiently documented and multifaceted work of talk within modernist narrative and, by extension, narrative more generally. It is my hope that the benefits of this approach become apparent, as my analyses, by placing dialogue under new kinds of critical pressure, yield new insights about much-studied works, and about a foundational yet overlooked feature of the novel.

CHAPTER 1

# Dialogue and Its Discontents

THAT PREVIOUS STUDIES have failed to account for the transformational shift that took place in the twentieth-century novel's treatment of talk is only one indication of dialogue's chronically deprecated status within literary theory. Despite Mikhail Bakhtin's suggestion that "the speaking person and his discourse is . . . what makes a novel a novel, the thing responsible for the uniqueness of the genre," commentators agree that dialogue remains curiously undertheorized, a "largely neglected topic" and a "largely unquestioned element within fiction" (*Dialogic* 333; Mepham, "Novelistic Dialogue" 411; Middleton 33). "To the degree that readers of the novel have listened for the sound of the narrator's voice," Dan Coleman has argued, "they have turned a deaf ear to all other kinds of talk that make novels, novels" (52). More recently, Bronwen Thomas begins her book *Fictional Dialogue*—one of the few full-length studies in the field—by remarking that talk remains something of a topic *non grata* among scholars. "While considerable critical attention has been paid to the representation of speech and thought in narrative," she observes, "the emphasis of late has swung much more in favor of thought than speech" (1).[1]

---

1. Although her book addresses fiction's capacity to emulate the dynamics of talk, rather than render instances of it, per se, Irene Kacandes also makes a related point: that "propensities . . . to denigrate talk" have led to an overall reduction in scholarship's exploration of the various ways textuality intersects with orality (xii).

The central goals of this study, then, are to help correct this critical imbalance and to supplement existing accounts of fictional speech which, despite important interventions like Thomas's, remain limited in both number and scope. In particular, this first chapter aspires to challenge two of the presuppositions about fictional dialogue that have helped to obscure its rich rhetorical and aesthetic potential: namely, that it exists to express character and that its most meaningful analogue remains real speech.

Particularly representative of this first position is Norman Page's influential early study, *Speech in the English Novel* (1973, 1988), which examines the role of dialogue in the eighteenth- and nineteenth-century British novel. Though he identifies a number of possible functions that speech might serve—"to further plot, to develop character, to describe setting or atmosphere, to present a moral argument or a discussion"—he argues that "the most important . . . and certainly the most productive of interest and variety" is undoubtedly "the presentation and development of character" (55). To this end, Page devotes much of his book to elaborating the ways in which authors employ talk as a mode of characterization, whether to distinguish characters as individuals (through the use of idiolect) or as members of group (through the deployment of dialect).

In this way, Page distills what has long been the default argument about fictional speech: that it ought to serve as a "badge of identity," at once an emblem and a prop of fictional subjecthood (16). In *Forms of Speech in the Victorian Novel*, for instance, Raymond Chapman similarly foregrounds dialogue's individuating dimension, "its power to reveal character" (1).[2] Further attesting to the ubiquity of this view is the entry devoted to "dialogue" in the *Routledge Encyclopedia of Narrative Theory*, which notes that it "fulfills the important narrative functions of characterisation and advancing the plot" (105). It's a conception of dialogue's capacities that has proven as indelible in practice as it has been in theory. Take, for instance, the development of punctuation techniques, which, as literary historians have shown, evolved to bind speech more closely to speakers.[3] Writing handbooks have played a similarly instrumental role in consolidating our understanding of talk as an extension of character. As Peter Middleton demonstrates, a central tenet of such "how-to" manuals is that "speech always, always, always reflects a character's back-

---

2. As the titles hint, Chapman's book parallels Page's study and at times strangely echoes it. Especially odd is Chapman's decision to begin his study in an identical manner to Page's—by using the same citation from *Alice in Wonderland* ("And what is the use of a book without pictures or conversations?") to attest to dialogue's importance—without acknowledging the overlap.

3. For more on the historical development of quotation practices in the novel, see Jonathan Rée, Mark Lambert, and Marjorie Garber. See also Lennard Davis, especially chapter 5.

ground and . . . inner reality" and that "for revealing character, there is no substitute for the voices of the characters themselves"[4]—the implication being that "to represent yourself, all you need to do is speak" (34).

Given the persistence of such beliefs in both critical discourse and the popular imagination, it is hardly surprising that the presumption of a bond between one's self and one's speech should be as central to reading dialogue as it is to writing it. As Stephen Ross notes in his study of voice in Faulkner's novels, it has historically been imperative for readers that "voice [be] an index of personal identity" (*Inexhaustible Voice* 85). To violate this literary obligation, then, is to substantially disrupt audience expectations, a sensation that might be further heightened by what critics suggest is readers' unusual degree of investment in dialogue, the subject of one of Henry James's well-known laments:[5]

> "Dialogue," always "dialogue!" I had seemed from far back to hear them mostly cry: "We can't have too much of it, we can't have enough of it, and no excess of it, in the form of no matter what savourless dilution, or what boneless dispersion, ever began to injure a book so much as even the very scantest claim put in for form and substance. (AA 382)

James's offhanded dismissal of readerly values notwithstanding, fictional dialogue's effect on and reception by audiences is a topic deserving of a greater amount of critical scrutiny that it has previously received.[6] One could argue that, as framed in James Phelan's terms, dialogue appears to have long been governed by a particular and particularly powerful "ethics of the telling": an understanding that fictional talk will obey certain unspoken laws of attribution and individuation (*Experiencing Fiction* 11). Indeed, Roland Barthes goes so far as to suggest that this particular constraint—the need to preserve a

---

4. The examples Middleton quotes come from Rita Mae Brown's *Starting from Scratch: A Different Kind of Writer's Manual*, p. 86, and *The Complete Guide to Writing Fiction*, p. 67, authored by Barnaby Conrad et al., respectively.

5. See James's preface to *The Awkward Age* for the entirety of his remarks, which include the complaint that readers slaver for dialogue, but only of a very particular and, to his mind, degraded and formulaic kind: "One had seen good solid slices of fiction, well endued, one might surely have thought, with this easiest of lubrications, deplored by editor and publisher as positively not, for the general gullet as known to them, made adequately 'slick'" (AA 382).

6. While much work remains to be done on readers' relationship to dialogue, critics have often taken for granted their exceptional interest in the "dialogue portions of . . . fiction," noting anecdotally that "it is the *speech* of . . . characters . . . that is most often remembered" (Page 1). See Chapman for more on the "readerly approach to dialogue" in the Victorian novel, especially chapter 11. See also Richard Beach, who explores readerly responses to literary dialogue in a pedagogical context and considers how it prompts inference-making among students.

"natural," one-to-one ratio between voices and bodies—has played a hugely formative role in the development of prose fiction, "classic" instantiations of which are "always haunted by the appropriation of speech" (41). Here, again, the locus classicus of such anxieties might be Melville's "Bartleby," whose narrator becomes increasingly discomfited by the encroaching of the scrivener's speech on his own.

In short, so deeply entrenched has this idea of "characterization through speech" been to the historical development and decipherment of narrative fiction that Page provocatively suggests it is "not altogether . . . a matter of convention" (98, 17). Certainly, Jacques Derrida demonstrates that the Western metaphysical tradition has been heavily indebted to (and instrumental in disseminating) a conception of voice as a conduit of presence:[7] thus the strong association between speech and subjectivity that has persisted in linguistic and psychoanalytic theory as well as literary theory. This association is exemplified by Ferdinand de Saussure's opposition between the unique, personalized *parole* and the generalized *langue,* or by Lacan's identification of the voice as one of the *objets* (*a*), which he calls "the 'stuff,' or rather, the lining . . . of the very subject that one takes to be the subject of consciousness" (315). Whether one treats speech's relationship to fictional selfhood as natural or conventional, it's difficult to dispute the central role this relationship has played in the evaluation of novelistic talk.

The problem is that true as such assessments of dialogue might be in the eighteenth- and nineteenth-century novel—the focus of both Page's and Chapman's studies—they are noticeably *less* true, or less universally true, of the twentieth-century one. At the risk of invoking the overworked opposition between realism and modernism, this study will document a tendency within fiction since categorized as modernist to unsettle traditional voice-body relations by sharing or "recycling" among multiple characters what would seem to be highly distinctive words or phrases, and, in the process, vitiating talk's individuating function. The results manifest in texts ranging from James's late fiction, in which the characters seem unaware of the fact that they all speak the same idiosyncratic language, to *The Waves,* in which Woolf allows her characters a limited ability to discern and comment on idiomatic overlap among speakers. Outside the Anglophone tradition, one might also think of the increasingly conversational second half of Franz Kafka's *The Castle,* in which K complains to Frieda, "In the account you gave I couldn't

---

7. In *Of Grammatology,* Derrida demonstrates the mechanisms that have resulted in the voice's metaphysical primacy and contributed to the privileging of the "pneumatological" over the "grammatological" (17). See also Mladen Dolar's discussion of phonocentrism in *A Voice and Nothing More* (36–42).

always distinguish your opinion from the landlady's" (156). At the same time, there is also a discernible lessening of features that distinguish characters' discourse from the implied author's, even in (and sometimes especially in) those texts largely composed of such discourse: *Lord Jim*, for example, or *Absalom, Absalom!*, a novel that may go furthest in justifying the complaint leveled at Faulkner by his friend Phil Stone, that "all the characters [in his novels] talked like William Faulkner" (Blotner 465).

It's a development that is particularly interesting in light of the late nineteenth-century novel's demonstrable fascination with regional dialects,[8] since by this metric, the texts considered here would seem to be noticeably less invested in reproducing linguistic diversity. That is not to suggest that modernist fiction—so strongly associated with polyphony—is uninterested in the operation or representation of locutionary difference; one need only think of Faulkner's phonetic reproduction of his speaker's idiolects (Anse Bundren's "hit" for "it," the Reverend Shegog's "I got de ricklickshun en de blood of de Lamb!") or Joyce's attempts, in the Nighttown episode of *Ulysses*, to make good on the claim advanced earlier in the novel, that "everything speaks in its own way" (*The Sound and the Fury* [hereafter SF] 295; (*Ulysses* [hereafter U] 7.177). Conversely, I don't want to overstate the degree to which individuation is achieved in the premodernist novel (or any novel) through dialogue alone; apart from Dickens or Twain, say, few writers seem either inclined or able to ensure that every character speaks distinctly. (Proust, in Genette's estimation, constituted a notable exception.[9]) Instead, it is generally quotation marks and speech tags, rather than quirks of diction or phraseology, that do the work of differentiation. What is most striking, however, is the marked absence in many canonically modernist texts of even the *pretense* of differentiation, of even pretending to personalize character speech. As concerned as many nineteenth-century authors appear to have been with language differences, the twentieth-century writers considered here show themselves to be at

---

8. Many have argued that interest in regional speech patterns and differences peaked in the late nineteenth century; for more on the "craze for dialect literature" in the US, see Gavin Jones's *Strange Talk*, especially chapter 1 (1). See also Chapman's first chapter for more on the growth of dialect representation in Victorian-era British fiction.

9. Genette notes that while "it would be excessive and hasty to say that all Proust's characters have an idiolect . . . nearly all of them do present, at least some time, some eccentric characteristic of language, an incorrect or dialectical or socially imprinted turn of phrase, a typical acquisition or borrowing, a blunder, howler, or tell-tale slip, etc." (184). By way of evidence, he offers "Odette's Anglicisms, Basin's improprieties, Bloch's schoolboy pseudo-Homerisms [and] Saniette's archaisms," among other examples (184).

least as interested in what is variously presented as the promise—or threat—of linguistic sameness.[10]

A more accurate account of dialogue in the novel, then, would need to reflect its distinctive status and deployments in modernist texts like these, which are not uniformly concerned with the lifelike portrayal of character. Indeed, it is significant that Page and Chapman limit their studies to the pre-twentieth-century novel, as if to acknowledge the qualitative differences in dialogue presentation that are discernible in subsequent fiction. Thomas makes more explicit reference to this shift, noting that it was during the early twentieth century that "novelists . . . experiment with dialogue in a more overtly self-conscious way, making this a key period in the development of the technique" ("Dialogue" 81). Such experimentation is evident in everything from Hemingway's telegraphic, even stichomythic, conversations, to Faulkner's breathlessly long monologues; cumulatively, such instances would seem to signal an interest in at once revitalizing one of the novel's most overlooked narrative mechanisms and, in the process, recalibrating the role played by audience. Thus, for instance, Ryan Bishop suggests that Joyce's *Dubliners* should receive credit for inaugurating conversations that, in their "naturalness," also placed unprecedented demands on readers, who were forced to grapple with "interruptions, incomplete sentences, and utterances that fade into the silence whence they emerged, all qualities not frequently found in texts before Joyce" (65).[11]

At the same time, fiction of the period featured not only new modalities of speech but also new attitudes toward it. John Mepham, for one, has intriguingly proposed that talking was accorded new primacy in twentieth-century Anglo-American fiction as the direct result of the "invention" and eventual diffusion of the "therapeutic speech situation" ("Psychoanalysis" 105). Indeed, as Mepham argues elsewhere, so substantively different is modernist dialogue in its priorities and presentation that it deserves a different designation altogether. On the one hand, Mepham proposes, there is the "Standard" form of dialogue, codified by the 1820s and still the "default manner of marking and laying out dialogue" ("Novelistic Dialogue" 412). In it, he explains that "quoted (direct) speech is clearly marked off from other textual matter by quotation

---

10. Though it lies outside the scope of this study, it would be interesting to consider this apparent shift in relation to contemporaneous cultural developments, such as the emergence of cinema, which was frequently touted as a "universal" language—epitomized, for instance, by the opening of Dziga Vertov's 1929 film, *Man with a Movie Camera*, which declared that it "aim[ed] at creating a truly international absolute language of cinema."

11. This claim, however, should be qualified by acknowledging the existence of other pioneers outside the Anglo-American tradition, perhaps most notably Fyodor Dostoevsky.

marks," and "each new speech begins on a new line and is indented as a new paragraph so that it is very easy for the eye to pick up the information wherever there is a change of speaker" (412). By contrast, the "Modernist" form is far less concerned with "marking" and preserving speaker differences; it is not narratively or typographically distinguished in the same ways, and as a result, it often results in some obfuscation between "external and internal speech" (414).

It is an argument reminiscent of Barthes's view, referenced above, that the readiness with which speech can be attributed is a good index of a text's "classic" or "modern" status. In the "modern" novel, Barthes implies, voice may cease to serve a characterizing function and in fact may not be linked to specific characters at all, such that "any reference becomes impossible" (41). "By contrast," he notes, "in the classic text, the majority of the utterances are assigned an origin, we can identify their parentage, who is speaking: either a consciousness (of a character, of the author) or a culture (the anonymous is still an origin, a voice: the voice we find, for example, in the gnomic code)" (41). Framed in Barthes's terms, one could say that most previous accounts of dialogue have focused primarily on the "classic" or *readerly* text (41). In the process, such accounts may have skewed our understanding of dialogue's function by grounding their claims in assumptions that may not be as universal as the authors imply. If, as Monika Fludernik has suggested, the act of discerning a "function" is itself an interpretive act, the prevailing focus on the characterizing dimension of dialogue would seem to reveal a critical blind spot, an attachment to an interpretive system in which the novel's diverse narrative resources, dialogue included, are invariably routed toward the creation of plausible individuals (*Fictions* 334–35). In other words, the failure to openly acknowledge how often the novel has harbored "other than mimetic ambitions" may deter readers from considering the more heterogeneous ends that dialogue might have been designed to serve (Mepham, "Novelistic Dialogue" 411).[12]

Of course, there are theorists besides Barthes whose work addresses the novel's capacity to disassociate speech from character. In Bakhtin's work, for instance, such a possibility is implicit in his conception of discourse as inescapably "interindividual," which militates against the idea that utterances could exclusively belong to single speakers (*Speech Genres* 121). Indeed, if Bakhtin's best-known work emphasizes the discursive heterogeneity of the

---

12. Mepham borrows the phrase "mimetic ambitions" from M. B. Parkes; see Parkes's *Pause and Effect: An Introduction to the History of Punctuation in the West*. He notes that "poetic, aesthetic, and symbolic ambitions have also been at work" in the novel (Mepham, "Novelistic Discourse" 411).

novel, his later writings place new emphasis on the ways in which an individual's discursive autonomy is inevitably constrained. In *Speech Genres,* for instance, Bakhtin underscores the extent to which the *parole* is shaped by the *langue* in the guise of "speech genres," those larger discursive forms that circumscribe and predetermine the utterances of any individual speaker. Despite his reputation among critics as a "genius of pluralism" and an advocate for the novel's "democratic rather than demagogic" priorities, it is important to recall that for Bakhtin, then, there was never any such thing as entirely *free* speech (Fogel 16; Davis 166).[13] As he wrote,

> the single utterance, with all its individuality and creativity, can in no way be regarded as a *completely free combination* of forms of language, as is supposed, for example, by Saussure (and by many other linguists after him), who juxtaposed the utterance, as a purely individual act, to the system of language that is purely social and mandatory for the individuum. (*Speech Genres* 81)

The problem, Bakhtin suggests, is that Saussure "ignores the fact that in addition to forms of language there are also *forms of combinations* of these forms, that is, he ignores speech genres" (81). In challenging Saussure's binary, Bakhtin implies that speech needs to be reconceived as not just inter- but also extra- (or perhaps super-) individual, since it will always to some extent precede the subject speaking. Thus, if Bakhtin's work has encouraged many to equate dialogue's presence in the novel with a degree of "characterological autonomy," this positivist reading should not occlude speech's powerful association—for Bakhtin, and perhaps also for the modernist writers who were his contemporaries—with *non-*autonomy (Hale 93).[14]

More recently, Sharon Cameron has challenged the conception of the novel as a stronghold of characterological sovereignty. In *Impersonality,* she uses Herman Melville's *Billy Budd* as a case study in character's capacity to "ope[n] to what lies outside of it" (181). Specifically, she argues that "character does not seem to be an autonomous or independent entity" in the text; instead, "characters . . . share traits we might have thought exclusively the property of one or the other" (181). Substantiating this claim through a close reading of Melville's novella, she demonstrates that the peaceable Billy comes

---

13. See Aaron Fogel for more on Bakhtin's association with a tradition of what he calls "dialogue idealism" (260n).

14. See Dorothy Hale, who suggests that Wayne Booth, for one, would extrapolate from Bakhtin the idea that "characterological identity is most authentically represented as self-expressive speech: the 'freedom [of characters] to say what they will, in their own way'" (93).

to swap "traits" with the violent Claggart, and notes that "it is not clear what . . . individuation would mean when a character is dispossessed of the attribute that most distinguishes him, which is converted to its antithesis" (181). Though Cameron here is speaking of "attributes" and not idioms, a survey of modernist dialogue reveals something analogous to the kind of ontological "sharing" she describes: a tendency for characters not just to "share traits" but, as I've suggested above, to share tongues.

Following Cameron and Bakhtin, then, what the following chapters suggest is not simply that many seminal examples of modernist fiction evince an increased willingness to present characters' autonomy as compromised, but that their dialogue frequently functions to at once reflect and respond to this state of affairs. This capacity for such "real-time" commentary is one that Marshall Berman, for one, has seen as the special purview of modernism, whose products ought to be understood as "at once expressions of and protests against the process of modernization" (235).[15] It is a thesis that undergirds recent studies like Sam Halliday's *Sonic Modernity,* which documents the relationship between nineteenth- and twentieth-century audio technologies and the representations of sound in contemporaneous texts. On the one hand, writers such as Woolf, Joyce, Conrad, Faulkner, and Hemingway had strong ideas about the voice as an affordance (or hindrance) for the modern subject—ideas that reflect varying degrees of engagement with the forms of technological innovation Halliday describes. Yet while Ivan Kreilkamp locates within Victorian culture a "nostalgia for a pure orality," representatives of modernist culture appear demonstrably more ambivalent (5). It is precisely the writers' variegated attitudes toward the voice that leads me to avoid a strong technological determinist reading of modernist speech representation. At the same time, it is impossible to ignore the historical factors that might have shaped the configurations of talk that occur in these works.

Indeed, it's difficult to imagine that inventions like the telephone and gramophone would *not* have created for twentieth-century writers at least a heightened awareness of speech's newfound ability to become detached or otherwise attenuated from the human body, as Halliday's study suggests. In this light, it makes sense that modernist fiction should reveal a propensity for generating what Genette has called "emancipated" discourse, whose defining characteristic is less its interiority than its appearance of freedom "from all narrative patronage" (174). By this logic, the modernists were merely taking their cues from the modes of vocal "emancipation" taking place around them.

---

15. Berman's statement reflects the "symptomatic" conception of modernist aesthetics broadly shared by theorists including Fredric Jameson and Andreas Huyssen, among others.

Thus, readers of *Ulysses* find Bloom whimsically imagining the dead revivified by auditory means: "Have a gramophone in every grave or keep it in the house. After dinner on a Sunday. Put on poor old greatgrandfather Kraahraark! Hellohellohello amawfullyglad kraark awfullygladaseeragain hellohello amarawf kopthsth" (U 6.963–66). More ambiguous, however, are some of the other moments Halliday alludes to in his study, such as Marcel's reflections on the uncanny quality of the telephonic voice in *The Guermontes Way*; Marlow's awed invocation of Kurtz's disembodied voice in *Heart of Darkness*;[16] or, I would add, Marlow's similarly solemn reflection in *Lord Jim* about the "weird power of the spoken word" (174). The possibility that modernist writers were both more attuned to and anxious about the voice's "power"—inspired, perhaps, by the technologies being used to amplify and transform it—might help explain how the traditional relationship between voices and bodies, which had for so long been taken for granted in the novel, came to undergo such a radical alteration during this period of literary production.

## I. "REAL TALK"

If one limitation of previous literary historical accounts of dialogue has been the extent to which they have taken for granted speech's inextricable and generally subordinate relationship to character—a relationship that, as the above discussion implies, would grow intermittently strained in the twentieth-century novel—another limitation has been the perceived relationship between fictional and "real" talk. This perception has been particularly instrumental to linguistic approaches to character dialogue, which import to the study of fictional discourse the terms and techniques appropriate to the analysis of "actual" conversation and discourse.[17] Some of the most suggestive work in this mode has been done by Michael J. Toolan, who in the past decades has examined the dynamics of fictional conversation using tools derived from discourse and conversation analysis, subfields of linguistics that emerged during the 1960s. In the process, he has offered a compelling defense of "literary linguistics" or "linguistic criticism" as a methodology, arguing, in response

---

16. See Halliday's reading of this dynamic in *Heart of Darkness* (*Sonic Modernity* 36–38).

17. For representative examples of this approach, see Bishop; Toolan, "Analysing Fictional Dialogue," "Analysing Conversation," and *The Stylistics of Fiction*; Burton, *Dialogue and Discourse*; and Herman, "The Mutt and Jute Dialogue." See also Herman, "Dialogue in a Discourse Context," which applies an "interdisciplinary approach" to reading "scenes of talk" in Woolf's *To the Lighthouse* so as to "develop a contextualist and functionalist approach to fictional dialogues" (75).

to Stanley Fish's attack on stylistics, that any method is subject to the charges of interpretive "fallibility" and bias (*Stylistics* 23). Undergirding Toolan's approach, and that of literary linguistics more generally, is the conviction that "the theories and principles developed by linguists and conversation analysts for the systematic study of discourse and natural conversation may be illuminatingly applied to the stylistic and structural study of a fictional conversation within a literary text" ("Analysing Conversation" 393). Buttressing this claim is the broader tradition of "extend[ing] to literary discourse ideas about language and communication" derived from linguistics, sociolinguistics, and speech act theory, as embodied by the work of such scholars as Mary Louise Pratt, Ann Banfield, J. Hillis Miller, and, more recently, David Herman (Herman, "Mutt and Jute" 219).

While the comparisons enabled by linguistic approaches to literature can be illuminating, they can also be misleading. Most problematic, perhaps, is the fact that such an approach perpetuates a false parallelism between fictional and natural conversation: the notion that talk in fiction is (or should be) at least vestigially linked to the real. As Herman puts it in his analyses of conversational exchanges in *Finnegans Wake*, "Literary dialogues . . . stage the principles and mechanisms of dialogue in general" and in the process "forc[e] us to reflect on our canons for conversational coherence" (219). Though Herman accounts for many uses of dialogue, he fails to allow for the likelihood that literary dialogues may just as easily *not* stage those "principles and mechanisms," or might otherwise disobey the rules of "conversational coherence." Put another way, it is true that linguistic terminology can help to *describe* the locutionary phenomena encountered in fiction; indeed, the following chapters occasionally draw on such terms by applying Bronisław Malinowski's notion of "phatic communion" to conversational interactions in James's fiction, for instance, or suggesting that certain of his or Hemingway's speakers violate H. P. Grice's "cooperative principle." But the risk is that such terminology also *proscribes* those phenomena by implying that the speech of fictional characters should be subject to the constraints of Malinowski's theories, or Grice's, or any other rules governing communication in social as opposed to literary contexts. It's true that some literary contexts are more hospitable to that kind of rule-breaking than others, and the high modernist texts that comprise my corpus may be extreme cases in this regard. Yet the risks of relying too heavily on the metric of naturalism remain, even if the fictional conversation in question only minimally departs from the rules of "real" talk.

To their credit, many practitioners of the linguistic approach have also been among its most astute critics. Indeed, Toolan himself identifies one of the most damning criticisms of this method: that it might help readers to name known textual phenomena, but not necessarily to identify new ones. Thus, he concedes, "literary linguistics may be a procedure for confirming interpretations or reconstructing meanings, rather than a method of constructing meanings" (*Stylistics* 25). Toolan's reading of the Christmas dinner scene in *Portrait of the Artist as a Young Man* provides a good case in point ("Analysing Conversation"). On the one hand, it makes apt and interesting use of concepts like "turn-taking" and the conversational unit of the "move." But do we really need such analysis to tell us that, in Thomas's paraphrase of Toolan's argument, there is "growing tension among those present" or that "'topic suppression' is an important structuring element in the talk"? ("Multiparty Talk" 660).

Perhaps the most vigorous critique of this methodology, and the one most salient to this study, comes from narratologists like Brian McHale, who have historically been suspicious of the linguistic approach. It is true, of course, as McHale concedes, that "conversation in novels may indeed reflect the 'rules' of spontaneous real-world conversation," as critics from Toolan to Thomas have suggested (McHale 438–39). But as he points out,

> at a finer-grained level, speech in the novel appears utterly unlike real-world speech. Novelistic speech is always highly schematized and stylized, depending for its effects on very limited selections of speech-features, many of them derived *not from actual speakers' behavior but from literary conventions, linguistic stereotypes, and folk-linguistic attitudes.* (439, italics mine)

McHale's insight exposes the essential misconception that has both motivated and frequently justified the application of linguistic techniques to the analysis of represented speech: namely, that such representations are modeled on "real-world" talk. In fact, as McHale argues, the template for novelistic conversation has always been more conventional than natural, more "literary" than "actual." (Indeed, Lennard Davis goes so far as to suggest that such conventions have even been the basis of so-called actual talk, such that "first came the literary conversation and then came the striving for real conversation" (163).) Stirling Haig, in his work on dialogue in Flaubert's novels, offers a similar argument, noting that "properly speaking, there is no oral style in literature at all, but an imitation, an oral convention" and that "this imitation is not of 'reality'; most often it is that of a *written* tradition" (2). The implication, then, is that it is written or literary models more than oral ones that we should be using to evaluate dialogue. Or, to put it another way, the tension with which we ought properly to be concerned is not that between factual and fictional speech but between *different models* of fictional speech. Building on McHale's insight, this book will contend that dialogue in the novel is best understood not in relation to "real" talk, but as an iteration of a relatively consistent set of literary conventions historically used to signify "talk." To this end, my analyses are less interested in assessing the realism or perceived feasibility of fictional utterances than in analyzing them in light of literary norms of speech presentation.

This line of argument has significant implications, given the extent to which commentary on represented speech has been dogged, and in some cases derailed, by discussions of its verisimilitude. As the *Routledge Encyclopedia of Narrative Theory* reports, debates about dialogue continue to "center on the extent to which novelistic dialogue is, or should be, mimetic of naturally occurring speech" (105).[18] It's not that there is nothing to be learned from considering dialogue in relation to "real life." Yet it seems strange that such mimetic appraisals should still predominate over, or be treated as necessary prerequisites to, other kinds of analysis. The result is that even scholars intent on debunking the analogy to actual conversations often begin, as Page does, by demonstrating how "tidied up" the fictionalized versions actually are (7–8). Why is it, in short, that critics seem compelled to revisit what each presents as a relatively settled and self-evident argument?

One possibility, already alluded to in the opening pages, is that the preponderance of protestation reflects a persistent devotion to the idea of dialogue's "realness." In other words, as Monika Fludernik has argued, readers continue to invest direct speech with "specious authenticity," a transparency it does not possess (*Fictions* 29). Similarly, Middleton has described, in slightly more neutral terms, the "pre-theoretical" knowledge that readers bring to the interpretation of novelistic speech, which includes the notion that, among other things, "the words are a reliably verbatim presentation of what is supposed to have been uttered" (32). Such convictions have been forcefully discredited by Fludernik as well as Meir Sternberg, who suggests that what he variously calls the "direct-speech fallacy" or "reproductionist fallacy" is still in circulation among readers (Sternberg, "Point of View" 68; "Proteus" 152). The problem with such "specious" or "fallacious" beliefs, however, is not the beliefs themselves, or that they reflect readers' naïveté. Rather, the more negative consequence of such beliefs is that they lend credence to the idea that dialogue is the product of comparatively minimal creative effort. Indeed, as Thomas has argued, as long as fictional speech is "approached as naturalistic,"

---

18. See also Chapman for more on the pervasiveness of the "debate about verisimilitude in fictional speech" in the critical literature (241).

generally speaking the "complexities of the interface between the dialogue and the framing work of the narrator are overlooked" ("Multiparty Talk" 661).[19]

An even more worrisome issue, however, is that the framing work of the author (implied or actual) has been similarly overlooked. I am not the first scholar to express concern that the authorial labor involved in crafting dialogue has been considerably effaced. Stephen Ross, for instance, has suggested that dialogue remains the site of the novelist's most unsung and least visible interventions:

> The assumptions underlying the portrayal of speech in fiction are among the strongest, and thus the least questioned, that authors and readers share. So crucial is imagined speech to our sense of a fictional world that we seldom ask how it comes to be. *Readers tend to treat quoted speech as a special kind of discourse that authors do not represent or imitate so much as lift directly from "life" into fiction.* (Inexhaustible Voice 68, italics mine)

Page and Haig report similarly dismissive treatment of dialogue among readers, noting the generalized resistance to the idea that the author is "present" in quoted speech; the consensus view, in other words, is that dialogue is a vacated space within fiction, the part of the novel in which "an author is theoretically absent" and in which his or her "presence appears (and it is again, of course, no more than appearance) to be least obtrusive" (Haig vii; Page 3). The question is whether professional readers have helped to reinforce the notion of dialogue as verbatim transcription rather than wrought convention (and whether the emphasis placed by some strains of narratology on the *narrator* has had the effect of denigrating the work of the *author*).

Brian Richardson, for one, does hold critics—and specifically narratologists—at least partly to blame for perpetuating this misconception. At issue, he argues, is that "traditional narrative theory" has been "typically based on the mimesis of actual speech situations" (*Unnatural Voices* 5). As a result, little work on poetics is derived from anything else, though evidence suggests that this state of affairs is changing. Recently, he notes, theorists of postmodern works "are beginning to describe a different, counter-poetics, one based on creative transformation rather than attempts at verisimilar representation: centered, that is, on *poiesis* instead of *mimesis*" ("Commentary" 701). Many of the works I consider here, while not "antimimetic" in the manner Richardson intends, are nonetheless "unruly" and certainly do not aim to render character

---

19. For more on dialogue's relationship to realism, see also the first chapter of Thomas's *Fictional Dialogue*, especially pp. 15–17.

voices with an eye to reproducing "actual speech" (701). Drawing on Richardson's work, then, one could say that the problem is that theorists have often treated even non-mimetically inclined texts as if the seamless reproduction of talk were their primary ambition and verisimilitude, the primary measure of their success.[20] Framed in this way, the fact that dialogue has historically failed to excite much critical scrutiny may be the result less of indifference than a more categorical misconception: that fictional talk is not truly the product of authorial design, but rather a feat of mimicry. Supporting such a hypothesis is the fact that, as David Lodge points out, it is rare to find literary scholars who quote dialogue. "When . . . we take what is deemed to be a representative passage from a novel," Lodge observes, "we invariably choose a passage of narrative that is either authorial or focalized through a character with whom the implied author is in sympathy" (76).[21]

The problem, to return to Richardson's terms, is that fictional conversation has come to be seen as a work of mimesis rather than poiesis: as something imitated but not truly *made*. It seems particularly telling, in this light, that much of the thinking on represented speech derives from what Aaron Fogel calls "handbook notions of natural, spontaneous conversation," since it reveals a tendency to think of dialogue-writing in terms of practice rather than theory: If you do it right, the logic goes, there should be no need to consider how it got done (260n). What makes modernist dialogue so striking is how forcefully it precludes such acts of interpretive dismissal by putting the poetic dimension of character speech conspicuously on display. If direct discourse has historically been deemed too unmediated, or transparent, to merit theorization, the opacity and idiosyncrasy of the dialogue considered in the subsequent chapters serves as something of a corrective—not only by making talk newly visible but by making it appear, in its oddness or excesses, to be a curiosity or even a *problem* in the text. In this way, modernist dialogue has the potential to interrupt readerly business as usual and to reinscribe the presence of an organizing authorial intelligence.

To date, James Phelan is one of the scholars who has done the most to describe the multifaceted rhetorical potentialities of character speech and to acknowledge the attendant "labor" involved in crafting it. If, as he suggests

---

20. Though Richardson in his study is focused more on narrating than specifically "speaking" voices, his observations are applicable to direct as well as indirect discourse. Without seeking to conflate the two, analogizing these two discursive modes seems continuous with his call to "move away from rigid typologies and Chinese box-type models of embodied speakers and toward an alternate figuration that stresses the permeability, instability, and playful mobility of the voices in nonmimetic fictions" *(Unnatural Voices* xii).

21. I am indebted to Coleman's article for directing me to this point (52).

in his work with Peter Rabinowitz, dialogue is still most regularly recruited for the purposes of "heighten[ing] our interest in the mimetic component" of a given narrative, it also possesses a greater reservoir of communicative potential, which might be exploited (or suppressed) over the course of a text (*Narrative Theory* 115). In particular, Phelan allows that character dialogue might function "thematically" (to represent ideas or themes) and "synthetically," that is, to call attention to the constructed nature of the narration. More broadly, Phelan also frames dialogue as a resource that, like the other elements of narrative, authors might deploy their own purposes. Thus, he proposes, "Character-character dialogue simultaneously works along two communicative tracks": operating not only as a form of "conversational disclosure"—fulfilling the more "standard functions of *narration*" (16)—but also as a form of "authorial disclosure" (*Somebody* 16).[22] The choice of the term *poetic* to describe modernist dialogue is intended to highlight its "made" quality and capacity to perform this authorially expressive function while underscoring its departure from mimetic conceptions of fictional talk.

That said, the notion that dialogue's more-than-mimetic capacities should require such underscoring is ironic, given that in the classical tradition, as Fludernik points out, it is so-called direct rather than indirect speech that was considered more rhetorically complex. If the *Republic*, for example, favors diegetic over mimetic modes of presentation and "privileges the narrator's rendering of speech events," Plato's hierarchy has since undergone a complete reversal; now, it is mimesis that occupies the "privileged position," and diegesis that is viewed as "intrinsically unreliable," thanks to its "equation . . . with mediation *tout court*" (*Fictions* 29, 27). Fludernik, for one, attributes this transvaluation to "misreadings" of Plato and his mimesis/diegesis distinction (28). While quoted speech, for Plato, was "characterized by a duality of discourse"—the author's and the characters'—contemporary readers are more likely to describe indirect or free indirect discourse as doubly inflected, thanks to the more recently theorized distinction between narrator and author (one that Plato, as Fludernik reminds us, did not recognize) (29). The result is that it is now mimetic speech that most readers experience as enunciated "in a single voice," and diegetic speech that we treat as "doubled" and thus epistemologically compromised (29). For Plato, one could say, dialogue was too mediated; for contemporary readers, not enough.

---

22. See Part One of Phelan's *Somebody Telling Somebody Else* for an extended theorization of character dialogue and its implications for prevailing conceptions of the narrative communication model.

Paradoxically, then, it may be the reflexive privileging of represented speech—readers' faith in its uncomplicated status—that has precipitated its critical neglect. And this perception, in turn, might be further shaped by the similarly unquestioned and historically contingent assumptions about the nature of "mimetic" representation. While contemporary critics tend to evaluate mimesis on the basis of how accurately an author imitates the words of another, Fludernik once again usefully contextualizes this value system, reminding us that for Plato, the goal was less the reproduction of particular words than the *quality* of those words. "If direct discourse imitates anything," she explains of Plato's position, "it is the (raw) manner of expression which one expects from real speech—there is certainly no implication of an imitation of *actual* words or sentences" (29). It was the ability to convey the general "manner" of spoken language, rather than the language itself, that was the original aim of mimesis. This legacy is visible, she argues, in the connotations of direct discourse, on the one hand—which has "com[e] to signify (or imply) empathy, specificity, realism, stylistic distinctness or reproductiveness"—and indirect discourse, which by contrast "tends to be read as distant, non-specific, non-realistic, stylized, and paraphrased" (29). In this way, Middleton suggests, novels may unconsciously perpetuate the kind of phonocentric bias Derrida discerns within Western culture, wherein "the spoken dialogue pretends to be the authentic, originating essence of self" and "the narrative writing . . . signals itself as secondary to such force, while all the time making it possible" (Middleton 47). In failing to question the authenticity of a novel's "spoken dialogue" while simultaneously approaching the "narrative writing" with suspicion, critics may inadvertently recreate the hierarchy poststructuralist criticism has sought to collapse (47).

The surprising implication, then, is that the greatest disincentive to theoretical work on fictional dialogue might not be the "widespread bias" against it, as some critics have argued, but rather the equally widespread if unrecognized bias *in its favor* (Coleman 52). Indeed, it is possible to speculate that one of the reasons there does not yet exist in literary studies the kind of account Sarah Kozloff has composed for film studies—a taxonomy of dialogic tropes and patterns, across various genres—is not only the daunting scale or methodological challenges posed by such a project, but also, despite the sophisticated theoretical inquiries into nearly all aspects of narrative, the extant presumption that dialogue is not truly deserving of scrutiny. It's a presumption that is forcefully contravened by the corpus of modernist writing, much of which conveys strongly the sense of dialogue's "madeness" through the inclusion of talk notable for its irregular quantity, for its quality, or for both. Without going so far as to suggest that dialogue in modernist texts is more deserving of inquiry, the fact that such texts draw attention to and so richly capitalize on this more submerged channel of authorial communication makes them particularly productive sites for considering its diverse rhetorical capabilities.

## II. MODERNIST DIALOGUE: A BRIEF OVERVIEW

An examination of modernist dialogue in situ makes especially clear both the need for new theoretical approaches and the limitations of previous ones. While the close analyses included in this study are designed to provide fuller illustration of this point, I believe they are usefully supplemented by a broader overview—a partial and provisional typology of dialogue in its modernist contexts. Whatever the limitations of such a schema, it may have at least heuristic value, prompting the further elaboration by others of the dialogic tendencies and "types" sketched below, whose concrete manifestations I explore in the following chapters.

At one end of modernist fiction's speech-representational spectrum lies what might be called *empirical* dialogue, so-designated because it takes its cues from and forcefully prioritizes language as it is "actually" spoken. The resulting talk might be described as phonocentric, inasmuch as it may sacrifice ready intelligibility for the sake of what presents, at least, as phonetic accuracy. Into this camp, one could recruit writers as diverse as Henry Roth, John Dos Passos, and Zora Neale Hurston, who, despite their multifarious styles and purposes in writing, all make it a point in much of their work to aggressively foreground the putative authenticity, spontaneity, and orality of their dialogue, in large part by rendering its sounds by means of "nonstandard" orthography. In so doing, these authors at once invoke real-world models of speech and estrange them by increasing readers' awareness of dialogue as a more material—and less transparent—textual element.

At first glance, it would be easy to see such strategies as continuous with those produced by American realist and regionalist writers such as Sarah Orne Jewett, Charles Chesnutt, Stephen Crane, or even Mark Twain, who all employed dialect to varying extents in their work. Yet whereas in *Huckleberry Finn*, say, or *The Country of the Pointed Firs*, the rendering of dialect serves the conventional functions of developing character or enhancing readers' sense of milieu, the "nonstandard" speech in the modernist texts mentioned above seems put to substantively different rhetorical ends. Consider, for instance, the opening pages of Dos Passos's *Nineteen, Nineteen*, which includes the following exchange between the protagonist, Joe, and a bar proprietor, Maria:

"Gimme two beers," Joe yelled through the door.

"Watta you wan', iho de mi alma?" asked Maria. "You savvy Doc Sidner?" "Sure me savvy all yanki. Watta you wan' you no go wid beeg sheep?" "No go wid beeg sheep . . . Fight wid beeg sonofabeech, see?"

"Ché!" Maria's breasts shook like jelly when she laughed. (3)

At first glance, Dos Passos's rendering of dialogue might appear to serve a characterizing function (an impression heightened by its lack of intelligibility, which seems to disqualify it for other narrative duties). Yet a closer examination suggests that it may be more closely linked to an authorial agenda. Here, the sonic quality of the language ends up competing with the semantic, such that we are reading not only to extract information (about characters, plot, or place) but to register the qualitatively different texture and tone of the speech itself. This is realism in excess of reality: a hypertrophic realism, which defamiliarizes not through the departure from, but rather from the excessive devotion *to,* mimetic praxis. Though such a passage may help provide "local color," conveying the ethnic tapestry of Dos Passos's New York, it serves a more extradiegetic function as well: attesting, through its sheer unorthodoxy, to the labor of the author, reestablishing his presence in what (as discussed above) has often been regarded as a "vacated" space. Framed in Phelan's terms, such empiricism elevates the experiential or "display element" of dialogue, the realism of which is offset by the readers' awareness of the effort involved in its production ("Imagining a Sequel" 248). The result is a kind of talk burlesque, a performance of "real" talk that never lets you forget the performer.

A similar showiness animates the dialogue in Henry Roth's *Call It Sleep,* a novel in which the renderings of early twentieth-century New York-ese, as spoken by Jewish immigrants, are so exaggerated as to strain credulity. As Alfred Kazin puts it in his introduction to the novel,

> Maybe street kids once talked this way, maybe not. The point is that Roth caricatures the terrible English of the street—a "foreign," external, cold-hearted language—in order to bring out the necessary contrast with the Yiddish spoken at home. This is the language of the heart, of tradition, of deeply felt togetherness. Just as Roth perhaps overdoes the savage English spoken in the street, so he deliberately exalts the Yiddish that he translates at every point into splendid, almost too splendid, King James English. (xv)

As in Dos Passos, it is the extremity, the "overdone" quality of Roth's dialogue—an impression produced by "caricature," on the one hand, and "exaltation" on the other—that distinguishes it from its antecedents in realist fiction.

Because such hyperrealist dialogue, despite taking more aestheticized form in these texts, nonetheless remains closest to dialogue in its more conventional manifestations, it can, to the reader less attentive than Kazin, appear unremarkable for anything other than its unusual presentation on the page. Suffice it to say that the mimetic appearance of such speech should not belie its richly synthetic and thematic nature. If Roth's rendering of talk seems designed, as Kazin implies, to dramatize the superiority of the Old World over the new, Hurston's might have an even more didactic function: to ensure that readers, thanks to her nonstandard orthography, contend with the speech of her characters with an attentiveness they might not normally bestow on marginalized subjects, or reserve for "authorial" passages. It's true, of course, that the dialogue of *Their Eyes Were Watching God* may appear to some readers under a completely different guise; as the novelist Zadie Smith notes, in her essay on the book, "Her conversations reveal individual personalities, accurately, swiftly, as if they had no author at all" (5). Yet that impression of transparency may, paradoxically, be underwritten precisely by the conspicuous display of artistry that undergirds the whole novel. Indeed, in each of the above-mentioned cases, one could similarly conclude that what motivates the departure from standard speech is less the conventionally realist aim of characterization than the more typically modernist goal of what for symmetry's sake might be called *authorization*: that is, the assertion and consolidation of an authorial presence and the extension of an authorially inflected or regulated voice into even the most seemingly off-limits areas of the diegetic frame.[23]

At the other end of the representational continuum, by contrast, are writers like Conrad, Woolf, and, at least in some instances, Faulkner—engineers of what I call *lyrical* dialogue, talk whose chief characteristic seems to be its strongly authorial flavor. If Dos Passos's, Roth's, and Hurston's novels appear to excessively particularize speech in their novels, Conrad's or Woolf's, one could say, lean just as strongly in the other direction, minimizing the distinctiveness of characters' language and conflating it with that of first- or third-person narrators: hence the analogy to the lyric, since these texts give the impression of suppressing "novelistic" polyphony so as to maximize expressivity or the sensation of addressivity. This more monologic orientation results not only in a homogeneous quality of voice but often in a highly literary style and diction, which militates against the successful recovery of putatively reported discourse as spontaneous character speech.

---

23. Along these lines, Carla Kaplan has suggested that the "framing conversation between Janie and Phoeby" be read less as a narrative means to an end—a "convenient, technical device for getting a life story across"—than as the end itself: Hurston's performative staging of a distinctive "politics of talk" (101).

On the one hand, both of these otherwise divergent approaches to dialogue—the empirical and the lyrical—represent, to varying degrees, departures from the norm. What makes the latter strategy especially provocative, however, is how forcefully it challenges the persistent if unspoken directive that a character's speech be differentiated not only from that of *other* characters but from that of the narrator. This is not to say that writers like Conrad or Woolf are uninterested in orality; like *Nineteen-Nineteen* or *Call It Sleep*, large quantities of novels like *Heart of Darkness*, *The Waves*, or *The Castle* are contained in quotation marks, presented as "spoken."[24] In the case of *Lord Jim*, for instance, Conrad even opens the novel by acknowledging its verbosity, noting that "[some reviewers] argued that no man could have been expected to talk all that time, and other men to listen so long. It was not, they said, very credible" (5). Conrad defends this decision on realist grounds, explaining that "men have been known . . . to sit up half the night 'swapping yarns'" (5). Yet the stronger defense may be that we are not intended to take this talk fully at face value, given that there is often only a vitiated sense that someone other than an implied version of Conrad, Kafka, or Faulkner is doing the "talking." At issue, once again, is whether the authors' (considerable) capacity for characterization might be competing with an equally strong or stronger drive toward authorization. While Woolf, for one, would actually worry over this aspect of her prose—wondering aloud in her diaries about whether she lacked that "reality gift" necessary for producing characters who, in Arnold Bennett's phrase, "vitally survive in the mind"—other writers evince less concern with disclosing the "synthetic" aspects of dialogue that the novel has traditionally worked hardest to conceal (*Writer's Diary* [hereafter WD] 56).[25] Consider the excerpt of *Lord Jim* in which Marlow, having just begun to compose a letter of introduction on Jim's behalf, pauses to consider the moral consequence of his actions:

"There was nothing but myself between him and the dark ocean. I had a sense of responsibility. If I spoke, would that motionless and suffering youth leap into the obscurity—clutch at the straw? I found out how difficult it may be sometimes to make a sound. There is a weird power in a spoken word.

---

24. In his afterword to *The Castle*, for instance, Pasley notes the "predominantly oral quality of [Kafka's] narrative style": "He is known to have judged his own stories above all by the effect which they had when read aloud" (321).

25. Bennett's remarks appear in his review of Woolf's novel *Jacob's Room*, published in *Cassell's Weekly*, March 28, 1923. They would subsequently spur an extended rebuttal from Woolf in her essay "Mr. Bennett and Mrs. Brown."

And why the devil not? I was asking myself persistently while I drove on with my writing." (105–6)

At first glance, what is most notable about the passage is how little it (like much of Marlow's account) seems to resemble the kind of extemporaneous talk that it purports to reproduce; in this sense, *Lord Jim*—like *Heart of Darkness*, with which it shares this trait—seems to require a suspension of readerly disbelief. More interesting, however, may be the way in which it seems to complicate the relationship between speaking and writing, between the "spoken word" and the written one. Even as Marlow clearly distinguishes between these discursive modes—between speaking, or "making a sound," and writing a letter—the novel itself appears to conflate them by so elevating the diction and syntax of allegedly voiced narration. Notwithstanding Conrad's considerable success in characterizing Marlow and staging a persuasive scene of telling,[26] it is also the case that the highly wrought quality of Conrad's prose might lull readers, in the long stretches between quotation marks, into forgetting that they are meant to be reading an unrehearsed account, delivered viva voce, rather than a writerly reconstruction. In this sense, the "authorial" dimension of speech that must be actively recovered in the case of Hurston or Roth here must be suppressed for the sake of maintaining the mimetic illusion.

Finally, somewhere in the middle of these representational extremes are writers like Henry James, Ernest Hemingway, and Gertrude Stein, whose texts feature dialogue perhaps best described as *mannerist* in its emphases and idiosyncrasies, which combine to make it almost instantly recognizable. Like empirical examples, the mannerists cull from actual speech while at the same time lyricizing those borrowed elements, lending them a more explicit authorial imprimatur.[27] Thus, even as such dialogue confronts readers with indelible proofs of an (implied) author's presence—in the form of, say, Stein's extremely restricted vocabulary,[28] Hemingway's relentless parataxis, or James's oddly placed adverbs—it also retains the underpinnings of "real" speech. Put another way, one could say that these authors specialize in the stylization of actual discursive features: highlighting speakers' documented tendency to

---

26. See Phelan's "dialogue essay," "Charlie Marlow, Narrative Theorist, Discourses on 'Youth,'" for a suggestive exploration of Conrad's construction of Marlow as a character narrator.

27. See Sarah Campbell's unpublished dissertation for a reference to a study by Richard Bridgman, *The Colloquial Style in America*, which hypothesizes a drift toward "colloquial" speech in the writing of several authors, including the three mentioned here (Campbell 5).

28. As Janet Malcolm notes in her account of reading *The Making of Americans*, so hermetic is Stein's vocabulary that "when she uses a new word it is like the entrance of a new character. It is thrilling" (*Two Lives* 136).

repeat themselves, for instance, or to affect the rhetorical tics of others, and making it an obsessive fixture of their prose. The mileage of such a strategy will vary; it might result, alternately, in the "unspeakable" language present in James's later work or in a language, like Hemingway's, that gives every appearance of being spoken. Yet even the speech in Hemingway's screenplay-like texts is less "real" than it initially seems; it may be more accurate to say instead that it effectively *signifies* the real. A corollary example might be found in the work of contemporary screenwriter Aaron Sorkin, who in discussing his own much-praised dialogue, acknowledges only his talent for "phonetically creat[ing] the sound of smart people talking."[29] So successful is Hemingway at similarly reproducing the "sound" of talk that readers may not realize how synthetic its substance remains.

What the Hemingway and Sorkin examples serve to further illustrate, however, is that conversational realism—what readers or viewers perceive to be an accurate facsimile of "people talking"—constitutes an aesthetic at once historically contingent and medium-specific. It is a truth perhaps best illustrated with reference to a well-known episode in American film history: namely, the difficulties encountered by Billy Wilder and Raymond Chandler in their attempt to adapt James M. Cain's novel *Double Indemnity* (1934) for the screen. On the page, Wilder and Chandler agreed, Cain's dialogue—much like Hemingway's—*looked* and *read* like a screenplay, as though the lines could be lifted verbatim. As it turned out, however, they couldn't; spoken aloud, Cain's words fell flat. As a result, the movie's dialogue was rewritten and uttered aloud to ensure the lines corresponded to norms of cinematic rather than literary talk (which are, in turn, distinct from those governing actual talk).[30] The question, of course, is how those norms come to be and how they maintain their hegemony. In other words, why—given how few people could ever approximate the tough, terse, yet impressively poetic, verbal stylings of, say, Jake Barnes or Walter Neff—did readers experience this particular stylization as that which best approximated the real? (And what does it say, moreover, that much of the speech most frequently framed as "real" is also that which tends to be coded as masculine—in its themes, its tone, or its stoical qualities?) These are questions that exceed the boundaries of this study but which nevertheless serve as a powerful reminder of the nonrealism of even the most

---

29. See Sorkin's interview with NPR from July 16, 2012.

30. For more on this episode, see Gene D. Phillips's *Creatures of Darkness*, pp. 170; and William Hare's *Early Film Noir*, pp. 27–28. See also Sara I. Rauma's unpublished study, *Cinematic Dialogue*, for a more comprehensive study of "dialogue metamorphosis" in novel-to-film adaptations, which provides additional context for the Cain example discussed above.

seemingly verisimilar speech, not to mention the nontransparency and noninevitability of verisimilitude itself.

Considered side by side, these three general tendencies—toward empiricism, lyricism, and mannerism—would seem to reflect a central tension within the modernist novel: between the desire to dramatize vocal plurality and reality, on the one hand, and the artistry required to produce its impression; that is, between "doing the police in different voices," to paraphrase Eliot's working title for "The Wasteland," and the authorial residue such *doing* leaves on the voices rendered. It is the same tension David Bordwell observes in the genre of art cinema, which, in his view, is always balanced between realism and authorial expressivity.[31] It may be no coincidence, given the influence of modernist fiction on these filmmakers, that the novels I consider disclose a similar dialectic, most evident in moments when their authors take the byways of character—that is to say, when they deploy an element traditionally associated with realism for a more self-expressive end.

If these dialogic tendencies are driven by distinct rhetorical purposes, then they are also seemingly united by a common desire to question the assumptions and conventions that had previously circumscribed the presentation and reception of talk. If literary modernism has not to date been strongly associated with dialogue—perhaps as a result of having been so closely linked to the pioneering of indirect discursive forms—the quality and diversity of dialogic experimentation alluded to above, and analyzed in the following chapters, suggest that the role of the "spoken word" in the shaping of modernist aesthetics has been underestimated. While Kacandes, for one, sees the preoccupation with talk as a signal feature of late twentieth-century global culture, resulting in the phenomenon she calls "talk fiction,"[32] my findings suggest that this fascination could be traced back further, to the early part of the twentieth century and, as Ivan Kreilkamp has argued, the latter part of the nineteenth.[33] A review of fictional and autobiographical writing produced by the authors considered here reveals that they shared a concern with speech both in their

---

31. Bordwell first articulated this argument in "The Art Cinema as a Mode of Film Practice" (1979).

32. See the preface of *Talk Fiction*, in which Kacandes defines this subgenre as one that "contain[s] features that promote in readers a sense of the interaction we associate with face-to-face conversation ('talk') *and* a sense of the contrivance of this interaction ('fiction')" (x). In this way, she further suggests, "talk fiction" entails a "hybridity of orality and textuality" that simultaneously links it to earlier conceptions of the novel as "conversational," and to subsequent ones, which were shaped by the "talk explosion" catalyzed by twentieth-century technologies (x).

33. This preoccupation is one that I discuss at greater length in the following chapters. For additional accounts of the Anglo-American novel's fascination with regional forms of talk, in particular, see Gavin Jones and Debra Rosenthal.

private lives and (to varying extents) in their public ones. It should come as no surprise, then, that such concern filtered into their work, resulting in talk's becoming an arresting feature of their texts as well as a recurring theme.

## III. NEW PARADIGMS: DIALOGUE, DISTANT READING, AND THE DIGITAL HUMANITIES

If much of the theoretical work on dialogue to date fails to account for the innovative presentation of and preoccupation with talk that emerged in modernist texts, it is equally important to acknowledge those studies that *do* acknowledge this dimension of late nineteenth- and early twentieth-century writing. In particular, my own analyses are indebted not only to the pioneering work of the theorists of narrative and the novels mentioned above but to monographs concerning dialogue in the work of single authors. Fogel, Haig, and Lambert, for instance, have each produced compelling accounts of character speech in the work of Conrad, Flaubert, and Dickens, respectively, while also offering insights that advance the study of dialogue more broadly.[34] A primary example is Lambert's discovery, in his study of quotation in Dickens's work, of a discursive hierarchy in Victorian fiction, whereby the directness with which authors render their characters' speech becomes an important metric of his or her characterological importance. Thus, Lambert argues, quoting characters' words, as opposed to paraphrasing them, confers on them a special prestige. Equally suggestive is what this claim implies: that an author's choice of discourse (direct or indirect) should be seen not just as a "stylistic choice" but as an ideological one, "a choice between two attitudes toward the integrity of speech" (23).

Fogel, in his study of dialogue in Conrad's fiction, takes a similarly "metrical" and ideological approach, employing what he calls an "abstract proportional model" to consider both the quality and the quantity of talk, the "relative amount spoken" by various characters (6).[35] Even more intriguing are his claims that this method is transferrable and that all novels similarly contain and express distinct "ideas of dialogue," which are "made available to the

---

34. Similarly suggestive is Campbell's previously cited unpublished dissertation, *The Turn of the Ear*, which explores the exciting implications of attending to talk in James's work.

35. See also Phelan for a brief but significant allusion to the importance of conversational quantity as well as quality and the extent to which talk's "location and its duration are part of the authorial communication" ("Imagining a Sequel" 250). As he explains, "The longer the duration of the scene, the more the author is marking its significance within the economy of the whole narrative" (250).

reader through formal repetition" and whose manifestation can range from the "subtle" to the "deliberately highly outlined and visible" (13).[36] Although Fogel confines his analyses to Conrad's novels, this notion—that novels have "recognizable ideas of dialogue" that find expression in their formal structures—is congenial with my own interpretation of modernist writers as particularly attentive to the rhetorical potential of conversational forms (13).[37] Indeed, my chapters explore what Fogel might call the distinct "ideas" of dialogue that surface within and across canonical modernist texts.

It is a theory of dialogue that also resonates with the one Ross puts forward, though less explicitly, in his studies of Faulkner's use of voice. "Just as an author's style grows in part out of differentiation within his or her prose," he argues, "so an author will usually manifest habitual ways of verbally structuring and arranging speech acts in dialogue" (*Inexhaustible Voice* 78). As an example, he cites Faulkner's frequent "transitions from one speaker's utterances to another's through some affirmative signal of comprehension": "Words like 'yes,' 'all right,' 'I see,' often begin one character's answer to another's talk" (78). While Ross identifies this pattern of "affirmative transitions," he seems more hesitant to interpret it (79). Fogel, by contrast, puts forward a strong reading of one of Conrad's more habitual representational tendencies: his extremely disproportionate distribution of speech, which, he posits, "ask[s] the reader to think about dialogue as formal and proportional rather than simply excessive," and as an index of power within the world of Conrad's novels (19).[38]

In their emphasis on the "habitual" features of character dialogue, Ross and Fogel highlight the utility of a macrolevel approach to fictional talk—that is, one that focuses not just on discrete instances of discourse but on the larger discursive architecture that emerges in a given work. It is a methodology that in many ways seems to anticipate Franco Moretti's attention to "networks," as exemplified by his efforts in *Distant Reading* to map, say, characters' interactions within *Hamlet* as a means of visualizing (and ultimately generating new

---

36. Intriguingly, Fogel hints at the broader applications of his theory, alluding to major nineteenth-century novelists like Austen, Balzac, Tolstoy, Stevenson, James, and Dostoevsky, but he does not pursue these possibilities further (12).

37. Particularly interesting is Fogel's translation of the novels' dialogic structure into visual form. He refers, in particular, to the "striping" between "direct speech and narrative prose" that is visible on the page (10). See also Mepham, who similarly explores the "graphic symbolism" of modernist dialogue ("Psychoanalysis" 424).

38. Fogel argues of Conrad that "no other novelist makes the abstract proportional model (the relative amount spoken) a figure on the page to be seen so consistently, so forcibly, or with such cumulative effect, as Conrad does in his 'political' works" (6).

interpretations of) its plot.[39] Of particular interest is that for the purposes of Moretti's analysis, "an interaction is a speech act," making his attempt to determine the play's "plot network" also a de facto elaboration of its dialogic network as well (214, 230). As he points out, this tactic is more easily applied to theater—in which "a network of speech acts is a network of actions"—than the novel, in which "direct discourse covers only a part of the plot," making it far more difficult to extract and represent the sum total of discursive interactions between characters (230). A further limitation, of course, is that this approach captures *that* something was said but cannot reflect more granular data (qualitative or quantitative) about that "something." In other words, the emphasis remains on *who* speaks rather than on *how*, in *what ways*, or for *how long* they speak. In this way, Moretti's method at once reinscribes dialogue's connection to character at the same time that it usefully models a way of abstracting it, distancing it from its original diegetic contexts for the sake of a more holistic and less character-dependent reading.

Of course, the notion that fictional utterances (or their absence) could be meaningfully tabulated is not new: Characters' lack of speech, for instance, has often been treated as a textual symptom of their oppression.[40] But the sophistication and suggestive power of such quantitatively driven analyses have grown, alongside the emergence of the digital humanities and Moretti's applications of its methods to the novel genre in particular.[41] Alex Woloch's *The One vs. the Many*, for instance, although not primarily concerned with character discourse, illustrates the benefits of combining close readings with a more quantitative perspective. In particular, Woloch's emphasis on the "asymmetric structure of characterization" within the realist novel—which entails a "major" character arrayed against numerous "minor" ones—is in many ways analogous to Fogel's analysis of the "asymmetric" or "disproportionate" arrangement of utterances in Conrad's novels. If Woloch's focus is on narrative rather than on specifically discursive asymmetries, he also hints at some overlap between the two, noting, much like Lambert, that a character's status

---

39. See "Network Theory, Plot Analysis" in Moretti's *Distant Reading*, pp. 211–40. As Moretti notes in a recent interview, one of the experiment's more interesting findings was "how central Horatio was to the play," a discovery that in turn "disproves our thinking about characters in binary terms: i.e., they're either a protagonist or a minor character[;] . . . now there seem to be more positions along this continuum."

40. A phenomenon I explore and seek to complicate in my article "Refusal to Tell," pp. 104–5.

41. At the same time, critiques of distant reading have also grown, focused both on its methodological shortcomings—especially its failure to engage with questions of race, gender, and sexuality—and recently on the field's own structural inequalities, which have received renewed attention in the wake of the #MeToo movement. See Lauren Klein's remarks at the 2018 MLA Annual Conference, "Distant Reading after Moretti," for a summary of these debates.

will often be telegraphed by their mode of speaking. To this end, he cites Tony Tanner's observation that Austen's *Emma*, for instance, "has a wider range of discourse than anyone else in the novel. She can out-talk, over-talk, everyone"; minor-ness, by contrast, has the opposite function, serving to "catalyze . . . inadequate speech" (qtd. in Woloch 87; Woloch 26). Like Fogel and Moretti, then, Woloch embodies what is in many ways a central presupposition of this project: that dialogue can convey information not just about individual characters, but about the broader ambitions of the novels that contain them.

Where I diverge from Woloch and Fogel, however, is in their reliance on a rhetoric of competition, violence, and force to describe character (and thus speaker) relations. It is true that Woloch confines his study to the nineteenth-century novel, and Fogel, to the work of a single novelist. Still, the investment in discerning asymmetry, disproportion, and disequilibrium seems to run the risk of excluding other, equally valid, interpretive possibilities. In particular, this sort of competitive paradigm fails to account for the more collaborative, consensual, and deliberately symmetrical forms of narrative and discursive arrangement that also belong to the heritage of the twentieth-century novel, as chapters 4 and 5 will especially show. As Molly Hite writes of *The Waves*, one of the primary ways in which it challenges "familiar habits of reading" is by refusing to concede the minor-ness of any character, insisting instead on the "equal status" of all six (xxxix). Especially problematic in this light is Woloch's mobilization of Bakhtin to this particular argumentative end. Though it is fair to trace back to Bakhtin an individualist conception of the novel, in which "the speaking person and his discourse" must "[strive] for social significance . . . as one distinctive language in a heteroglot world," it does not necessarily follow that Bakhtin's account has universal purchase (*The One vs. the Many* 336). What if a speaker's language is *not* "distinctive"? Or if we read the "speaking person" in collaboration with others, as David Kurnick suggests we do when reading James's late fiction ("What Does")?

The possibility is one that may be finding increased reinforcement among modernist scholars, who have long had to contend with commonplace assumptions about the solipsism and presumed interiority of modernism's seminal texts. As critics as various as Peter Nicholls, Seth Moglen, and Melba Cuddy-Keane have recently suggested, modernist fiction might be far more committed to envisioning collectivity and less invested in private subjectivity than has been alleged.[42] In Nicholls's words, it is "worth emphasizing the [modernist] attachment to public values since modernism has so often been

---

42. For more on modernism's concern with community and collectivity, see the entry for "Common Mind, Group Thinking" in Cuddy-Keane et al.'s *Modernism: Keywords*.

defined in terms of a turn to subjectivity" (274). This is not to say that themes of social stratification and competition, which Woloch sees as central to the nineteenth-century novel, lose all traction in the twentieth-century one, but rather that there are critical payoffs to considering character relations through a wider array of interpretive lenses. Thus, while it may be productive to read certain texts in terms of *agon*—in the manner of Woloch, who describes a scene from *The Sun Also Rises* as "another illustration or figuration of competition between characters (within discourse) as a form of battle or violent conflict"—this book seeks to recognize the variety of *other* ideas that character discourse could be used to "illustrate" or "figure" ("Minor Characters" 319).

A subsidiary goal of this book, then, is to counter the prevailing view of modernism as singularly concerned with the individual at the expense of the community or collective;[43] or, put another way, to suggest that the novel post-Flaubert has not simply been set on a progressively inward trajectory. It seems particularly significant, in this light, that the accounts linking the novel's rise to the individual's (such as Ian Watt's or, more recently, Nancy Armstrong's) end around 1900.[44] It may be true, as André Bleikasten has argued, that modernist writers "created sharply interiorized fictional spaces in which the reader was made to feel individual psyches at work" ("Faulkner" 81). But it is also true, if less widely recognized, that they also created compelling *externalized* spaces, often through the orchestration of character speech. David Herman suggests as much when he notes of *To the Lighthouse* that "Woolf's representations of talk require rethinking of modernist narrative construed as a foregrounding of inner experience" ("Dialogue" 75–76). In fact, one could further argue that not only in its depiction of speech but in its attention to speaking *as an activity,* modernist literature reveals itself to be at least as concerned with public experiences as with private ones.

It is with all this in mind, then, that this book calls for and seeks to model a way of reading modernist dialogue less "for" subjectivity than beyond it.

---

43. Particularly representative of this position is Georg Lukács, who claims in *Theory of the Novel* that the "modern novel" entails the "immoderate elevation of the subject" (117). More recently, Armstrong similarly takes for granted modernism's obsession with the subject, arguing that its texts reflect the "aesthetic imperative" to "not only tell the story of the group as that of the individual" but to "also tell the story of the group from the perspective of that individual" (110). Linda Wagner-Martin confirms this reading by asserting that in contrast to collectively minded fiction of the 1930s, "most modernist fiction did not emphasize community" and instead focused on "a character's individual psyche" (*The Modern American Novel* 96, 106).

44. Both Watt's *The Rise of the Novel* and Armstrong's *How Novels Think* present the novel's "rise" as coeval with the individual's. As Armstrong argues, "The history of the novel and the history of the modern subject are, quite literally, one and the same" (3). For an alternative account, see J. Hillis Miller, who suggests that the novel is "the form of literature developed to explore the various forms intersubjective relations may take" (22).

At a glance, such a project might seem counterintuitive: To suggest that fictional speech (traditionally regarded as an ambit of individuating difference) might be read more synchronously and systematically—that is, as a system—might be as surprising as to suggest it could serve as an expression of something more than discrete characters. Yet such a reading, one that "studies connections" within novels' "large groups" of utterances, is both possible and potentially productive—and even, perhaps, a not-unexpected proposition for twenty-first-century readers accustomed to the ubiquity and power of networks (Moretti, *Distant Reading* 212). The key, I suggest, is a willingness to shift one's interpretive sights: to attend to inter- and extrasubjective configurations as well as single subjects; to treat direct discourse as seriously as discourse in its indirect or free indirect forms; and to consider what the general shape of discourse in the novel might disclose—what ideas or ideals it might enact—that specific instances alone cannot.

CHAPTER 2

# The Consensual Voice

*Fantasies of Reciprocity in James and Hemingway*

EARLY IN Henry James's novel *The Ambassadors* (1903), shortly after the protagonist, Lambert Strether, makes the acquaintance of Maria Gostrey, the two take a stroll through the streets of Paris. As they walk, they talk; in the excerpt of their conversation below, Maria speaks first:

"You're doing something that you think not right."
    It so touched the place that he quite changed colour and his laugh grew almost awkward.
    "Am I enjoying it as much as *that*?"
    "You're not enjoying it, I think, so much as you ought."
    "I see"—he appeared thoughtfully to agree. "Great is my privilege."
    "Oh it's not your privilege! It has nothing to do with *me*. It has to do with yourself. Your failure's general."
    "Ah there you are!" he laughed. "It's the failure of Woollett. *That's* general."
    "The failure to enjoy," Miss Gostrey explained, "is what you mean."
    "Precisely. Woollett isn't sure it ought to enjoy." (A 25)

What is striking about this excerpt is not so much what Strether and Maria are saying (though the "low semanticity" of their dialogue is of interest itself)

---

1. A term originated by linguists, and used by sociologist Fred Davis, to describe the communicative function of clothing (5).

but rather how they are saying it, and especially the high degree of parallelism present in their exchange. Although the two characters barely know each other, it is clear that they have already become what Ruth Yeazell calls "verbal collaborators" (68). As they converse, each integrates the words of the other (*enjoy, privilege, failure*) into their own responses, resulting in an ever-lengthening, if only ambiguously referential, locutionary chain. Even more interesting is that this pattern is far from exceptional. In fact, this phenomenon—what I call *consensual speaking*—is diffuse within James's fiction, particularly in his later novels, which turn up copious evidence of this tendency for characters to, in Yeazell's words, "echo and qualify" each other's words (68):

"To lie 'for' her?" [. . .]
   "To lie *to* her, up and down, and in and out." (*The Golden Bowl* [hereafter GB] 414)

"He has done everything."
   "Oh—everything! Everything's nothing" (*The Wings of the Dove* [hereafter WD] 99)

". . . yet at the same time I see it as bearing you up."
   "Oh it does bear me up!" Strether laughed.
   "Well then as yours bears *me* nothing more's needed." (A 47)

At times, this reiterative habit is taken to almost absurd extremes ("Kept her, on that sweet construction, to be his mistress?" "Kept her, on that sweet construction, to be his mistress") (GB 419). James, as if to indicate his self-awareness about this dimension of his writing, will occasionally employ the verb *echo* to describe his characters' conversational activity, as when Strether "could only after a moment re-echo Miss Barrace" (A 326).

Yet despite the ubiquity of this sort of consensual talk in *The Ambassadors, The Wings of the Dove,* and *The Golden Bowl,* relatively little has been written about its motive or function within James's fictional universe.[2] A major exception has been Yeazell, who along with Leo Bersani has attended to many of the more idiosyncratic elements of Jamesian conversation. In her essay "Talking in James," she addresses the collaborative, highly concatenated nature of

---

2. Although Sharon Cameron and George Butte, among others, have written extensively about the intersubjective orientation of consciousness in James—the prevalence of "supposedly separate characters with supposedly separate consciousnesses, which then dominate each other"—their focus has been primarily on interpenetrating thought rather than speech (Cameron, *Thinking* 29).

speaking in the late novels, noting that Strether's exchanges with Maria Gostrey give readers the impression that "they were not so much separate persons as parts of a single self" (68). It is an insight that lies behind David Kurnick's more recent study of the "performative universalism" in James's fiction: the fact (which he agrees has "largely escaped critical commentary") that James's "quite different characters" all speak more or less alike (215)—and, one might add, more or less *un*like any other speakers, real or fictional. Yet despite his suggestive analysis of the "striking verbal similarities that hold across the whole cast of Jamesian characters," his conclusion—that such "similarities" signify the characters' "shared purposiveness" and awareness of themselves *as* characters, engaged in creating a "larger fictional product"—is only one possible interpretation (215, 216). While I agree that the "stylistic indistinction" of the late novels points toward the intriguing possibility of style's "collectivism," Kurnick's next step, to attribute this "collective" impulse to the novels' *characters*, seems at once too utopian[3] and too totalizing, since the purposes of characters within the texts appear more varied than this metafictional reading allows (216). The questions raised by the consensual speaking in James's late fiction therefore persist: Why do the characters talk this way? What, to paraphrase the title of Kurnick's essay, does Jamesian conversation *want*?

Further complicating this question is the fact that James was not alone among early twentieth-century Anglo-American writers in dramatizing a consensual orientation among his novels' speakers. Ernest Hemingway, whose style is inimical to James's in so many respects,[4] is well-known for his novels' highly recursive diction, and his characters' is often no less so. So homogeneous is the lexicon employed by the speakers of *The Sun Also Rises*, for instance, that Hemingway permits protagonist Jake Barnes to comment upon it: "The English spoken language—the upper classes, anyway—must have fewer words than the Eskimo . . . One phrase to mean everything" (153). In fact, nearly all of the novel's characters, upper-class or not, talk a similarly synchronized language, leading to exchanges whose primary purpose seems to be to confirm the characters' cooperative achievement of discursive uniformity. In contrast to James's critics, Hemingway's have been less hesitant to assign a motive to this particular tendency in his writing, suggesting that his charac-

---

3. Similarly aspirational may be James Carlos Rowe's conclusions, based on his readings of James's essays on American speech, that James "celebrates the social and political powers of language" and "treats verbal communication as the chief basis for forming what a proper critical theorist would term 'class consciousness'" (*Other* 31).

4. An opposition epitomized by the contrast between Hemingway's stated ambition to "write books without any extra words" and James's deprecation of "American simplicity": "I glory in the piling up of complications of every sort" (*Ernest Hemingway: Selected Letters* [hereafter EHSL] 215, qtd. in Edel 687).

ters' circumscribed vocabulary is part of a broader mimetic program: a way of conveying the fact that, as Gertrude Stein put it, describing her own *The Making of Americans*, "everybody sa[ys] the same thing over and over again with infinite variations but over and over again" ("Gradual Making" 138). Typical of this position is Robert Lamb, who makes the case that the function of repetition in Hemingway's conversation is to "inves[t] it with verisimilitude" (467).

Yet Hemingway's repetitions may be no better explained as a reality effect than James's are understood as a metafictional one. Rather than understand their work's dialogue as either singularly imitative or primarily reflective of characters' purposes, this chapter seeks to read it rhetorically—as an authorially expressive structure, capable of conveying ideological and affective commitments that exceed the boundaries of a single character. In proposing such a reading, I do not mean to suggest that the conversations' consensual arrangement should be seen solely as the product of authorial intent; rather, my approach here, as in the following chapters, remains indebted to the tradition of rhetorical narrative theory which, as Phelan conceives it, involves less "an author . . . extending a multidimensional . . . invitation to a reader" than a "synergy occurring between authorial agency, textual phenomena, and reader response" (*Narrative as Rhetoric* xi–xii). By drawing attention to the ways James and Hemingway, like the other writers considered in this study, came to use character discourse as a channel of communication and representation, it becomes clear that dialogue's relation to authorial "agency" has been underestimated.

In the case of James's and Hemingway's fiction, such a rhetorically oriented reading of character dialogue reveals both the extent of its stylization and the ideas that such stylization is being made to perform. In particular, this chapter seeks to demonstrate that conversation, through its symmetrical and response-privileging structure, functions to convey a longing for the kind of reciprocity and consensus that remain elusive within the world of the novels. The notion that these authors, in particular, might have been especially invested in—or even personally susceptible to—such fantasies of reciprocity finds support in their nonfiction writing, which, like their novels, registers a preoccupation with the ubiquity and threat of isolation. Hemingway's letters, for instance, refer frequently if glibly to loneliness—to being "lonely as the deuce" or "lonesome as hell"—while James, for his part, once admitted that the "deepest thing" about him was "*the essential loneliness of [his] life*" (EHSL 53, 205; qtd. in Edel 511). Their novels tend to express doubts about the feasibility of human connection even more forcefully. As Robert Pippin observes, James frequently "situates his characters in a social world where various uncertainties in any common form of life, and the profound and unstable dependencies . . . characteristic of modern societies, have made much more difficult . . . basic elements of mutual understanding" (147). It's a state of affairs that James has his character Van register in *The Awkward Age,* when he casually dismisses "the existence of friendship in big societies" (AA 13). Significantly, such commentary anticipates the cultural criticism of James's contemporaries like Van Wyck Brooks, who, fifteen years after the publication of *The Awkward Age,* would offer his own pessimistic assessment of friendship's viability in the "vast Sargasso Sea" of modern America (149).

More recently, scholars have increasingly recognized how regularly Anglo-American modernist authors concerned themselves with the theme of endangered affinity. Seth Moglen, for one, has argued that American modernist fiction frequently reflects "a crisis in the capacity for social solidarity at the public level, and for emotional and sexual intimacy at the private" (5). Meanwhile, Jessica Berman, borrowing from Raymond Williams and Walter Benjamin, has suggested that the defining event of the early part of the century was precisely a dissolution of "knowable communities" or "communit[ies] of listeners,"[5] a shift not lost on its novels, in which often "the only community available seems to be the 'community of speech'" (2). Given the dissipation of such "knowable" social groups, it is perhaps not surprising that so many modernist texts contain what Peter Nicholls calls "images of a failed sociality" (22); or that *The Ambassadors,* like *The Sun Also Rises* (often positioned as a reluctant heir to James's novel)[6] is populated by characters centrally concerned with redressing this problem of social failure.

What this chapter seeks to highlight is the extent to which that concern manifests not only thematically but also at the level of discourse: in the texture and textual arrangement of the novels' conversations, which cumulatively function to express a desire for what could variously be called *mutuality, reciprocity,* or *consensus.* In this sense, James's and Hemingway's work could be seen to model an inter- or trans-subjective conception of speech in which talk—much, as Cameron has argued of character in modern fiction—"does not seem to be an autonomous or independent entity" so much as a collectively engineered product (*Impersonality* 181). At the same time, and perhaps more important, their fiction illustrates the way modernist authors might co-opt dialogue for the sake of at once theatrically dramatizing and covertly editorializing about a particular set of ideas. In so doing, I'll suggest, their work highlights the potential for fictional dialogue to serve in postrealist fiction as

---

5. For Berman, James is one of the writers to "engage directly with early twentieth-century historical and political transformations of community" and whose novels "return again and again to issues of commonality, shared voice, and exchange of community" (3).

6. For more on the novel's indebtedness to *The Ambassadors,* see Hays and Houston.

an authorial back channel: a means of smuggling into narrative the kind of "omniscience" and modes of direct address that had been tacitly discouraged in the modernist novel.

## I. THE QUESTION OF JAMES'S SPEECH

Although James had long been conducting "fictional exploration[s] of vocal culture,"[7] it was not until 1905 that he offered a more sustained commentary on the subject in a talk delivered to the graduating class at Bryn Mawr (Jones 97). Titled "The Question of Our Speech," the lecture, later published in book form as one of two essays, makes an impassioned, pedantic, and frankly xenophobic plea for the restoration of linguistic standards, which James, recently returned to the US after a twenty-year hiatus, found sadly deteriorated.[8] More specifically, he exhorted the students to create a "virtual consensus of the educated . . . in regard to the *speech* . . . they profess to make use of," without which the "educative process" and the "imparting of a coherent culture," would, he claimed, "never get under way" (*The Question of Our Speech* [hereafter QS] 6). To aid in the development of this educated "consensus," James proposed a program of verbal emulation and imitation: "Imitating, yes; I commend to you . . . the imitation of formed and finished utterance wherever, among all the discords and deficiencies, that music steals upon your ear" (QS 50).

Given the roughly coeval production of this essay and his late novels, it is tempting to assume that this work of "verbal criticism" could be used to "explain" the intentions behind the idiosyncratic conversational dynamics of *The Ambassadors*, *The Wings of the Dove*, and *The Golden Bowl*.[9] Indeed, so readily and regularly do characters in these texts take up the words of their interlocutors that it almost seems as if they are being made to model the verbal habits—the "conscious, imitative speech"—that James prescribed as the antidote to the many "discords and deficiencies" of fin-de-siècle American English (QS 50). Of course, to suggest that James's novels be read merely or even primarily as illustrations of his theories would be to do them a disservice: His fiction is hardly that didactic. Yet what does, as James might say,

---

7. James himself "trace[d] his ideas of language back to the early 1880s, just prior to his creation of *The Bostonians*" (Jones 83).

8. In no small part, James implies, owing to the effects of immigrants on the English language. See Edel for a description of James's trip to New York in 1904, during which he felt himself to be in the "'torture rooms of the living idiom'" (qtd. in Edel 613).

9. As Jones notes, "We should not forget that James's late style coincided with his most outspoken remarks on 'the question of our speech,' which place linguistic speculation firmly in a social and cultural context" (97).

*beautifully* survive in the contemporaneous novels, more than any of the essay's specific recommendations, is its conviction that speech plays a crucial role in the creation and cultivation of community. Framed in James's terms, they exemplify the belief that "the question of our speech" is always already a "question of our relations with each other" (QS 10).

In this sense, James's essay makes explicit an ideology implicit in later fiction like *The Ambassadors*, whose protagonist, Lambert Strether, is almost fanatical about sustaining verbal consensus. Indeed, when considered in light of James's critical statements, the character Strether might emerge less as a biographical surrogate for James[10] than an ideological avatar, a representative or "ambassador" for his stated aspirations for discourse—even if in the novel they manifest in substantially transmuted form. If James's stated goal in this lecture is to achieve a nativist cultural consensus, Strether, by contrast, appears more invested in attaining a personal or affective one. Put another way, one could say that in *The Ambassadors*, James's public ambitions for spoken language manifest as Strether's far more private ones. This kind of movement is very much in keeping with what scholars like Jones have seen as a greater trajectory within James's fiction, whereby "questions of speech" are increasingly "related less to the public problems of social and political identity than to the radically private problems of individual consciousness" (97).

Yet it's clear that the "questions of speech" raised by the novel cannot be explained solely with reference to Strether's "individual consciousness." Although it's true he and Maria Gostrey are principally "responsible" for the drive toward consensus in the novel, such consensus-seeking is also a more unconsolidated and less character-centered activity. In other words, it is not only in the response-oriented structure of Strether and Maria's exchanges that we can locate evidence of a consensual impulse, it is also in the presence of syntactic and lexical features so textually diffuse as to be unattributable to individual speakers. In this sense, speech—much, as Cameron has noted, like consciousness—resists being psychologized within James's novel.[11] Instead, I'll suggest, James uses it as a vehicle for the expression of more-collective drives and *desiderata*, in this case, a longing for reciprocity that if only obliquely expressed in the novel's content is emphatically broadcast by its dialogic structures. If direct discourse, then, has long been identified as an area of difficulty

---

10. A commonplace of James criticism. As Edel puts it, like *The Awkward Age*'s Mr. Longdon, "or the unnamed narrator of *The Sacred Fount*" before him, "the curious New England 'ambassador' Lambert Strether would re-embody a new, still slightly bewildered novelist" (477).

11. See *Thinking in Henry James*, in which Cameron argues that in James's novels "consciousness is disengaged from the self" and "reconceived as extrinsic, made to take shape—indeed, to become social—as an *inter*subjective phenomenon" (77).

within James's fiction—and an element of the novel about which James himself had conflicted feelings[12]—it is also treated, at least in the fictional world of *The Ambassadors,* as a potential avenue of interrelation and rapprochement.

## II. WISHFUL SPEAKING IN *THE AMBASSADORS*

Strether's conversations with Maria offer the most vivid example of the diegetic interest in verbal consensus-building, epitomized by the conversation excerpted at the chapter's start. Violating as they do both narrative economies and conversational ones,[13] the readerly lessons to be learned from such protracted yet content-poor exchanges is that speakers in *The Ambassadors* are less interested in communication per se than in the sheer fact of interaction: in achieving what linguist Bronisław Malinowski describes as "phatic communion," that "type of speech in which ties of union are created by a mere exchange of words" (285). Arrayed across the "mere laid table of conversation," as Strether puts it, neither he nor Maria can condone "forsaking the board" (A 19).

At first glance, it would be easy to conclude that the impulse toward verbal "communion" originates solely with Strether. Given what readers learn of his sentimental history, it's not hard to discern a psychological motive for his assiduity. "It had been," Strether reflects, "a dreadful cheerful sociable solitude, a solitude of life or choice, of community; but though there had been people enough all round it there had been but three or four persons *in* it" (61). Of these "three or four persons," two, his wife and son, have died. In retrospect, Strether now sees these tragedies as part of a greater pattern of relational failure: of his having "failed, as he considered, in everything, in each relation" (61). But if he has failed, he now realizes he has also *been* failed. Indeed, it is not until he has left this "life . . . of community" to travel abroad that he discovers how socially impoverished a "life," and how limited a "community," his has been. Only after his first conversation with Maria, for instance, does he "bec[o]me aware of how much there had been in him of response; when the

---

12. See James's comments about dialogue in the preface to *The Awkward Age,* p. 106, quoted in the previous chapter. Of particular concern to James was his suspicion that readers harbored narrow and unnecessarily rigid preconceptions about what constituted "good" dialogue: "that really constructive dialogue, dialogue organic and dramatic, speaking for itself, representing and embodying substance and form, is among us an uncanny abhorrent thing, not to be dealt with on any terms" (107).

13. Here, I am relying on the maxims underlying Grice's "cooperative principle," especially as it pertains to "quantity" in conversation: "Make your contribution as informative as required" and "Do not make your contribution more informative than is required" (26).

tone of her own rejoinder, as well as the play of something more in her face . . . seemed to notify him" (19). That Strether is so attentive both to Maria's "rejoinder" and his own (underutilized) capacity for "response" suggests his investment in dialogue as both a practice and a guiding ideal, one he seems to associate specifically with Europe. Compared to the singular "voice . . . of Woollett," Paris, with its "talk more or less polyglot," would appear the locale far better aligned with Strether's values (31, 109).

So anxious is Strether to access this sort of intersubjective ideal, in fact, that he will routinely subordinate his own voice to achieve it. When Maria labels Mrs. Newsome a "swell," for instance, he is only too ready to take up her term ("Oh yes, she's rather a swell!") (50). A page later, Maria offers a further revision ("She's just a *moral* swell"), and Strether "accepted gaily enough the definition": "'Yes—I really think that describes her'" (52). It is only one of innumerable instances in which Strether will eagerly "accept" the definition of another. From the opening pages of the novel, readers see widespread evidence of Strether's citational habit, his practice of off-handedly quoting others: "He's 'notoriously,' as he put it himself, not from Boston" (73); "it had been 'given him,' as they said at Woollett" (95); "Chad . . . was more than ever, in Miss Barrace's great sense, wonderful" (127); "what you call a *parti pris*" (230). Most famously, he will adopt Little Bilham's characterization of Chad's relationship as a "virtuous attachment" and thus quite literally take "his" word for it (112). Yet Strether's apparent deference to the discourse *of* others should not conceal what seems to be a competing desire: to have his own discourse acknowledged *by* others. In the novel's third book, we find Strether "waiting . . . to get back from [Maria] in some mirrored form her impressions and conclusions," not unlike Charlotte Stant, in *The Golden Bowl*, who waited "till [The Prince] spoke again with a gesture that matched" (A 86; GB 291). Short of "mute communication"—a mysterious prospect that is regularly held up as the *sine qua non* of intimacy in James's fiction—such "mirroring" or "matching" is often treated in the late novels (however mistakenly) as the greatest possible proof of fellowship (GB 139).

Even as Strether perceives conversation with Maria as a means of generating intimacy, however, the novel suggests that talk can also serve to forestall it and allow a character like Strether to shelter indefinitely in the realm of purely verbal relations. Particularly illustrative of dialogue's ambivalent status as at once a form of flirtation and a form of deferral is Strether and Maria's shared allusion to Waymarsh's "sacred rage." On the one hand, the phrase, which "was to become between them, for convenient comprehension, the description of one of his periodical necessities," would seem to testify to the pair's affective synchrony (41). Indeed, James is hardly alone in evoking a "private phraseology," as Maggie Verver calls it, to telegraph two characters' affinity (GB 359). One thinks of Proust's lovers, Swann and Odette, whose phrase, "Do a cattleya,'" having become for them

> a simple verb which they would employ without thinking when they wished to refer to the act of physical possession . . . survived to commemorate in their vocabulary the long-forgotten custom from which it sprang. (331)

Like "the sacred rage," to "do a cattleya" becomes a shorthand, even a shibboleth, for the couple, the sort of "esoteric vocabulary understood only by the members of a closed social world" (Yeazell 70). Yet while Swann and Odette's metaphor served to "commemorate" their love ("elle le commémorait"), such as it is, Strether and Maria's can only ever gesture, obliquely, toward the possibility of it. Unlike Proust's couple, James's never share a kiss, never consummate their flirtations.[14] Their phrase, in other words, does not "signify" or memorialize an event—it *is* the event. Behind this brief exchange, as behind perhaps all of Strether's conversations with Maria and her continental double, Marie, thus lies another aspiration: that shared language might be not just the *byproduct* of mutual understanding, as in *Un amour de Swann*, but its impetus. In this sense, the exchanges with Maria would seem to enact central fantasies of Strether's: that language is sufficient to engineer intimacy; that verbal intercourse might not just substitute for, but actually be superior to, its sexual variant, Proust's "act of physical possession." Put another way, one could say that Strether is engaged in *wishful speaking*: an attempt to realize, through talk alone, the "possibility of any mutuality" to which Pippin, for one, claims James was similarly committed (148).

What complicates this conclusion, however, is that such wishful behavior is not confined to Strether. Thus, alongside this psychological explanation for the novel's distinct locutionary tendencies dwell other, less characterologically determined ones. Attesting to the diffuseness of this fantasy is the fact that it undergirds James's novels beyond *The Ambassadors*, particularly the later novels, in which characters place (or misplace) similar hopes in speech. One thinks especially of John Marcher in "The Beast in the Jungle" for whom sharing the "real truth" with May Bartram is enough "to constitute between them a sensible bond," or *The Awkward Age*'s Mr. Longdon, for whom "talking on a bench" is the greatest intimacy to which one can aspire, and who imagines, like Marcher, that a shared "secret" or "hope" could qualify as "[the thing]

---

14. This is very much in keeping with E. M. Forster's famous observation that James's characters "are incapable of fun, of rapid motion, of carnality. . . . Their clothes will not take off" (*Aspects* 229).

that will have drawn us together" (*Collected Short Stories* [hereafter CS] 747; AA 147, 247). That Strether invests so much in his verbal rapport with Maria only to turn down the possibility of a physical or conjugal one at the end suggests strongly that when he extols the need "to live," he may mean less "to live sexually," as Peter Brooks has suggested, than to live emotionally, intellectually, relationally (114). Certainly, there is an undercurrent of desire animating his and Maria's tête-à-têtes. Yet the fact that Strether, like Longdon and Marcher, similarly settles for talk alone suggests that James's male protagonists make a habit of imbuing speech with magical sublimating properties.

While it is Strether, then, who may most prominently embody this attitude, there is also evidence that the fantasy of verbally orchestrated intimacy is more widely distributed both within *The Ambassadors* and beyond it, in the fiction James produced shortly before and after. Indeed, the dialogue-heavy novels that followed James's foray into theater seem to be constructed with this ambition in mind: represented speech becomes increasingly elliptical, vague, and incomplete, thus inviting (even demanding) further elaboration or interrogation by the fictional listener.[15] In *The Turn of The Screw*, for instance, the governess's conversations with Mrs. Grose are characterized by a disproportionate number of open-ended statements whose construction, even when not in interrogative form, necessitates that the interlocutor supply the missing object: "But not to the degree to contaminate—" (11); "But aren't they all—?" (10); "Then you *have* known him—?" (11); "That was the great reason—" (48); "You leave him—?" (65); "and I can't think wherever she must have picked up—" (74); "Then in spite of yesterday you *believe*—" (75). It is as if James had discovered a means of dramatizing, through the syntax and punctuation of his characters' speech, the hunger for response—for the experience of "withness"—that haunts many of the characters in his later fiction.[16]

And, perhaps, haunted James himself. One can't help thinking here of the author's own desire for public recognition, his "disappointment in the marketplace as well as the world of letters" (Edel 396). As Edel puts it, "He had felt so many times in his life that the world did not want his art and did not recognize his genius" (684). In 1908, still stung by the disastrous reception of *Guy*

---

15. See Cynthia Ozick, who argues that after "the 1895 crux" of *Guy Domville*, James "would never again write the kind of novel he had written during his earlier years, before he began playwriting" (xiv; Edel 434). Instead, as Edel points out, he now "imported the stage into his novels" (434). See also Kurnick's *Empty Houses*.

16. On the subject of "punctuation's ability to convey meaning beyond a grammatical or syntactical function," see Elizabeth Bonapfel (79). The other reference here is to the propensity of characters in James's later fiction to seek others willing to "watch," "wait," or "act" *with* them. It is a desire that reaches an apotheosis in "The Beast in the Jungle" (1903), which is centrally about Marcher's hope that May should "watch with" him (CS 746).

*Domville*, James was doubly shocked by the poor sales of *The New York Edition*: "The non-response of *both* sources," he wrote to his agent, James Pinker, "has left me rather high and dry" (qtd. in Edel 663). It may be no coincidence, then, that some of his most biographically proximate characters seem similarly sensitized to the experience of nonresponse. Thus it is not only Strether, the "perfectly equipped failure," but his earlier iteration, Mr. Longdon, who expresses this note of frustration: "I was no success as a young man. I mean of the sort that would have made most difference. People wouldn't look at me" (A 40; AA 20). "Well, we shall look at you," Vanderbank responds (AA 20). The worst fate, such evidence implies, is that of being *not* looked at, *not* responded to. It is almost as if in his fiction James anticipated the idea Bakhtin would formulate in his later theories: that "for the word (and consequently, for a human being) there is nothing more terrible than a lack of response" (*Speech Genres* 127).

And nothing more desirable, perhaps, for James's fictional subjects than the presence of one. It is in this light that it becomes possible to suggest that the synchronicity among James's speakers is best explained neither as a stylistic provocation nor as a reflection of James's "social Utopianism" (Rowe, *Other* 17). Instead, it might most plausibly be read as the manifestation in textual form of certain aspirations—to recognition and reciprocity—with which James himself identified. Indeed, by portraying a linguistic landscape at once so conspicuously uniform and so uniformly unnatural, James essentially signals his intention to use dialogue as an expressive rather than simply "reflective" device. At a moment when many of his contemporaries in American letters were engaged in reproducing real dialects,[17] James was more focused on inventing one: on using dialogue to communicate aspirations that the plots of his novels would fail to sustain.

### III. "MAKING OUT," "TAKING IN," "KEEPING UP": JAMES'S ASPIRATIONAL PHRASEOLOGY

To understand both the impetus and the ends of James's unmimetic talk, however, requires a closer look at its mechanics. For what we find is that dialogue in *The Ambassadors* is marked not only by its degree of symmetry but also by a number of equally estranging and revealing mannerisms. In addition to the textual phenomena discussed above (echolalia, compulsive citation, con-

---

17. See Jones, who argues that "late-nineteenth-century America was crazy about dialect literature" and the vocal difference it dramatized (1). The result, as he argues in his first chapter, was that writers attempted to record and "redact an astounding variety of cultural voices" (4).

catenated speaking), there are other recurring features of character discourse whose idiosyncrasy and contravention of verisimilitude seem to require "explanation." Most distinctive, perhaps, is the use of phrasal verbs, those compounds of verbs and modifying particles that are so typical of Jamesian conversation. In *The Ambassadors* alone, characters regularly take in, take out, take from, or take up; come in, come on, come out, come down, or come up. Historically, the linguistic category has been of great interest to lexicologists, from Samuel Johnson to James's near-contemporary William Pearsall Smith, who noted that "there is hardly any action or attitude of one human being to another which cannot be expressed by means of these phrasal verbs" (254).[18] Yet they have not roused the interest of literary critics, despite the fact that such collocations pullulate in his fiction, sometimes to almost comical extent. Take, for instance, Maria's introductory gambit to Strether:

> If you'll only come on further as you *have* come . . . you'll at any rate make out. My own fate has been too many for me, and I've succumbed to it. I'm a general guide—to "Europe" don't you know? I wait for people—I put them through. I pick them up—I set them down . . . I take people, as I've told you, about. (A 25–26)

Here, Maria describes her activities almost exclusively by means of these verbal formula: in terms of "coming on," "making out," "waiting for," "putting through," "picking up," "setting . . . down," and "taking about." In this case, the primary function may be self-mockery—Maria's deflation of her importance as a "general guide." But given the frequency with which these constructions appear in characters' speech, it seems likely they have another, less ironic functionality. If Smith, for one, praises the expressive power of such compounds, James's characters seem to take advantage of the degree to which they *don't* express: their capacity to leave events and actions deliberately underdetermined. What does it mean, after all, for Maria to "pick people up," "set them down" or "put them through"?

Even more important than whether readers understand, however, may be the implied presumption that other *characters* will. Like the "language of enigmatic praise" in which James's characters speak, or the "high generality of [their] diction," these constructions have the benefit of both heightening the impression of intimacy and, just as important, allowing the greatest possible margin for error between speakers (Yeazell 69; Levenson 15). In this

---

18. Johnson, for his part, bemoaned the difficulty of indexing this "kind of composition, more frequent in our language than perhaps in any other," in which we "modify the signification of many verbs by a particle subjoined" (12).

sense, the phrasal verbs that recur in *The Ambassadors* may be designed less to mean than to place-hold: to signal the characters' desire to map out some maximally neutral, and thus easily shared, verbal terrain. Thus, these formulas seem to attest less to the impossibility of referential meaning (as others have suggested)[19] than to the characters' affected confidence in its certainty: that is, their commitment to preserving the illusion that so inevitable is successful signification that their conversations can sustain even the use of such thin and barely meaningful signifiers.

Similarly suggestive in this regard is the characters' use of what might be called *pseudo-idioms*: codified expressions that have been tweaked just enough to destabilize their clichéd status. Indeed, it can be difficult to locate within *The Ambassadors* a cliché that *hasn't* been emended in some way, whether by the insertion of an adverb ("as if you wanted one immediately to know the worst") (24); a prepositional phrase ("We've tired out, between us, her patience"; "there at any rate it *is*") (187); or some other qualifying clause ("But there—as usual—we are!; "He can bear it—the way I strike him as going—no longer"; "You're looking, this morning, as fit as a flea"; "I don't do it, for instance—some people do, you know—for the money") (247, 192, 186, 26). At other times, however, the deviation from fixed expression is more elaborate, and the effect, more ambiguous. After dispatching a message to Woollett, for instance, Strether considers that his gesture was at best "a sort of whistling in the dark":

> It was unmistakable moreover that the sense of being in the dark now pressed on him more sharply—creating thereby the need for a louder and livelier whistle. He whistled long and hard after sending his message; he whistled again and again in celebration of Chad's news. (196)

The following paragraph further embellishes on this figure, though it soon becomes clear that ownership of this riff might have passed from Strether to the narrator, who refers to "the increase of his darkness . . . and the quickening, as I have called it, of his tune" (197). What makes the ambiguous nature of attribution so interesting here is what it implies about the narrative's complicity in the characters' verbal schemes. As with phrasal verbs, the goal of these pseudo-idioms seems less to "mean" than to demonstrate mastery of language designed to maximize ambiguity. By deploying, with only the most minimal revisions, these agreed-upon phrases, characters showcase their capacity for

---

19. I am thinking here of what scholar Margery Sabin calls Bersani's "dismissal of referential meaning in the book," but also of Cameron, who argues that in *The Golden Bowl* "speech is emptied of significant implication" (Sabin 96; Cameron, *Thinking* 85).

nonpragmatic discourse—their facility with talk designed to obfuscate, rather than communicate, in the interest of safeguarding the promise of *eventual* signification.

The manifest and undifferentiated status of what would otherwise seem to qualify as highly idiosyncratic linguistic traits has several implications. On the one hand, this feature of the novel would seem to dramatize James's ideas about language's dynamism and its social power. It is not, after all, until after speaking with Little Bilham that Maria can declare him to be "one of *us*!," a conclusion that Strether takes less as an indication of tribalism than as proof of language's consolidating potential; to his mind, "a quick unanimity between the two appeared to have phrased itself in half a dozen remarks" (83). From Strether's perspective, then, Maria and Chad, within the space of just a "half-dozen remarks," are on the verge of realizing the sort of "virtual consensus" that James called for in his lecture and that Strether himself has so doggedly pursued.

Yet readers will recognize that such discursively produced "consensus" is hardly an unmitigated good; indeed, *The Ambassadors* makes clear the costs (personal as well as ethical and political) of privileging unanimity—namely, the attenuation of difference. "In Little Bilham's company," Strether notes at one point, "contrarieties in general dropped" (83). Much the same, however, could be said of almost any character in the novel, though it is Strether who seems most inimical to contrariety. Confronted with or, in James's words, "sinking . . . up to his middle in the Difference," Strether almost inevitably strives to neutralize or assimilate it (*Complete Notebooks* [hereafter CN] 562).

Of particular concern is his failure to register the fundamentally divergent stakes of seeking to minimize locutionary difference—as he does in his conversations with Maria—and his suppression of other forms of diversity. This impulse is particularly evident during his encounter with the potentially "unfamiliar phenomenon" of Marie de Vionnet (129). Though he anticipates a *"femme du monde,"* once they begin to talk, Strether is almost immediately reassured: "She—oh incontestably, yes—*differed* less; differed, that is, scarcely at all—well, superficially speaking, from Mrs. Newsome or even from Mrs. Pocock" (129). Indeed, by the end of their conversation, he is convinced of her "common humanity": "She did come out, and certainly to his relief, but she came out as the usual thing" (129).

As the novel eventually reveals, however, this assessment could hardly be less precise: Madame de Vionnet does "differ"; she is not the "usual thing." And the implication is that Strether, desirous of finding something "usual," has simply persuaded himself that he *has*: aided in this effort both by the epistemological generosity of his claims and by the kinds of verbal formulas ("come out") that function to muffle the slightest intimation of difference. Significantly, they do the same for Madame de Vionnet, a native French speaker who nonetheless speaks the same strangely idiomatic English as the novel's Anglophones: "It's just there that, since you've taken it up and are committed to it, it most intensely becomes yours," she explains to Strether, during their colloquy in Notre Dame (183). It is only when Marie's ontological "difference" asserts itself—when she is exposed as unvirtuous—that her verbal difference suddenly does, too: Then, for the first time in the novel, Marie begins to speak French. This change, Strether reflects, had the "odd" effect of "fairly veiling [Marie's] identity, shifting her back into a more voluble class or race to the intense audibility of which he was by this time inured" (312). Though he may couch it in heavily qualified, almost incomprehensible, language, what is clear in this moment is that Marie is being *punished* for her difference: demoted, in Strether's mind, from a privileged class to a "more voluble" one, and from an embodiment of a cosmopolitan ideal, to a representative of a single "race." By choosing to synchronize her shift in language with her shift in "class" and "race," James implies that the price of consensus might be conformity—of identity and ethnicity, as well as ideology.

In this way, *The Ambassadors* reveals how radically the fantasies of community Strether harbors are out of touch with its lived reality, as represented not only by the repressive (and openly satirized) regime of Woollett, but also by what the concluding chapters show to be the perhaps equally exclusionary society of Paris. Far from endorsing the consensual ideal James endorses in his speech, then, *The Ambassadors* reveals itself to be an illumination of its perils. In straining toward consensus, Strether has imagined it where it did not exist and has overlooked it where it did—most notably, between Marie and Chad. Indeed, the novel goes so far as to suggest that Strether's pursuit of mutual understanding might be nearly as dubious (ethically, epistemologically) as Woollett's policy of isolationism. To accept unconditionally the words of another may be to promote a superficial understanding, but it is also to minimize the chance of reaching a more profound one. Enamored as Strether is of what Barthes calls "the discourse of others," he fails to vet such discourse adequately for truth (S/Z 184). "*Do* take it from me," Little Bilham assures Strether, who of course does (A 112). But at some cost; for in adopting Little Bilham's characterization of Chad's relationship as a "virtuous attachment," Strether recuses himself from the task of having to characterize it for himself. In this sense, the phrase becomes not only a "simplifying rubric" but a stultifying one (P. Weinstein 131).

James's fiction thus seems to significantly complicate the assertions of his criticism by suggesting that codified language may have less a unifying effect—serving to galvanize community—than an enervating one. This idea is epitomized, perhaps most poignantly, by an early passage in the novel, when Strether refers twice in the space of one paragraph to the death of his "little dull boy" (61). As becomes clear, this epithet has served to perpetuate a possibly false image of his son, who may be quite different than this memorializing language would imply.[20] It is only when he belatedly interrogates the cliché, however, that Strether begins to consider what it may have disguised: "It was the soreness of the remorse that the child had in all likelihood not been dull— had been dull . . . mainly because the father had been unwittingly selfish" (61). In this light, it is significant that James himself relied on a similar technique in the wake of his friend Constance Fenimore Woolson's suicide, when he "came to rest in a conventional and distancing judgment—'fundamentally tragic being!'" (Ozick xx). However incidental, such an anecdote reveals the affective power rhetorical formulas may have held (however unconsciously) for James, as well as for his characters, and the corresponding risk of self-delusion run by those who rely too heavily upon them.

There may be no better illustration of the epistemological risks of uncritically adopting linguistic formula than Strether's use of the phrase "let oneself go." Strether not only hopes to "let himself recklessly go"; he prescribes the same course of action to Waymarsh ("*Let* yourself, on the contrary, go") and playfully bemoans to Mrs. Pocock his failure to follow his own advice: "Oh, I've not let myself go very far. . . . I'm only afraid of showing I haven't let myself go far enough" (118, 275, 222). It is something of a comic punch line, then, that Strether should share this seemingly unobjectionable ambition with a character who is perhaps his antithesis in modernist fiction: Joyce's Molly Bloom. When, during her closing monologue in *Ulysses*, she wishes of her lover that "he was here or somebody to let myself go with," her intended meaning could hardly be more different from that of the prudish Strether, who is shocked when confronted with proof of precisely the sort of unvirtuous behavior Molly is proposing (U 18.584–85). But it only goes to show how radically nonconsensual even the most seemingly centripetal language may be. It is a fact that James was, perhaps, able to admit only in his fiction. In his lecture "The Question of Our Speech," James asked his audience

> to take it from me, as the very moral of these remarks, that the way we say a thing, or fail to say it, fail to learn to say it, has an importance in life that it is impossible to overstate—a far-reaching importance, as the very hinge of the relation of man to man. (QS 21)

---

20. For more on the way tropes in James's fiction work to promote magical thinking, see Yeazell, who argues that metaphors act as "ways of mediating . . . dangerous knowledge"; or Kurnick's discussion of the mystifying effects of the image of Kate's analogy of Milly to a "dove" (Yeazell, *Language* 39; Kurnick, "What Does" 219).

That even James's hyperconscious speakers may fail to think about "the way [they] say a thing" is only a testament, then, to the difficulty of securing the "relation of man to man": of ensuring the sort of verbal and social consensus that James's fictions at least intermittently continue to long for.

## IV. HEMINGWAY'S RHETORIC OF DISAVOWAL

If *The Ambassadors'* characters retain faith in conversation's capacity to realize consensus, however misguided, the cast of *The Sun Also Rises*, by contrast, openly scorns such possibilities. Unlike James's characters, Hemingway's express few hopes that their exchanges could "do" or mean anything. When early in the novel Jake asks Robert Cohn, "What was the matter?" Cohn responds, enigmatically, "talking" (21). His answer is in many ways paradigmatic of attitudes throughout the novel, which is rife with similar disparagements of speaking: "Well, let's shut up about it" (34); "Yes, it's a rotten shame. But there's no use talking about it, is there?" (55); "Let's not talk. Talking's all bilge" (62); "Don't let's ever talk about it" (247); "You'll lose it if you talk about it" (249). Repeatedly, Jake and Brett admonish each other not to "talk like a fool"; Jake, at one point, confesses to having done so ("when I'm low I talk like a fool") (30, 34, 88, 63). In this light, one could say that if James uses dialogue to dramatize a collective longing for reciprocity, Hemingway, at least at first glance, seems to position it antithetically—as an obstacle to real intimacy and authentic exchange.

Considering historical context, it may be hardly surprising that Hemingway attributes to characters a sense of speech as devalued currency. As James Dawes has noted, World War I was widely believed to have "initiate[d] a semantic crisis, a crisis of meaning premised upon disbelief in language's ability effectively to refer to and intervene in the material world" (131).[21] Indeed, James himself—writing just over a decade after publication of *The Ambassadors* and a year after the onset of the war—would reach a strikingly similar conclusion in the pages of *The New York Times*:

> One finds in the midst of all this as hard to apply one's words as to endure one's thoughts. The war has used up words; they have weakened, they have deteriorated like motor car tires; they have, like millions of other things, been more overstrained and knocked about and voided of the happy sem-

---

21. See Paul Fussell for a comprehensive study of the war's transformative effects on language, as well as Vincent Sherry.

blance during the last six months than in all the long ages before, and we are now confronted with a depreciation of all our terms, or otherwise speaking, with a loss of expression, through increase of limpness, that may well make us wonder what ghosts will be left to walk.[22]

In its lament for the condition of the English language, James's comments represent a grim reversal of the message he offered at Bryn Mawr; here, he raises "the question of our speech" only to foreclose on the possibility of an answer. That a similar pessimism, and a similar rhetoric of "deterioration" and "depreciation," find their way into *The Sun Also Rises* is not surprising. As is widely known, Hemingway transcribed this excerpt of James's essay onto a typescript page of *A Farewell to Arms*, a novel whose hero famously decries "abstract words such as glory, honor, courage, or hallow": "those big words," as Stephen Dedalus called them, "which make us so unhappy" (*A Farewell to Arms* [hereafter AFTA] 185; U 2.264). In this context, it would be easy to conclude that the denigration of speech in *The Sun Also Rises* is meant to provide textual confirmation for the idea that words were "used up,"[23] with the characters' radically diminished diction serving to reflect a verbally impoverished, postwar reality.

Yet a closer examination of dialogue's presentation suggests that its chronic deprecation by the novel's characters exists in tension with Hemingway's own investment in direct discourse as a channel of authorial communication. Put another way, even as the novel presents a narrative of speech as failed, it provides copious evidence to the contrary: offering, through the abundance and prominence of dialogue, proof of both diegetic and extradiegetic faith in talk's expressive potential. Thus, at the same time that his characters discredit the capacity of discrete words to mean, they continually, even compulsively, turn to conversation and thus, like James's characters, reveal their reliance on the mechanisms of dialogue to sustain a sense of affinity and social cohesion widely perceived in the world of the novel to be lost.

Hemingway himself was frank about the book's elegiac quality: the fact that it was about a "lost generation," metonymically represented by protagonist Jake Barnes, who suffers from "the loss or atrophy of certain non-replaceable parts" (EHSL 223). And it is haunted equally by the loss of affective possibility, by both "failed efforts at heterosexual connection" and the "fragility . . . of

---

22. Preston Lockwood, "Henry James's First Interview."
23. Zoe Trodd, for one, has recently argued that Hemingway's style should be understood as a calculated response to linguistic depreciation, noting that his "limited vocabulary, few adjectives, and concrete descriptions of specific objects all countered with minimalism the problem of 'used up' words" (8).

male homosocial friendship," as well as by the more generalized "isolation" which finds "all of the major characters . . . searching for acceptance and a sense of community" (Moglen 29; Helbig 85).[24] In this light, it is notable that language in *The Sun Also Rises* should be a demonstrably communal property, "implicitly and explicitly shared," rather than "purified through a single consciousness," as David Humphries has argued (117). Faced with the absence or infeasibility of naturally occurring forms of consensus, characters try to manufacture their own. In this sense, the dwelling on talk's "failure" should be read more as ritual behavior than as a meaningful disavowal—especially in the context of what, I'll suggest, is dialogue's consistently ironic functionality within the text.

What is "failed" or "used up," in other words, is less talk in general and more a specific *type* of talk: language that asserts its capacity to signify in a literal, straightforward way. In this sense, one could say that the characters' approach to dialogue reproduces Hemingway's own, as reflected in the conversation in his novels, whose superficially naturalistic qualities have often functioned to conceal (or at least distract readerly attention from) their underlying stylization. Like James, then, Hemingway departs from the mimetic tradition of dialogue use to craft a highly mannered discourse that, cumulatively, conveys a set of ideas at once omnipresent yet never explicit in the rest of the novel. It is only by reading dialogue *across* speakers that this message about language's capacities becomes evident. In this way, Hemingway's writing, like James's, attests to dialogue's capacity to signify not just locally in the narrative, but globally—at scale. In contrast to *The Ambassadors*, however, *The Sun Also Rises* also illustrates one additional readerly lesson: the importance of being attentive both to dialogic synchronies and to characters who depart from them. In the case of Hemingway's novel, it is Robert Cohn who emphatically diverges from the discursive norm and who embodies modes of expression that are linked, temporally, to the prewar era and, ideologically, to the kinds of idealism, abstraction, and individualism that are increasingly revealed to be not just in tension but actually incompatible with the other speakers' discursively manifested values. Historically, the perceived realism of Hemingway's dialogue—the fact that it has so frequently been esteemed primarily for its mimetic achievements—may have functioned to obscure its more synthetic capabilities. As with James's work, however, making a deliberate effort to holistically consider his dialogue reveals the ideological priorities informing its highly unnatural symmetries.

---

24. Unlike Helbig, I would argue that the novel's language is not a "confessional discourse" so much as a collective one that serves to engender a sense of affiliation.

## V. "LET'S UTILIZE IT": LANGUAGE AND COLLECTIVE ETHICS

The fact that utterances in Hemingway's novels tend to signify in aggregate, rather than in isolation, is a lesson dramatized by any number of episodes throughout the narrative. Take, for instance, the seemingly insignificant exchange that takes place during Jake, Bill, and Harris's fishing trip to Burguete:

> "Isn't that a pub across the way?" Harris asked. "Or do my eyes deceive me?"
> "It has the look of a pub," Bill said.
> "It looks to me like a pub," I said.
> "I say," said Harris, "let's utilize it." He had taken up utilizing from Bill.
> (133)

As the scene continues, Harris and Jake will increasingly "take up" Bill's word ("I say. You know this does utilize well"; "Come on and utilize another glass"), much as Strether did Little Bilham's (*The Sun Also Rises* [hereafter SAR] 134). Perhaps because Jake comments explicitly on the phenomenon ("he had taken up utilizing from Bill"), and because the repetition is so emphatic, the episode has often been frequently celebrated as an example of "how language can create a community" (Humphries 117). At the same time, it also exemplifies how *authors* can create the impression of community, through the curation and distribution of character talk.

On the one hand, the sharing of language does serve a diegetic function, most frequently by offering proof of fellowship. When Jake and Georgette discuss being "sick," or when Brett and the Count riff on the word *joke,* or when Jake and Montoya debate who is and is not "*aficionado,*" the message is that words can constitute a meaningful shorthand, telegraphing a whole range of values, and, as in *The Ambassadors,* allow for the rapid sifting of "us" from the "them" (SAR 23, 65, 136). Even more determinative than characters' use of particular words is their embrace of certain, more generic verbal formulas or syntactical arrangements. Take, for instance, the use of the first-person plural imperative *Let's*: Counting Harris's exhortation ("let's utilize it"), it appears forty-seven times within the text, making it one of the most frequently occurring words in the characters' collective idiom (*nice,* by contrast, appears forty-three times; *tight,* twenty-four; *hell,* fifty-three). And *Let's* is one of the most evenly distributed; it is something of a common lexical denominator among the characters, voiced by everyone from Bill ("Let's find the gang and go down" [137]; "Let's translate Brett to the hotel" [163]); to Mike ("I say, Brett, let's turn in early"; "Let's take a drive" [85, 234]; to Jake ("Well, let's shut up about it" (34); "Let's have a drink, then" [63]); and especially Brett who tends toward negative formulations ("Don't let's go there" (211); "Don't let's ever talk about it" [247]). Considered in tandem, then, it becomes clear that readers are encountering more than the sum of character-based emanations, but a more cumulative effect, what Phelan calls "authorial disclosure across conversations" ("Conversational" 9, 10).

In this light, it seems especially important to consider the one character who does not make regular use of this construction or participate in the kind of deliberate verbal uptake on display in the episode above—to consider, in other words, what Robert Cohn's discourse might "disclose." Compared to the novel's other speakers, who regularly invoke the collective, Cohn is far more likely to speak in the singular, a discrepancy highlighted in the exchange below:

> "Well, Bill and I will go up right after lunch," I said.
> "I wish I could go. We've been looking forward to this fishing all winter." He was being sentimental about it. "But I ought to stay. I really ought. As soon as they come I'll bring them right up."
> "Let's find Bill."
> "I want to go over to the barber-shop." (106)

It is not only that Cohn fails to agree to Jake's plan or to respond in kind. More significant is the emphasis he places on his individual desires ("I wish . . ."; "I want . . .") in contrast to Jake's more collective orientation ("Bill and I will go"; "Let's find . . ."). His openly ambitious and egocentric speech is an anomaly in the novel, and even his "we," in Jake's assessment, is incorrect—a sign of self-indulgent "sentiment."[25] In short, Cohn's self-interest runs completely counter to what the novel increasingly reveals to be a group mentality. When at one point Bill jokes to Mike, "Don't you ever detach me from the herd," he makes explicit a sensibility the novel's dialogue has already done much to disclose (145).

In this sense, one could say that Cohn functions to reveal the existence not only of a verbal and social consensus but of the ethical one that underlies it: one that privileges reciprocity over singularity, collectivity over "self"-expression. This collective ethics manifests in a number of other discursive features, not only the inclusive predicates and shared diction but also the sort of parallel speaking practiced in *The Ambassadors*. When Bill first meets Brett,

---

25. As Doris A. Helbig points out, Cohn is both an inveterate misuser of "we" and an overuser of "I" (97–98).

for instance, it does not take long before they've subordinated semantics so as to maximize synchronicity:

> "Vienna," said Bill, "is a strange city."
> "Very much like Paris," Brett smiled at him, wrinkling the corners of her eyes.
> "Exactly," Bill said. "Very much like Paris at this moment." (80)

And a few lines later:

> "So that's the way it was in Vienna," Brett said.
> "It was like everything in Vienna." (81)

This exchange exemplifies the sort of "discourse of non-specificity" which proliferates in the novel and in which Hemingway's speakers are almost universally proficient (Tomkins 751). And, like the "high generality of the diction" in *The Ambassadors*, the use of "non-specific" language in *The Sun Also Rises* seems designed to maximize opportunities for concurrence among speakers (Levenson 15; Tomkins 750). Indeed, it is Bill's proficiency in this language, his willingness to prioritize consensus with the other over expression of the self, that is the measure of his belonging. Just as Maria must exchange "a half-dozen remarks" with Chad before declaring him "one of us," so, too, must Brett hear Bill speak and establish with him something like Maria and Chad's "quick unanimity" before quickly expressing her approval: "Brett smiled at him again. 'You've a very nice friend, Jake'" (A 83; SAR 81). While Jake, then, may try to make such discursive congruence sound casual ("When you were with the English, you got into the habit of using English expressions in your thinking"), the novel repeatedly implies that such overlap—much like the "work" Jake will never be caught doing—is very much by design, the product of concerted effort by the characters (SAR 153, 19).

Once again, Cohn is the one character who actively resists the reciprocal mandate: who fails to "take up" the word of others, as Jake and Harris take up Bill's, or respond to verbal cues, as Bill does Brett's. (That he is spoken differently *about*—by his full name rather than just his first one—is just one textual manifestation of his difference.) His exceptional status is especially evident in one of the novel's early scenes, when Jake, having been asked by Cohn for his opinion of Brett, responds that she is a "nice girl." Cohn speaks first:

> "She's a remarkably attractive woman."
> "Isn't she?"

"There's a certain quality about her, a certain fineness. She seems to be absolutely fine and straight."

"She's very nice."

"I don't know how to describe the quality," Cohn said. "I suppose it's breeding." (SAR 46)

In *Our America*, Walter Benn Michaels observes that the full measure of Cohn's difference from Jake is registered in their diction: "'Breeding' is the term used by people who don't really have any; 'nice' is the term used by people who do'" (26). Yet even more revealing than Cohn's choice of words is his deafness to Jake's: his refusal to accept Jake's assessment of Brett—that she is "nice" or "very nice"—in favor of his own.[26] If, before falling in love with Brett, Cohn "never . . . ma[de] one remark that would, in any way, detach him from other people," as Jake alleges, the implication is that now his remarks do "detach" him: they have that power (SAR 52).

It's one instance of a broader tendency in the novel: to frame Cohn's verbal contrarianism as grounds for his social expiation. Take, for instance, Jake's excoriation of the telegram Cohn sends to Burguete ("Vengo Jueves Cohn"): "What a lousy telegram! . . . He could send ten words for the same price. 'I come Thursday.' That gives you a lot of dope, doesn't it?" (SAR 133). On the one hand, Jake's withering critique could be taken as another symptom of the more generalized antipathy toward Cohn or as an expression of his well-documented "difference." Yet Jake's comment might also be seen to suggest the inverse—that Cohn's deviation from rhetorical norms *justifies* his marginalization rather than results from it.[27] What's interesting is the way in which Jake's critique seems to provide cover for the seemingly prejudicial exclusion of Cohn, and for derision of him, alternately, as "pitiful," a "moron," and a "kike." Thus, while Jake may insist there is "no password" among *aficionados*, it seems clear that talk can still function as shibboleth—or, in this case, an alibi for anti-Semitism. According to this logic, Cohn's estrangement has less to do with his Jewishness than with what Jake implies is his more diffuse rhetorical and ideological nonbelonging.

The question is whether the novel endorses Jake's assessment, which is to say, whether it sanctions the characters' casual anti-Semitism and construc-

---

26. Helbig makes a similar point in Bakhtinian terms, noting that this dialogue "more closely resembles a monologue," given Cohn's apparent "deafness" to Jake's response (95).

27. See Woloch, who has argued that a character's minor status might "catalyze . . . inadequate speech" (26). I am arguing the opposite: that inadequate speech might catalyze a character's minor-ness.

tion of Cohn as an antagonist. Regardless, it's clear that by suggesting Cohn is excluded less for what he *is*[28] than for what he *says*, and how he says it, Hemingway offers readers (and perhaps himself) an "out" for their antipathy. And yet Cohn's language *does* attest to his ideological difference. Framed in the terms René Girard introduced in his book, *Deceit, Desire, and the Novel*, Cohn is a Romantic hero in a "romanesque" world: convinced of the originality of his desires despite the unassailable fact of their mediation. Mark Spilka was only the first of many critics to highlight Cohn's adherence to a prewar "code,"[29] and it is a sensibility that manifests in his speech as well as his behavior. Even his brief exchange with Jake relies on what Frederic Henry might call "abstract" words, though more romantic than militaristic: "love," "best friend," "honest woman" (46–47). Like Strether's blind faith in Chad's "virtuous attachment"—or even Jay Gatsby's quixotic devotion to Daisy—Cohn's rhetorical inflation of Brett is meant to telegraph his attachment to outmoded ideals. Moreover, it suggests that he takes at face value terms that the novel's other characters reflexively deflate or ironize. Thus, in the conversation above, Jake's "girl" is Cohn's "woman," and Jake's understated "nice" is amplified by adverbs into Cohn's "remarkably attractive" and "absolutely fine and straight."

In short, Cohn talks precisely the kind of talk that characters in the novel, like Hemingway himself, are most concerned to disavow. It is in his speech, then, that we recognize the target of the novel's opprobrium: language of the standardized, institutionalized, or otherwise "abstract" variety. When in Burguete with Bill, Jake excoriates Cohn for speaking "with an air of superior knowledge that irritated both of us," there is more at stake in their accusation (101). For such "superior" speaking contravenes the deliberately understated mode of communication epitomized by the characters' telegraphic way of talking, which like Hemingway's own style, privileges economy. Bill, in particular, tends to talk as if he were paying by the word: "Must bathe"; "might do that"; "Beautiful lady . . . going to kidnap us" (80). It is well known that Hemingway emulated the "language of cables, which had entranced him since his newspaper days," and Fussell suggests he may have similarly learned from the "Great War style of British Phlegm" adopted by many of the soldiers writing home from the front (EHSL xi; Fussell 181). That the majority of his characters seem

---

28. The Davidsons, for instance, see Cohn as one of "those excluded others" who "are required to define the code" (93); Benn Michaels examines his expulsion in historical context, as the product of Nativist and anti-Semitic sentiments.

29. Spilka describes Cohn as "the last chivalric hero, the last defender of an outworn faith" (109); more recently, Lori Watkins Fulton calls him "a romantic type basically untouched by the war" (71).

to mimic this style conveys the impression that they, too, are cultivating a similarly phlegmatic style and a commitment to the ironic and pragmatic that can be both performed—and preempted—by discourse.

## VI. "DO YOU JOKE HIM?"

Unlike James's novel, then, it is clear that in Hemingway's, not all interlocutors are created equal. If, as we noted, *The Ambassadors'* speakers produce the same oddly structured English, foreign speech in Hemingway's novel often retains traces of its origins: hence Georgette's comment "This is no great thing of a restaurant" (24) or Jake's question, to a waiter in Spain, "How does one eat inside?" (236). Yet there is a far more significant discrepancy that emerges than the one between "native" and "foreign" speakers. A closer analysis reveals a structuring opposition between the majority of speakers, who treat language with suspicion; and those few, mostly Spanish or ethnically distinct speakers—Cohn, Pedro Romero, Montoya—who maintain serious, unironic stances toward it. That this difference is meant to be understood in generational terms more than ethnographic ones, however, is strongly suggested by the fact that these speakers are also the novel's noncombatants and thus do not qualify as members of Stein's *génération perdue*. "In those days," Hemingway explained in *A Moveable Feast*, "We did not trust anyone who had not been in the war" (MF 82). If for James, in 1905, a "common" tongue was still the product of a common national identity, Hemingway makes it clear that solidarity is now to be founded on experiential rather than ontological or geographical grounds. Thus the "question of our speech" that James raised had for Hemingway become also and inevitably a question of "our time."

Within the world of the novel, however, this verbal dichotomy is more often staged not as an explicit clash between pre- and postwar sensibilities but as a more submerged tension between irony and sincerity. When, during a debate with Jake, Cohn insists, "I'm serious," readers realize he is one of the few speakers within the novel who could make such a claim. Perhaps another is the Italian general who visits Jake's bedside: "Then he made that wonderful speech. . . . What a speech! I would like to have it illuminated to hang in the office. *He never laughed*" (39, italics mine). By contrast, Jake maintains a posture of what sometimes seems like obligatory bemusement. Thus, as if following Bill's mock injunction "to be ironical the minute you get out of bed," he will repeatedly laugh off his injury: "It's supposed to be funny"; "It seemed like a hell of a joke"; "I suppose it was funny" (119, 34, 38). Similarly, when Brett assures the count that she and Jake don't "joke" each other, it is a reminder of just how exceptional *not joking* is (65).

As the novel ultimately makes clear, however, joking is less a sign of nihilism than it is a mark of submerged feeling. As he reflects in *A Moveable Feast*, following the news of a friend's suicide, "They say the seeds of what we will do are in all of us, but it always seemed to me that in those who make jokes in life the seeds are covered with better soil and with a higher grade of manure" (104). It's a metaphor that suggests that Hemingway's impetus for assigning to his characters the habit of ritual deprecation may be to attest to their quality, with their joking surface vouchsafing for the existence of feeling depths. In *The Sun Also Rises*, then, to assume a posture of irreverence toward something—to "make jokes" about it—is, simultaneously, to disclose one's capacity for emotion. If Hemingway himself seemed surprised by the reviewers' failure to recognize the novel's "depths" of feeling ("If you went any deeper inside they couldn't read it because they would be crying all the time"), it may be a testament to how convincing a surface, a "jazz superficial" story he had created (EHSL 226).

One could go so far as to say that "joking" is presented as the preferable discursive modality to "talking": If the latter is "all bilge," the former, by contrast, emerges as a way of articulating emotion. Indeed, it may be only by "being ironical" that one can still hope to convey real sentiment. It is no coincidence that Bill, who spends more time joking than any other character in the novel, is also most prone to expressions of feeling. As he confesses to Jake while fishing, "Listen, you're a hell of a good guy, and I'm fonder of you than of anyone on earth. I couldn't tell you that in New York. It'd mean I was a faggot" (121). Here, it is the homophobic joke that seems to "cover" for—and thus ensure the sincerity of—the sentiment that precedes it, just as being "hard-boiled about everything in the daytime" purchases Jake relief from that posture "at night" (42). Similarly, it is no coincidence that Cohn, the character taken least seriously in the novel, is generally humorless. Part of what makes him so "wonderful"—that is, "awful"—is his inability to understand the transvaluation of language that has taken place, whereby what is tragic (Jake's accident) could perhaps only be talked about as "funny" (34). For this reason, he is unable to participate in the comic mishandling of language that Bill excels at or to consider, more generally, the possibility that words, like his fling with Brett, might not "mean anything" or signify as he thinks they should (185).

In short: a holistic assessment of dialogue in *The Sun Also Rises* suggests that Cohn remains committed to "talking" in a novel whose other characters are committed to "joke." Or, put another way, Cohn speaks with the goal of self-expression, while Jake, Brett, and the rest share with Hemingway himself what could be called a *postpsychological* conception of speech: of talk (fictional or otherwise) not as natural, spontaneous emanation, but as highly stylized construction. There is no room, such a style makes clear, for the sort of "wordy, sentimental" expression embodied less by Cohn than by the literary antecedents of whom James was certainly one (EHSL 129). Indeed, it may be no accident that Hemingway assigns to the hapless Cohn a speech that sounds very like the one Strether delivered to Little Bilham:

> "Listen, Jake . . . Don't you ever get the feeling that all your life is going by and you're not taking advantage of it? Do you realize you've lived nearly half the time you have to live already?" (19)

What in James's novel was a revelation—an exhortation to the reader, as well as Little Bilham, "to live all you can"—is presented in Hemingway's as a banality (A 132). And the implication is that ideas that can be openly, if vaguely, expressed in James's novel can only be smuggled into Hemingway's, transmitted in a highly wrought code.

And yet the expulsion of Cohn's voice and the nonironic modality it represents is not sufficient to ensure consensus among the remaining characters. As the ending implies, even the novel's two most like-minded characters, Jake and Brett, cannot sustain the sort of synchronicity that, as the count suggests, would seem to be inevitable ("Why don't you get married, you two?" [68]). Like the similarly editorial remark in *The Ambassadors*—that Maria and Strether "might have been brother and sister"—the count's comment underscores the novel's ultimate disclosure: that even the most fated and seemingly natural of connections may nevertheless fail to endure (21). While some commentators have suggested that it is touch, not talk, that serves as the more powerful vehicle for interconnection,[30] the evidence seems to mitigate against it. The affirmative "touch" Jake shares with Montoya does not prevent them from falling out; Jake's touch might "turn [Brett] all to jelly," but it's not sufficient to sustain a relationship (34). And neither, the novel finally suggests, can language, which may no longer provide even a comforting simulacrum. In the novel's conclusion, Brett famously suggests to Jake that they "could have had such a damn good time together" (251). Although Jake concedes the "prettiness" of the sentiment, he knows it to be false; by the novel's conclusion, he

---

30. See Frederic Svoboda, who speaks for many critics when he observes the importance of "the ritual touch" in the novel: "The *corrida* must *touch* Jake before they are willing to believe him as a fellow *aficionado*" (30, 46).

has realized that there may no longer *be* a sincere core of emotion underlying his and Brett's ironic displays. In this light, talk emerges as less a choice, as in James's fiction, than the only remaining alternative—and a poor one at that. As Jake's reply suggests, even the most perfect verbal synchrony can't compensate for more complete forms of intimacy that Hemingway's protagonist, unlike James's, knows to be superior.

## VII. THE MUTE CONSENSUS

Both novels, then, could be said to end with scenes of noncoincidence: with the surprising failure of the two couples—Strether and Maria, Jake and Brett—most adept at the sort of reciprocal speaking practiced in each text. Even if James's pair come closer than Hemingway's to achieving reciprocity, it's hard to tell how close they *do* come, since even Strether's concluding remark is limited to a statement of the most frankly deictic and ambiguously Jamesian sort: "Then there we are!" (347) (a strategy perhaps not lost on Woolf, who concludes *Mrs. Dalloway* with Peter's similar mock-epiphany: "For there she was") (194). Yet even more tragic than the prospect of incomplete or failed consensus, both novels imply, is the false presumption of it where it does not exist. More often than not, such a presumption is the product of silence, paradoxically held up in both texts as the highest proof of intimacy—an indication that so complete is the characters' affinity that talk has been rendered superfluous. In *The Ambassadors,* Strether continually extols the expressive powers of muteness: "had he been able to put into it anything so handsome as so much fine silence"; "Her silences were never barren, nor even dull"; "It ended by being quite beautiful between them, the number of things they had a manifest consciousness of not saying" (A 31, 106, 232). As Leo Bersani points out, this idealization of silence and suspicion that "dialogue . . . compromises intimacy" is diffuse in James's later work (154). And *The Sun Also Rises,* as demonstrated above, registers a similar preference for not talking or for using a radically curtailed speech over more effusive variants.

Yet a survey of these texts reveals that mute understanding often conceals *mis*understanding. One could call it a case of mistaken intimacy or unverified consensus. In both novels, such delusion is generally the result of silence or scant communication, which may be precipitated by the speakers' (misplaced) belief in their similarity. Cosmopolitans like Strether and Little Bilham, after all, shouldn't require more than the barest phrase to understand each other; *aficionados* such as Jake and Montoya can affirm their bond with a single "touch." That both of these ostensibly solid relationships are revealed to be friable discloses the dangers of presumed reciprocity, which is shown, again and again, to be profoundly unstable. As Ralph Touchett remarks (ironically) to Henrietta Stackpole, "I'm sure you understand everything and that differences of nationality are no barrier to you" (*The Portrait of a Lady* [hereafter PL] 139). The comment, far more applicable to Ralph himself than Henrietta, bespeaks a sort of cosmopolitan hubris that James, in particular, portrays as the basis of perilous miscalculations.

If an expatriate's incomplete knowledge of their "host" culture and eagerness to assimilate make them particularly prone to error, these novels suggest that the danger is open to anyone inclined to this sort of romantic thinking. (Even Jake, who may believe himself inoculated against this kind of gaffe, indulges in something similar on the subject of Spain.) In fact, it is a subsequent work of American modernism, William Faulkner's *Absalom, Absalom!*— a novel examined in the fourth chapter—that may feature the most tragic iteration of this trope. Speaking of Sutpen and Judith, the narrator tells us that they have achieved the kind of mutuality to which James and Hemingway's characters would seem to aspire: "They were too much alike. They were as two people become now and then, who seem to know each other so well or are so much alike that the power, the need, to communicate by speech atrophies from disuse" (96). Henry and Bon similarly engage in a "dialogue without words, speech" (88). Idealized though they might be, such mute exchanges actually attest not to intimacy but to distance. Though Henry and Bon, like Sutpen and Judith, may be genetically "alike," this belief in their "likeness" ends by being a blind, in both cases, for tragic forms of misunderstanding. Talking, of course, might not have forestalled the tragedy. But unlike silence, it could not have hurt.

CHAPTER 3

# The Exceptional Voice

*Joyce, Faulkner, and the Dream of Autonomy*

IN THE OPENING paragraphs of "The Dead," before the beginning of the "Misses Morkan's annual dance," readers learn a bit about its two hostesses:

> Though their life was modest they believed in eating well; the best of everything: diamond-bone sirloins, three-shilling tea and the best bottled stout. But Lily seldom made a mistake in the orders so that she got on well with her three mistresses. They were fussy, that was all. But the only thing they would not stand was back answers. (176)

At first glance, the excerpt is worth remarking because it shares the "leaden ring" of the story's famous first line ("Lily, the caretaker's daughter, was literally run off her feet") and betrays the idiosyncrasies of syntax and diction that Hugh Kenner has identified as a trademark of Joycean free indirect style (*Joyce's Voices* 175).[1] In this case, it is Lily's limited vocabulary and repetitive cadence that give her away: Those two "bests," for instance, and the insistence

---

1. See *Joyce's Voices*, in which Kenner identifies the "Uncle Charles Principle" as a salient feature of Joyce's style, which holds that *"the narrative idiom need not be the narrator's"* (18).

on starting sentences—not once, but twice—with a *but* suggest hers is the orienting voice and vision in this passage.²

More striking than Joyce's feat of ventriloquism, however, is the irony inherent in this remark; for even as Lily claims that the Misses Morkan cannot abide "back answers," this passage gives the impression of "answering back" just the same. Indeed, this aside—with its self-rationalizing tone, its *but*s, its willingness to pass judgment, however mild, on Lily's two employers ("They were fussy, that was all")—suggests the narrative is offering, in sublimated form, precisely the sort of reply that Lily is prohibited from speaking aloud. Even more suggestive is that hers is hardly an isolated case. Similar retorts surface repeatedly and far more vocally in "The Dead," from playful rebuttal ("West Briton!"), to sharp dissent ("And why couldn't he have a voice too?"), to moments of far meeker protest ("I hadn't a bad voice as voices go") (190, 199, 194).³ So marked is this phenomenon of "back answers"—a term I use to connote the full range of verbal responses described above—that it seems possible to say of Joyce's characters what Bakhtin has said of Dostoevsky's: that their "every thought . . . senses itself to be from the very beginning a *rejoinder* in an unfinalized dialogue" (*Problems of Dostoevsky's Poetics* [hereafter PDP] 32).

In this sense, "The Dead," at first glance, would appear not only to exemplify Bakhtin's theories of dialogism,⁴ expounded at greatest length in *The Dialogic Imagination,* but also, more important for the purposes of this project, to reproduce some of the locutionary patterns typical of James's and Hemingway's novels as discussed in the previous chapter. Though the speech of Joyce's characters is less distinctively concatenated or co-constructed than that of their counterparts in *The Ambassadors* and *The Sun Also Rises,* the quantity and quality of dialogue within "The Dead" suggest a similar investment in the principle of reciprocity. Yet despite the value apparently assigned to verbal exchange, closer examination suggests that the story also manifests a conflicting set of priorities: a conception of talk and its potentialities that differs markedly from the one which emerges in James's and Hemingway's novels and which emphasizes its socially divisive properties over its consensus-building ones. As the above excerpts begin to indicate, there is a comparatively high degree of dissent—of *non*consensus—among the text's fictional speakers. But

---

2. For an alternative reading of this passage, see Margot Norris, who claims that these sentences do not reflect Lily's voice so much as they reveal the appropriation of her idiom by a "bourgeois agenda"—namely, that of the Morkans or the Conroys (216).

3. Norris, too, analyzes the story's repeated "back answers," but through a more narrowly feminist lens: She reads them as a subversive "disruption[s]" to the status quo by marginalized, largely female voices (480).

4. As do other stories in *Dubliners*. See R. B. Kershner for further application of Bakhtin to the book.

there is also the incongruous behavior of its protagonist, Gabriel Conroy, who throughout the story manifests both an un-Jamesian ineptness at dialogue and an un-Joycean aversion to it. Far from participating in the construction of a shared or collectively normed language, Gabriel seems consistently more concerned with preserving the sanctity and exceptional status of his own.

That a similar dynamic surfaces in William Faulkner's 1929 novel *The Sound and the Fury* provides further evidence that modernist texts might encompass a paradigm of verbal expression that competes with the one on display in James's and Hemingway's work. A conspicuously "polyphonic" text that, like Joyce's, has often been read in light of Bakhtin's theories,[5] *The Sound* contains, in the character of Quentin Compson, a fictional subject whose attitude toward and practice of speech show him to be, like Gabriel, forcefully opposed to dialogic ideals. Because Quentin has so frequently been compared to Stephen Dedalus,[6] his parallels to the less superficially analogous Gabriel, another artist figure and author surrogate, have been largely overlooked. Yet the characters' attitudes toward spoken language—their philosophies of self-expression—seem uncannily alike. Both, as I will demonstrate, consistently favor monologic over dialogic modes of discourse, and both, when dialogue does occur, treat it as a site of confrontation rather than an opportunity for collaboration. At the same time, each character practices a distinct type of dialogic resistance: If Gabriel tends toward chronic speechlessness, Quentin reveals a marked preference for "subvocal speech" over the actually uttered (Richardson, *Unnatural Voices* 61). The question is: What are readers to make of these sorts of rhetorical habits and the texts' emphasis on them? Why should Joyce and Faulkner choose to insert into their multiply voiced fictions characters so committed to cultivating vocal exceptionalism?

On the one hand, it is possible to read this pattern as evidence of a more general shift in literary aesthetics: from a fictional universe in which everyone speaks in more or less the same way (as they tend to do in Hemingway's and James's work) to one in which, as Joyce reminds readers of *Ulysses*, "everything speaks in its own way" (U 7.177). But it may also reflect an important shift in thematic concerns: away from issues of community and consensus and toward the more familiar modernist problematics of subjectivity and selfhood. Having suggested in the first chapter that James's and Hemingway's deployment

---

5. For some of the more recent applications of Bakhtin to Faulkner's work, see Charles Hannon, pp. 1–17; and Richard Godden, especially the introduction.

6. The comparisons are almost too commonplace to count. See, for instance, Kenner, who claims that the characters share "'aesthetic' affiliations" (*Joyce's Voices* 195); and André Bleikasten, who refers to Quentin as Faulkner's own "portrait of the artist as a young man" (*The Ink of Melancholy* 104).

of dialogue telegraphs a distinct set of ideas and ideals, here I will argue that the very different speech habits of Joyce's and Faulkner's protagonists convey divergent, even antithetical, aspirations: for autonomy rather than reciprocity; and for singularity rather than communal identity. Instead of striving, in the manner of James's and Hemingway's characters, to echo their interlocutors, Joyce's and Faulkner's speakers go out of their way *not* to talk like, or even to, each other; to delineate and differentiate their own voices and, in the process, to consolidate their intellectual as well as verbal autonomy.

As in the case of James's and Hemingway's texts, there is evidence to suggest that the characters' ambitions are meant to dramatize, at least to some degree, their authors' own. Indeed, it can be tempting to overstate the extent to which biographical factors—namely, Joyce's and Faulkner's similarly conflicted relationship with their native regions—can be seen to inform their work.[7] Yet it seems safe to say that for both writers, "community" constituted less a fantasy than a fact of life: one that Joyce expatriated to leave behind and one that Faulkner would increasingly resent as he became "stuck to—or stuck with—an extended family of as many generations of relatives as happened to be around at a given time" (Woodward 267). Indeed, it is no coincidence that both "The Dead" and *The Sound* are noticeably *noisy* texts, full of voices and talk about voices; and that both take place in the thick of "more than . . . nuclear" families (Woodward 267). One could go so far as to say that Faulkner and Joyce use conversation to stage the same tensions between self and other that are anatomized in James's and Hemingway's work, but that here, those tensions are scrutinized from an inverse angle: from the perspective of writers for whom the norm was not deracination, or a lack of relations, but an oppressive superabundance of them.

This is not to imply that Joyce and Faulkner endorse their characters' self-absorbed outlooks. On the contrary, both texts are ruthless in undercutting their protagonists' pretensions to specialness: Faulkner, for one, consistently undermines Quentin's differentiation from other speakers in *The Sound,* while "The Dead" similarly disrupts Gabriel's illusion that he is free of romantic and rhetorical debts. At the same time, the fact that these individualist agendas are associated with "major" characters—rather than, as in *The Sun Also Rises,* a "minor" one like Robert Cohn—signals an interest in airing them, even if only to better repudiate them. Similarly suggestive in this regard is the fact that both Joyce and Faulkner choose in their texts' conclusions to preempt diegetic voices so as to center ones more closely identified with the (implied)

---

7. C. Vann Woodward is reacting to this critical tendency when he cautions, "If the comparison is not carried too far, William Faulkner's relation to the South resembles James Joyce's relation to Ireland" (265).

authors' own. If Joyce, in the last, lyrically concentrated passage in "The Dead," seems to override the story's other speakers, Faulkner similarly—though at far greater length—unfurls in the final section of *The Sound* a more unabashedly authorial idiom.[8]

To suggest that two such canonically modernist authors end their work by reducing possibilities for discursive pluralism may seem anathema, particularly given how often both have been recruited into Bakhtin's camp. Rather than assign a single ideological motive to this reassertion of authorial voice, however, the goal of this chapter is to consider the dialectic catalyzed by its reemergence, as well as its implication for readers, who are forced to navigate this tension between the characters' dreams of autonomy and the textual demonstration of their rhetorical indebtedness.

Compared to James and Hemingway, then, Joyce and Faulkner seem more frank in their co-option of character discourse for authorially expressive (and specifically critical) ends, inasmuch as they use dialogue to convey the kinds of ideas from which they might reasonably seek to distance themselves. In the case of *The Sound*, Faulkner assigns to his characters discursive tendencies—to monologize, to self-attribute—that reflect an investment in outmoded logics of patriarchy, hereditary authority, and dynastic succession. Meanwhile, in "The Dead," Gabriel's verbal panic, when faced with female interlocutors, reflects anxieties of sexual and intellectual obsolescence that would find fuller and far more sympathetic expression via Bloom's stream of consciousness in *Ulysses*. In this way, dialogue in both texts becomes not simply an *additional* channel of communication—amplifying, as in James's and Hemingway's words, authorial concerns—but a more frankly dissident one: a space for the staging of certain unpalatable but still persistent preoccupations.

## I. *O*s, *AND*s, AND *BUT*s: ANSWERING BACK IN "THE DEAD"

Reading "The Dead," it is easy to collect evidence of Joyce's "powerfully dialogical imagination" (Kershner 18). On the one hand, there is Joyce's propensity for actual literary dialogue, which, as R. B. Kershner notes, "gradually supplants narration" as *Dubliners* progresses, allowing Joyce to show off his "miraculous ear for verbal nuance" (Kershner 95; Burgess 46). In the relatively brief span of "The Dead" alone, Joyce showcases via his characters an encyclo-

---

8. See Bleikasten, who reads this section as unambiguously "authorial": "Free of the restrictions of the interior monologue, Faulkner now seems to speak in his own person, and a richer, denser, more ceremonious style comes to unfold. Previously held in check or fraught with ironic intent, Faulkner's rhetoric now bursts into full flower" (*Ink* 132).

pedic array of speech practices: from mimicry, imitation, and parody to allusion, quotation, and paraphrase. If *Ulysses,* then, has been called "a thesaurus of Bakhtinian discourse types," "The Dead" may provide a similarly comprehensive if more condensed index (Lodge 86).[9] Particularly suggestive is the proliferation of *and*s and *but*s at the beginnings of sentences, along with interjective *O*s. While one might assume that the *but*s in the opening excerpt are specific to Lily's idiolect—the product, perhaps, of what Bakhtin calls "character zone"[10]—it soon becomes clear that this linguistic tic is far more widespread (*The Dialogic Imagination* [hereafter DI] 234). A brief survey reveals that introductory *but*s appear more than thirty times within the text, both in directly reported speech and in *skaz*: "But she liked the review immensely"; "But you will come, won't you?"; "But there's such a thing as a common everyday politeness"; "But she had no right to call him a West Briton"; "But she never would be said by me" (189, 195, 191, 194). In the aggregate, these interjections testify to the importance the text's speakers assign to the act of rejoining: of not just talking, but talking *back*.[11]

Of all the characters in the story, it is Gabriel who most consistently contravenes this dialogic imperative. He does so most notably over the course of three verbal exchanges which have come to be known as the "three rebuffs" and which, though exhaustively examined, have historically been seen as indices of Gabriel's other problems—with women, with Ireland, with nationalism—rather than his problems with language per se.[12] Recently, such "problematic" readings of Gabriel have themselves been cast as a critical problem, evidence of an ungenerous bias against a character whose very sin, in readers' eyes, has been his lack of generosity.[13] To clarify, then, I am not singling out Gabriel for punishment so much as remarking on the extent to which the *story* singles him out: both in the way it talks about him[14] and in the way it makes him talk. In the course of these conversational set pieces, it becomes clear (as

---

9. Here I diverge from the view that "The Dead" is only narrowly dialogic and that the narrative responds "preeminently to the protagonist's voice, only infrequently allowing subsidiary characters to affect its tonality" (Kershner 151).

10. Best understood as "areas of linguistic influence surrounding characters in a novel" (Kershner 19).

11. Though Norris, too, has noticed this pattern, I am less inclined to see these voices as uniformly disruptive to "prosperous and happy domesticity, social harmony, and refined culture" or to claim them on behalf of progressive ideologies (480).

12. See Free, p. 299n, for the ways in which critics have tabulated these "rebuffs." She also provides a useful overview of symptomatic interpretations of them; see also Norris and Vincent J. Cheng.

13. See Free, especially pp. 277–84, for examples of this sort of critical "misprision."

14. Free suggests that the "story's narrative technique . . . negatively distinguish[es] Gabriel from his fellow revelers" by "relentlessly trespassing on his—and most only his—pri-

it did with Hemingway's Cohn) just how broadly Gabriel deviates from the diegetically determined conversational norms.

The first of these conversations occurs early in the story, when Gabriel, following Lily to the cloakroom, attempts a bit of pleasantry:

—Tell me, Lily, he said in a friendly tone, do you still go to school?
—O no, sir, she answered. I'm done schooling this year and more.
—O, then, said Gabriel gaily, I suppose we'll be going to your wedding one of these fine days with your young man, eh?
The girl glanced back at him over her shoulder and said with great bitterness:
—The men that is now is only all palaver and what they can get out of you. (177–78)

Though the exchange begins with Gabriel's "friendly" inquiry, it ends with Lily's "bitterness"; in this sense, it is paradigmatic, since nearly all of Gabriel's conversations are characterized by similar disjuncture. Here, Lily's choice of words is especially revealing. According to the *OED, palaver* connotes not only "unnecessary, profuse, or idle chatter" but also "talk intended to cajole, flatter, or wheedle"—just the sort of "talk," in other words, with which Gabriel has been (however "gaily") plying Lily. In this sense, it may not be too much to suggest that Lily's "bitterness" is at least partly directed at him and that her response qualifies as a doubly "back answer": at once correcting Gabriel's misconception about "the men that is now" and consigning him to their company. But even more revealing than Lily's response is Gabriel's lack of one. For the first time, but not the last, he is rendered temporarily speechless; unable to reply in words, he instead "coloured, as if he felt he had made a mistake" (178). Indeed, the narrative voice, as if colluding in his embarrassment, segues to a character description—giving Gabriel, as it were, time to regain his composure. To make up for his error and to differentiate himself from those men interested only in "what they can get," Gabriel decides to "give": to make Lily the present of a coin for "Christmas-time" (178).[15] Yet it is clear that this financial transaction cannot compensate for his failure to sustain a verbal one. Nor, significantly, can it help Gabriel recover the sense of social and cultural

---

vate thoughts" (279). By this logic, however, any novel focalized through a single character is guilty of a similar transgression.

15. I am not the first to notice this: Free, too, notes that Gabriel, to differentiate himself, "abandons small talk and gives to, rather than takes from, the young woman whose unexpected behavior disarms him" (284).

superiority that at once motivated his attempt at "palaver" and condemned it to fall short.

His encounter with Molly Ivors may serve as an even better mise-en-scène of Gabriel's difficulties with dialogue. Teased by Molly about his recent contributions to an antinationalist newspaper, Gabriel is again unnerved, a fact telegraphed through a series of clichés: he "colours," once again, "tries to smile," and "knit[s] his brows" (188). As Burgess has pointed out of "The Dead," "where cliché occurs, cliché is intended," and in this light, the recourse to trope may signal Gabriel's paucity of language resources at the moment (46). This time, however, he cannot "buy" his way out of his difficulties; he cannot "risk a grandiose phrase" or gesture with Molly as he did with Lily. The result is to finally force an unguarded response from Gabriel:

—O, to tell you the truth, retorted Gabriel suddenly, I'm sick of my own country, sick of it!
—Why? asked Miss Ivors.
Gabriel did not answer for his retort had heated him.
—Why? repeated Miss Ivors.
They had to go visiting together and, as he had not answered her, Miss Ivors said warmly:
—Of course, you've no answer. (190)

Here, what is worth remarking is how thoroughly Gabriel fails to keep up his end of the conversation: He enters into debate, only to retreat; he offers a "retort," only to clam up. His reticence leads Molly to conclude, quite rightly, that Gabriel "has no answer"—as apt a summation of his discursive behavior as any we receive within the story. He may be Molly's intellectual and social peer, but rhetorically he cannot match her. What is interesting is that this asymmetry—the *form* of their conversation—may tell us as much about the speakers' compatibility as its content. In this sense, the lopsidedness of Gabriel and Molly's exchange, much like the parallelism of Strether and Maria's, emerges as an important interpretive metric, an index of rapport.

All of this is not to suggest that Gabriel is not extraordinarily sensitive to discursive issues; in fact, like James's and Hemingway's characters, he is an extremely self-conscious speaker and continually deliberates over matters of style and register. In questioning Lily, for instance, Gabriel tries to affect at least a certain concern for what Bakhtin calls the "apperceptive background" of his listener (DI 282). And he works even more strenuously on his after-dinner speech, "integrating in advance," to borrow Tzvetan Todorov's phrase, the reactions of his audience:

Then he took from his waistcoat pocket a little paper and glanced at the headings he had made for his speech. He was undecided about the lines from Robert Browning for he feared they would be above the heads of his hearers. Some quotation that they would recognise from Shakespeare or from the Melodies would be better. . . . He would only make himself ridiculous by quoting poetry to them which they could not understand. . . . He would fail with them just as he had failed with the girl in the pantry. He had taken up a wrong tone. His whole speech was a mistake from first to last, an utter failure. (179)

Considered in the context of Gabriel's earlier conversational sallies, this passage attests to Gabriel's concern with the reception not just of this particular speech but of his speech more generally. In his apprehension about "his hearers," or what Bakhtin calls the "specific conceptual horizon . . . the specific world of the listener," and careful parsing of their cultural literacy, Gabriel shows himself willing to adjust his verbal and intellectual coordinates (DI 282). Yet despite attempts to "integrate" his audience, he seems almost inevitably to alienate them: to ask the wrong question, choose the wrong pitch, tell the wrong joke.

Among the most common critical explanations for Gabriel's poor conversational record has been that he cannot tolerate the speech of female interlocutors.[16] And clearly there is much to support this thesis, for if Gabriel pretends to be the injured or "discomfited" party, it is clear he harbors lingering resentments against both partners—dismissing Lily as "the girl in the pantry" and mentally demoting Miss Ivors to "the girl or woman, or whatever she was" (179, 191). Yet I would argue that such hostility is more by-product than cause of his strained exchanges and that he may be less threatened by women per se than by their comparatively high capacity for other-oriented talk. Gabriel, as documented above, is excessively affected by other people's words, both psychologically and physiologically. Minutes after speaking with Lily, he is "still discomposed by the girl's bitter and sudden retort"; and though it has presumably been years since his mother's death, her "slighting phrases . . . still rankled in his memory" (178, 187). Considered cumulatively, these comments, along with those to Molly, suggest that Gabriel is unnerved not by any

---

16. John Paul Riquelme's view is representative here: "Women speak in response to Gabriel's provocations throughout the story in ways that he neither anticipates nor intends, and their speech causes him discomfort" (126). See also Norris and Kershner, the latter of whom takes a similarly negative view of Gabriel's "expectation of the dialogical position of women": that "the woman should be silent or at least provide perfect counterpoint to his own inner monologue" (144).

particular "phrase" or "retort" but by the business of retorting—of having to retort—more generally.

In short, Gabriel's problem is not that he can't talk but that he can't talk *back*: cannot engage in the sort of reciprocal, almost Jamesian, intercourse of which women, in the narrative economy of "The Dead," are usually the initiators and in which they are shown to be expert. (Men, by contrast, are far more likely to lapse into overly familiar, "sharply" spoken, or simply "rude" speech, to judge by the behavior of Mr. Browne, Freddy Malins, and Bartell d'Arcy) [182, 199, 212].) In this sense, it is not fair to say, as Gabriel does of himself, that he has "poor powers as a speaker"; instead, it seems more accurate to describe him as a poor *responder* (203). It's no accident, after all, that Gabriel's most successful rhetorical moment is the delivery of his pre-prepared speech, for it is his one real occasion for monologue in a dialogue-rich world. Yet it is clear that he treats even this speech occasion less as a collaborative venture than a competition, one that can end alternately with triumph, or—as was the case with his previous exchanges—with "mistakes" or "failure." And in his nervous concern with "his" speech, he does not truly listen to anyone else's, as Richard Ellmann, among others, has noted.[17] While the balance of Joyce's characters may speak for the purposes of identifying common ground, Gabriel, by contrast, approaches conversation as an opportunity to self-particularize.

Framed in theoretical terms, part of the problem may be Gabriel's faith in what Bakhtin calls a "unitary language," a belief that for Bakhtin is inevitably misplaced, given that

> only the mythical Adam, who approached a virginal and as yet verbally unqualified world with the first word, could really have escaped from start to finish this dialogic inter-orientation with the alien word that occurs in the object. Concrete historical human discourse does not have this privilege. (DI 279)

Yet if Gabriel entertains fantasies of verbal escape,[18] the text repeatedly undercuts them through its marked emphasis not only on actual dialogue but on what Bakhtin calls the "internal dialogism of the word" (DI 279). As Kristina Clark and Michel Holquist have pointed out, the utterance for Bakhtin is best understood as a zone of conflict, a "place where struggles between centrifugal and centripetal forces are fought out in miniature" (291).

---

17. Ellmann notes, for instance, that Gabriel "does not listen to the words" of his aunt's song, but "only watches his wife listening" ("Backgrounds" 178–79).

18. See Vincent P. Pecora for a more extended discussion of the "desire to escape at all costs" that characterizes "The Dead" and indeed much of *Dubliners* (233).

In fact, even the most seemingly "centripetal" moments in "The Dead" tend to reveal evidence of discursive centrifuge. In addition to the conscious quotation (from Browning, from Shakespeare) and self-citation ("if I may use the phrase, a thought-tormented age") present in Gabriel's address, it also registers less obvious influences (204). When Gabriel is worrying over his speech, for instance, "an idea came into his mind and gave him courage. He would say . . . Ladies and gentlemen, the generation which is now on the wane . . ." (193). Significantly, however, this idea may not be wholly "his" so much as Lily's: for his turn of phrase, "the generation which is now," seems strangely indebted to Lily's, "the men that is now." The correspondence might seem slight, yet given that Gabriel might just as easily have omitted the pronominal phrase altogether ("the generation now on the wane"), it seems possible to suggest that Lily's idiom, in this moment, may "overlap and infect" Gabriel's own (Bakhtin, DI 320).

Indeed, the text furnishes additional support for this possibility. Still stung by Lily's "retort," Gabriel responds by looking immediately at the "headings he had made for his speech"—a gesture that implies an opportunity for her words to interpenetrate his (179). And even before beginning his chat with Lily, Gabriel "looked up at the pantry ceiling" and toward the guests milling about—suggesting he saw this salvo with the caretaker's daughter as a dry run for the after-dinner performance to come (177). Indeed, it's intimated that his discourse is inflected not only by that of other characters but by Joyce's as well. As Ellmann points out, "There are several specific points at which Joyce attributes his own experiences to Gabriel," and, arguably, he also "attributes" some of his own language to the character (*James Joyce* [hereafter JJ] 246). A case in point may be the wording of Gabriel's final reverie: "His soul swooned slowly as he heard the snow falling faintly through the universe" (225). According to Ellmann, "'swooning' was a word, and an act, of which Joyce was fond" (JJ 132n). In a sense, then, Joyce was assigning "his" word, if not directly to Gabriel, then to the narrator who is charged with externalizing his thoughts in this moment and whose language we might choose to see as shaped by *both* the author's predilections and the character's pretensions.[19]

It is not, then, that the discursive situation within "The Dead" is so different from the one on view in *The Ambassadors* or *The Sun Also Rises*, which similarly (if more explicitly) divulge language's "interindividual" standing: the vocal mingling of character with character, character with narrator, character and narrator with author. What has changed, however, are diegetic *attitudes*

---

19. Significantly, Joyce would also bequeath this word to Stephen, who experiences a "swoon of sin" in the second chapter of *A Portrait of the Artist as a Young Man* (Ellmann, JJ 132n).

toward this situation—its valence within the text and the affective response it appears to generate within the characters. Thus, if verbal overlap was actively cultivated by the characters in James's and Hemingway's novels, Gabriel's pursuit of it is far more ambivalent—not only because he generally fails to achieve it, but because even being *successfully* in relation, one suspects, might threaten the sustainability of more private and self-authored pleasures. While waiting for Gretta to leave the party, for instance, he "long[s] to be alone with her" and imagines a moment

> when the others had gone away, when he and she were in their room in the hotel, then they would be alone together. He would call her softly:
> —Gretta!
> Perhaps she would not hear at once: she would be undressing. Then something in his voice would strike her. She would turn and look at him. (215)

It is significant that Gabriel's fantasy does not include the sound of Gretta's voice but focuses exclusively on the "striking" quality of his own. Unlike Strether, say, who avidly anticipates Maria Gostrey's "impressions and conclusions," Gabriel takes pleasure in imagining Gretta's physical and gestural rather than verbal response—that is, by envisioning the moment *before* she hears and speaks (A 86). In this sense, his erotic fantasy seems to bespeak a more existential one: that he might still plausibly transcend the reach of other voices; that he might find some space or "room" in which his voice remains, if not entirely alone, then dominant and supreme. Significantly, it is only after his climactic confrontation with Gretta that he is finally disabused of the illusions, romantic and rhetorical, under which he has been laboring. By telling him about Michael Furey, then, Gretta could be seen to provide the story's definitive "back answer." For what it forces Gabriel to acknowledge is not only the nature of his wife's romantic past but the sheer fact of its past-ness: the existence of a narrative that precedes and exceeds his. As Todorov reminds us, "It is impossible to avoid encountering the discourse previously held upon [an] object [of speech]," the fact that it has "always already been said" (62). And here Gabriel must face up to the fact that this "previously held" discourse, that of a dead man, may be far more powerful than his own.[20]

---

20. Cf. Kershner, who sees Gretta, rather than Michael, as Gabriel's primary discursive competitor; as he argues, "The two are speaking different languages, and Gretta's is the more powerful" (141).

## II. "THE LIVING AND THE DEAD"

In this light, "The Dead" would seem unambiguously to discredit the fantasy of autonomous speaking or writing. To imagine one can ever be the "single author" of one's speech is, the text's treatment of Gabriel implies, to be at best profoundly deluded. Pecora, for one, sees the ramifications of this discovery at the heart of both "The Dead" and *A Portrait,* in which, he claims, Joyce's use of free indirect discourse enacts "Stephen's most intimate reflections: are my words *my* words, *my* thoughts my thoughts?" (235). "The Dead" would appear even more efficient in its performance of this proto-poststructuralist message: that, as Pecora writes, nobody is ever the "the sole owner and producer of the language and the intentional structures he or she uses" (235). Indeed, this message is conveyed not only through the story's dialogic structures but at the level of theme. However invested Gabriel may be in the distinction between the "new generation" and the one that is "now on the wane," it is not one "The Dead" ever pretends to uphold. It's no surprise that Gabriel would find such a binary reassuring, since to delineate a "now" from a "then," a new generation from an old, is to insulate one's self from a line of antecedents and forerunners, those "dead and gone great ones whose fame the world will not willingly let die" (204). But while Gabriel may declare his refusal to "linger on the past," it becomes clear that the past lingers on him, in the form not only of Michael Furey, but in the appearance of an undistinguished horde of "the living and the dead" (225). The final paragraph, by this logic, can be seen to enact the fear of usurped individualism, of selfhood overrun by others. Gabriel's discourse begins to merge with Joyce's and lose its specificity until, like the snow, it has become almost "general."[21]

Yet in its final pages, the story also does something of an about-face. Many critics have remarked on the stylistic shift that takes place near the close of "The Dead" and have noted in particular the way in which "the distinctness of Gabriel's individual voice is submerged in the concluding passages of free indirect style" (Riquelme 125). But even as Joyce seems to dramatize this theme of dispossession—of being, or having one's discourse, dispossessed—he himself makes what in the story's final pages could be described as gesture of *re*possession. Compared to the previous portion of the story, the final section

---

21. See Elizabeth Bonapfel for an account of the way this thematic is conveyed by the story's punctuation. In particular, she argues that Joyce's use of dashes rather than inverted commas to offset dialogue "blurs boundaries between narrator and speaker"; as she puts it, this "'dialogue between the dashes' defamiliarizes the very boundaries of speech, and . . . interrogates the assumption that we can easily distinguish among the 'voices' of character and speech, narrator and description" (82, 83).

is conspicuously single-voiced: focalized through Gabriel but manifesting a recognizably Joycean idiom (not to mention a Bloomian one: "Yes, yes: that would happen very soon," Gabriel thinks—a phrase that forecasts Bloom's own thought in "Calypso": "Be near her ample bedwarmed flesh. Yes, yes" (224; U 4.239)). If Joyce, then, spends much of the text cultivating polyphony—suppressing his voice for the sake of amplifying others"[22]—in the final pages he seems intent to assert it over the characterlogical din.

Alternatively, however, it may be as plausible to interpret the final passages as *Gabriel's* bid for lyrical supremacy: his attempt to author a poem, or "song," more powerful than even Michael Furey's.[23] Even as we're told that his "own identity was fading into a gray impalpable world," it also seems buttressed by this reverie, as if he were attempting to rhapsodize about his suffering, in real time (Riquelme 225). In this way, it's possible to read the concluding paragraph, replete with snow imagery, as an expression of Gabriel's desire to overwrite, to white out, the historical palimpsest with which he has recently been confronted—and to interpret those final passages, more generally, as an attempt to engage in a more unabashedly Romantic mode of authorship. Whether we attribute this pursuit to Gabriel, or Joyce, or both, may be of less consequence than the fact of its textual presence and the longing for an unexpurgated lyrical voice it seems to imply. If we accept the stance attributed to Bakhtin by Holquist—that "single-voiced discourse is the dream of the poets; double-voiced discourse the realm of the novel"—the finale of "The Dead" could be seen as a dramatization of this poetic "dream" (DI 434). In fact, one need not agree with this (perhaps deliberately oversimplified) dictum in order to discern the *fantasy* of single-voicedness being performed in these final passages, a performance that, paradoxically, features as many as three comingled voices: of character, narrator, and author.

Even intimating that the text could harbor such monologic ambitions runs counter to popular conceptions of Joyce, the arch-polyphonist. At the same time, it helps unsettle this storyline, which casts Joyce as default champion of disenfranchised voices. It's telling that critics have tended to focus almost exclusively on the subversive aspects of the story's vocal pluralism; Jon Thompson, for one, considers it a tool "to de-privilege the dominant forms of authority in fin-de-siècle Dublin" (80). Bakhtin's texts, meanwhile, have been subjected to similarly idealized readings.[24] Yet one function of the story's

---

22. David Lodge sees this as a Bakhtinian strategy, whereby "the author, like a ventriloquist, is a silent presence in the text, but his very silence is the background against which we appreciate his creative skill" (36).

23. I am grateful to André Aciman for this suggestion.

24. Exemplary of this attitude is Hannon, who claims, apropos of Faulkner, that "dialogization ensures the representation of suppressed voices of dissent and confrontation" (6).

conclusion is to recall awareness to the presence and impact on discourse of more-centripetal forces. By so radically shifting the emphasis from fictional voices to a conspicuously authorial one, Joyce draws attention to the discursive hierarchy that is an inescapable if often invisible premise of novelistic prose, at the top of which sits the author and supreme discourse-generator. In usurping Gabriel's voice and implying that he in turn may borrow Lily's, Joyce dramatizes what is for Bakhtin the defining characteristic of novelistic composition. In this sense, "The Dead" doesn't just feature heteroglossia; it is to some extent also *about* it. It's a claim justified not only by the displays of dialogism but by the unusual attention paid to actual voices within the text—their diverse registers, timbres, and qualities—and the ways in which their reception in the world is inevitably mediated by the speakers' gender, class, and race. Yet the surge of lyricism at the story's conclusion suggests that at least for Joyce, polphony does not tell the whole of novel's story.

Of course, Joyce's subsequent work confirms that he was hardly stumping for monologism or a revival of authorial omniscience. Nonetheless, "The Dead" speaks to the allure of expressive autonomy, its continued pull within the most seemingly decentralized of modernist spaces. Indeed, Franco Moretti, in his provocative analyses of the oscillations between many- and single-voicedness in modern fiction, has argued that some of the nineteenth century's most famously polyphonic works trend surprisingly in the direction of monologue. Writing of *Moby Dick,* for instance, he describes the novel as the "story . . . of a lost polyphony," noting both the "reduction of polyphony within the plot" and "a second reduction, at the level of discourse," thanks to "the monologic device" first of Ishmael's voice and finally of Ahab's, which comes increasingly to dominate all others (*Modern Epic* 61, 62). The accumulated evidence of "The Dead" suggests it is possible to read Joyce's text somewhat analogously, though with a greater sensitivity to the ways in which the text (much, I'd suggest, like Melville's) undermines such impulses and succeeds in keeping monologic dominance at bay. In this light, "The Dead" might emerge not so much as the story of a "lost" polyphony than a polyphony resented and contested, if ultimately affirmed.

## III. "NO MAN IS HIMSELF": CUMULATE SUBJECTS IN *THE SOUND AND THE FURY*

What Gabriel Conroy comes with some difficulty to discover in "The Dead"—that he is not the sole author of his speech, or himself—is something that within the fictional world of Faulkner's novels tends to be presented as a given. Faulkner himself was particularly emphatic on this point. As he once told an audience in response to a question posed during his residency at the University of Virginia:

> To me, no man is himself, he is the sum of his past. There is no such thing really as was because the past is. It is a part of every man, every woman, and every moment. All of his and her ancestry, background, is all a part of himself and herself at any moment. And so a man, a character in a story at any moment of action is not just himself as he is then, he is all that made him. (qtd. in Gwynn and Blotner 84)

Though the purpose of Faulkner's response was to explain his use of "the long sentence," it may serve nearly as well to elucidate other aspects of his style. Even a casual reader of Faulkner's work will recognize the relentlessness with which it forecloses on the sorts of distinctions—between *is* and *was,* self and other, *now* and *then*—that many of his characters, like Gabriel, repeatedly insist upon. In *As I Lay Dying* (hereafter AILD), for instance, Darl will fall back on the past-present binary to syllogistically confirm his mother's absence: "Because if I had one, it is *was*. And if it is was, it cant be *is*. Can it?" (101). That the deceased Addie will speak contemporaneously with the novel's other characters is just one indication of the futility of such logic. Like Thomas Sutpen or John Sartoris, Addie Bundren is a character whose function in the novel is, among other things, to affirm, as Faulkner famously wrote in *Requiem for a Nun,* that "the past is never dead. It's not even past" (73). Framed in more positive terms, such figures could equally be said to express "the persistent Faulknerian themes of the interconnectedness of all times, peoples, and actions" (Bunselmeyer 330).

In *The Sound* these themes emerge not only at the level of plot but through the construction of its "monologues," each of which turns out to contain a congeries of voices. The pattern has not escaped critical scrutiny. Writing of Benjy's section, for instance, Bleikasten goes so far as to suggest that it qualifies as more "polylogue" than "monologue"; similarly, he notes of Quentin's that "the speech attributed to him can hardly be called *his,* for it is not any more than Benjy's the discourse of a single person. . . . Many voices, past and present, are heard, and within this polyphonic ensemble Quentin's own enjoys no special privilege" (*Ink* 57, 74). If Bleikasten's claim seems to minimize the factors, textual and paratexual, that ensure Quentin's privileged status, Stephen Ross offers the more measured observation that "so much do voices dominate Quentin's consciousness that his mind seems like a room jammed with chattering people" (*Inexhaustible Voice* 252). Arnold Weinstein notes, along similar lines, that the novel succeeds in conveying the "stereophonic" quality of a single mind (322). Viewed through this lens, Faulkner's work would appear, like Joyce's, to teach the same unimpeachably polyphonic lessons.

Yet even as *The Sound* works to dispel the illusion of autonomy, its characters—particularly Quentin, and to a lesser extent Jason—struggle to maintain it. Like Gabriel, both Compson brothers approach conversation primarily as a site of potential conflict. But what manifested in "The Dead" as an aversion presents in *The Sound* as a more pathological condition: a fear, in Quentin's case, of contamination by the other's words; and in Jason's, of the co-option of his own words by another. Put another way, if Quentin is interested, not unlike Gabriel, in escaping the "loud world," Jason is intent on outmatching it; he is less concerned with the incursion of other people's voices than with broadcasting his own. What the brothers' locutionary strategies have in common, however, is that they serve similarly to sustain illusions of their "exceptional" status—ones demonstrably contradicted by their lived realities. That Quentin, in particular, is invested in preserving the fiction of his own alienation, despite the consequences, is a testament to how seductive this ideation is intended to be.

Indeed, a careful analysis of character discourse suggests that the novel's fictional subjects are even less individuated and more cumulate than has previously been acknowledged. Even as characters in the novel appear to diverge, ideologically, intellectually, and psychologically, their idioms, by contrast, continue to overlap. While scholars have commented extensively on the form and function of voice in Faulkner's work,[25] this particular phenomenon—the presence of submerged yet meaningful discursive synchronies among characters—is one that remains comparatively underexplored. On the one hand, this pattern of what we might call *involuntary homology* among the novels' speakers has clear implications for our reading of it, since it suggests that Faulkner's text may stage—more forcefully and at greater length than Joyce's text—the obsolescence of a certain mode of autonomous subjectivity, at least as the Compson brothers envision it. But it may also have broader implications for the reading of modernist narrative more generally. By challenging the assumption that fictional utterances must originate with a single, discrete speaker, the novel also undermines the usefulness of interpretive paradigms predicated on notions of ownership, attribution, and possession.

---

25. Ross's *The Inexhaustible Voice* remains the definitive study of "voice" in Faulkner's fiction; see also Bleikasten and John T. Matthews.

## IV. QUENTIN'S "LOUD WORLD"

In his essay on Faulkner, "The Last Novelist," Kenner argues that American modernists conceived of language largely as a "code" rather than, in the mode of early twentieth-century European novelists, as a "heritage." What distinguishes modernist literary production in America, he suggests, is precisely

> the assumption . . . that Language is something arbitrary, something *external* both to the speakers who use it and to the phenomena they hope to denote. Its norms are not imposed by history, they are elected, and if they turn out to be misleading us we can elect new ones. (213)

This assumption—"that a language may be less a heritage than a code . . . that we are free to change"—has, Kenner acknowledges, "been suspected in other times and places, but never so much as in America has it been felt in a whole people's bones" (213). It is a compelling thesis, one that harmonizes well with my reading of James's and Hemingway's fiction in the previous chapter, in which I propose that a perceived lack of linguistic heritage emerges as both a theme of and a possible explanation for the idiosyncratic expressive regimes of the novel's characters. One way of making sense of the strangely vague and exploratory conversations that emerge in *The Ambassadors* and *The Sun Also Rises,* in other words, is as an attempt at negotiating new verbal standards.

Yet as illuminating as Kenner's theory may be for an understanding of American modernist writers, it does not seem to account for the full range of "assumptions" about spoken language that surface in their fiction. Faulkner, for instance, may perceive himself to be a writer liberated from inherited norms, but his characters don't seem to enjoy a similar freedom. Unlike Frederic Henry, for instance, there is no evidence that Quentin Compson feels "free to change" language, though this does not mean he does not recognize it as "arbitrary." That Quentin may experience language more as monolithic history than as manipulatable code is forcefully attested to, for instance, by the sense of helplessness he feels in the face of his sister's "unvirgin" status (*Sound* [hereafter SF] 78). While Stephen Dedalus, say, comes independently to the conclusion that "paternity may be a legal fiction," or God, a "shout in the street," Quentin needs his father to tell him that "virginity" is a word and concept "invented" by men (U 9.844, 2.386; SF 78). Similarly illustrative are the form and the shape of his monologue: Though Quentin is capable of beautiful neologisms, his section of the novel reflects a preference for repeating the words of others rather than inventing his own. A typical excerpt of his stream of consciousness, for instance, features no less than four other voices:

The displacement of water is equal to the something of something. Reducto absurdum of all human experience, and two six-pound flat-irons weight more than one tailor's goose. What a sinful waste Dilsey would say. Benjy knew it when Damuddy died. He cried. *He smell hit. He smell hit.* (90)

Here, Quentin recalls words from several incongruous sources: Dilsey, T. P., his freshman-year physics and Latin classes at Harvard. Much like Joyce's handling of Leopold Bloom's trains of thought, Faulkner's montage-like presentation of these voices suggests that Quentin doesn't bother enclosing them in quotation marks—an indication of not only the banality and regularity of this sort of discursive traffic,[26] but also its degree of interpenetration with Quentin's own thoughts.

The extent to which Quentin may be overmastered by what Barthes calls "the discourse of others" (rather than, as in the case of Bloom, an opportunistic recycler of it) is further indicated by the disproportionate time the chapter devotes to hearing, an activity that seems more involuntary than it does deliberate (*S/Z* 186). As critics like Ross have noted, the section begins with his "hearing" his watch, Shreve's slippers, the clock; and ends, suggestively, when the clock's "last note sounded" (*Inexhaustible Voice* 76; *SF* 178).[27] Yet the sheer proliferation of both newly perceived and recollected sounds in the chapter, coupled with the record of his attempts to silence them (as with Caddy: "You shut up you shut up you hear me you shut up are you going to shut up"), implies that such listening may be an unwelcome compulsion rather than proof of aural receptivity (*SF* 158). If Benjy's section can be read as an extended "trying to say," one could classify Quentin's as a trying to *not* hear, to not let others (people or things) "say" (Bleikasten, *Ink* 67). This effort culminates in the chapter's concluding passages, when Quentin confesses to his father that he would like "to isolate [Caddy] out of the loud world so that it would have to flee us of necessity" (*SF* 177). It seems clear, however, that Quentin's real ambition is to isolate himself as much as (or more than) Caddy, whom he is using as a placeholder for his own desires (just as Faulkner, famously sound-phobic, could be using Quentin as a conduit for his own[28]).

---

26. Though stream of consciousness represents an innovative formal technique, its contents, as Moretti has demonstrated apropos of *Ulysses,* are often conservative and tend toward cliché; Bloom's monologues, for instance, follow a rhythm he describes as "two or three stimuli, one commonplace, two or three stimuli, one commonplace" (*Modern Epic* 163; see also pp. 149–67).

27. For more on Quentin's listening habits, see Ross, "The 'Loud World' of Quentin Compson."

28. Faulkner was famously sensitive to sound; he prohibited his daughter from owning a phonograph and drove at least one local restaurant to the "practice of unplugging the gaudy jukebox whenever Faulkner entered" (Blotner 476).

Quentin's suicide may be the most acute narrative consequence of this longing for silence, since it connotes for him "that sense of water swift and peaceful above secret places, felt, not seen not heard" (136). But his isolationist fantasies are reflected in his language as well as his behavior and manifest most strongly in his documentable preference for monologic forms of expression. It may not be a stretch to say that Quentin specializes in nonreciprocal communications, like the suicide notes he "wrote . . . and sealed" for Shreve and his father, or the one-sided conversation he carries on with the young Italian girl, who may or may not "spika" English (81, 132). As the chapter makes clear, Quentin consistently favors silent or socially "subordinate" interlocutors, like Deacon, or the little girl, or the man on the mule on whom he bestows a coin, in a gesture very much reminiscent of Gabriel's with the "caretaker's daughter," Lily:

"Hey, Uncle," I said. "Is this the way?"

"Suh?" He looked at me, then he loosened the blanket and lifted it away from his ear.

"Christmas gift!" I said.

"Sho comin, boss. You done caught me, aint you."

"I'll let you off this time." I dragged my pants out of the little hammock and got a quarter out. "But look out next time. I'll be coming back through here two days after New Year, and look out then." I threw the quarter out of the window. "Buy yourself some Santy Claus." (87)

Like the gift of the bread to the "little sister" he meets in the bakery, this gesture is at once unsolicited and unanswered. Most important, it assures him of having the last and definitive word, as his other conversations in the novel reveal he generally does not.

Indeed, the exchanges Quentin does have or recalls having had during the course of the chapter are almost uniformly contentious. Ross has pointed out that "all of Quentin's major experiences, as remembered on his last day, take the form of verbal confrontations: arguments between this mother and father, arguments with Caddy, with Herbert Head, with Dalton Ames, with his father" ("'Loud World'" 252). But it seems likely that for Quentin, nearly all conversations are associated or strongly equated in his mind with confrontation. Looking through the window of the watch repair shop, for instance, he imagines each of the clocks "contradicting one another," each "with the same assertive and contradictory assurance"; later, listening to the young boys fishing at the bridge, he reports that "they all talked at once, their voices insistent and contradictory and impatient" (SF 85, 117). The equivalence between speech and *agon* seems so strong that Quentin can even confuse the fantasy of "shooting Herbert" with "shooting his voice," a phrase so ambiguous that it allows readers to imagine both Quentin figuratively "shooting" his own voice "through the floor" or, alternatively, Herbert, metonymically reduced to his voice, being "shot" (105). Far from the benevolent force it was in James, then, or the criterion of value it remained in Joyce, the speaking voice in Faulkner's text has become an instrument of violence. It is worth noting that Faulkner himself was notably ambivalent on the subject, by turns "honor[ing] the speaking voice" in his novels and excoriating it in other personal writings (Matthews 28). "What the hell can I do?" Faulkner wrote in a letter to Malcolm Cowley. "Goddamn it I've spent almost fifty years trying to cure myself of the curse of human speech, all for nothing" (*Selected Letters* 234). He expressed a similar sentiment in a letter to Hemingway: "I have believed for years that the human voice has caused all human ills and I thought I had broken myself of talking" (*Selected Letters* 251–52).

It is a conviction that Quentin—who in the novel *has* largely "broken [him]self of talking"—seems partly to share. Indeed, the negative connotations that accrue around "human speech" in his chapter make it possible to see his abstinence from it as a strategic, even self-defensive, maneuver. As John Mepham argues in his account of modernist speech representation, "Stream of consciousness and interior monologue" should be classified not just as "literary techniques" but also as "psychological strategies," adopted in response to new historical realities. More specifically, he argues, "they are what happens when the framework of intersubjectivity . . . the framework which makes verbal communication and mutual readability among people possible, are for whatever reason absent" ("Psychoanalysis" 118) On the one hand, *The Sound* would appear to illustrate perfectly the situation Mepham describes, one in which the conditions enabling "verbal communication and mutual readability" have broken down or becomes "absent." Yet Quentin's gravitation toward the subvocal may have less to do with historical contingencies than with personal ones. Like Mepham, readers of Faulkner have frequently considered how the characters' soliloquized chapters might reflect their psychological states: Bleikasten sees Jason's and Quentin's sections, for instance, as illustrative of "how alienation works within the recesses of a mind" (*Ink* 123). It seems equally possible to see the two brothers' confinement to their own consciousnesses not simply as a symptom of some preexisting condition but also as its *cause*. Put another way, Quentin's abstention from meaningful intercourse—his insistence on reporting and rehearsing past dialogue rather than engaging in it—might indeed derive from some underlying sense of "alienation." But it might just as readily catalyze it. If, as Nancy Armstrong has argued, "the modern individual could only define him- or herself as such in opposition to an engulfing otherness . . . that obliterated individuality," then this kind of staged dichotomy—between internal silence and an external, "engulfing" loudness—is for Quentin perhaps a self-sustaining fiction (25).

That it *is* a fiction is made evident by the number of voices that populate his consciousness. But even as the distinctions between Quentin's voice and those of competing egos erode, as they do especially in the section's concluding pages,[29] it is worth noting that inquits—those speech tags that identify speakers—remain to the very last, albeit in vitiated form. And their lingering presence suggests just how committed Quentin may be to the notion of authorship, of ownership over one's language. Even when all other formalities have been abandoned, the differentiation between subjects appears to remain, for Quentin, of paramount significance:

> and i you don't believe i am serious and he i think you are too serious to give me any cause for alarm you wouldnt have felt driven to the expedient of telling me you had committed incest otherwise and i wasnt lying i wasnt lying and he you wanted to sublimate a piece of natural human folly into a horror and then exorcise it with truth. (176–77)

A striking example of this phenomenon—the improbable persistence of speech tags in otherwise unconventional discursive environments—can be found in "The Bear," though there, the space that elapses between speakers raises different questions, to be considered in the next chapter. Like the habitual suppression of antecedents in Faulkner's work, the retention of speech tags when all other conventions for formatting dialogue have been foregone raises certain questions, since these contradictory tendencies seem to "belong" to so many of Faulkner's speakers. In particular, the lingering presence of inquits implies that the question "who is speaking?" retains central importance for Faulkner's speakers and that its obfuscation, a source of continued intellectual interest for narrative theorists, is for the novel's subjects a real cause for concern.

---

29. When asked why he began to "omit capitals on the names and on 'I' in the last part of Quentin's section," Faulkner responded, "Because Quentin is a dying man, he is already out of life, and those things that were important in life don't mean anything now" (Gwynn and Blotner 18).

Jason is, if anything, more invested than his brother in logics of ownership and attribution—not, like Quentin, for the purposes of safeguarding his voice but in the hopes of publicizing it. Especially revealing of his promotional agenda is the exchange with Dilsey he has later in the novel: "Did you hear me? Jason said. I hears you, Dilsey said. All I been hearin, when you in de house" (278). If Quentin is anxious about hearing, Jason is infinitely more concerned with *being* heard.[30] In the case of Caroline Compson, this priority has assumed such prominence that it seems to have completely occluded her ability *to* hear or to pretend any interest in the words or responses of others: "Dilsey, she called, without inflection or emphasis or haste, as though she were not listening for a reply at all. Dilsey" (267). Jason may be no more receptive to other people's speech, but he is still desirous of their recognition of his own. Particularly revealing here is his habit of self-citation and attribution: "Like I say blood always tells" (238); "because like I say blood is blood and you cant get around it" (243); "Well like I say they never started soon enough with cutting'" (263); and, perhaps most memorable, "Once a bitch always a bitch, what I say" (180). That this last line opens Jason's section seems designed to foreground not only some of his most loathsome traits—boastfulness, misogyny—but his own peculiar form of self-branding. As Ross has recognized, this pattern of "incessant 'I says' serves as one of many symptoms of egotistical self-assertiveness" (84). But it reveals something about Jason's ideology as well as his psychology: his beliefs that these words—that words in general—can belong to him and that language in general is a property to be owned and laid claim to.

The irony, of course, is that the very phrases Jason claims as "his" tend to be the most clichéd, and thus the least attributable, to him or anyone else. In this sense, his treatment of speech, like Gabriel's, might seem designed to illustrate the Bakhtinian lesson that even the language we think of as "ours" is not. Of greater interest than the truth content of Jason's authorship claims, however, is the fact that he insists on making them, that he thinks it necessary to make them. In this way, it's possible to see Jason's habit of possessive speaking as a symptom of his fear of *dis*possession—of his suspicion that one's words, without such preventive measures, would be subject to co-option: to precisely the kind of circulation that the novel reveals to be continually taking place.

---

30. It is perhaps for this reason that his section of the novel creates the most powerful impression of being spoken, even though it is "strictly speaking pure and uncommunicated *interior* discourse," since "many of Jason's characteristic verbal mannerisms . . . evoke a strong sense of communication, as if he were speaking out loud" (Ross, *Inexhaustible Voice* 77).

## V. "HE SMELL HIT"; "I SEES HIT"

Plenty of critics have mapped the narrative similarities between, say, Quentin and Benjy, or Quentin and Jason. Daniel Singal, for one, suggests that the brothers share "the calamity of being a Compson in a modern world," though they react to it differently: "Quentin by clinging to his inherited identity, Jason by violently repudiating his" (133). Bleikasten goes even further, arguing, apropos of the brothers' similar hostility to "others," that "Jason turns out to be in many ways Quentin's homologue" (*Ink* 109). Yet if scholars have discerned these sorts of thematic continuities, fewer have recognized the symmetries that emerge at the level of discourse through instances of represented speech and thought. Bleikasten is one of the few to acknowledge the prevalence of such locutionary coincidence; speaking of the novel's first two sections, he notes that "linguistically, there are obvious similarities between the two monologues[;] . . . especially when Quentin records 'present' actions and perceptions, he often uses strings of minimal sentences strongly reminiscent of Benjy's speech" (72). But he does not attest to the more diffuse pattern of similarities among the novels' putatively differentiated speakers, similarities that challenge not only the characters' ideals of autonomy but the interpretive conventions of speaker "differentiation" and "identification" central to readerly practice.[31]

An indication of how widespread such discursive synchronies may be emerges in the opening passages of the novel's second section, when Quentin reports, "Through the wall I heard Shreve's bed-springs and then his slippers on the floor hishing" (77). Though the sentence's content may be specific to his life at Harvard, its structure cannot help recalling the opening line of the novel and of his brother's chapter: "Through the fence, between the curling flower spaces, I could see them hitting" (3). Both begin with the same adverbial phrase ("Through the"), followed by a report based on sensation ("I heard"; "I could see"), and a concluding, aspirated gerund ("hishing," "hitting"). And while Quentin's formulation is clearly marked by more precise diction ("bed-springs"), there is actually not as much distance between their respective vocabularies as may initially appear: Earlier, Benjy alludes to his own "slipper" and to the "hissing," if not "hishing," of the fire Jason builds (73, 72). While Benjy's perceptions are arguably subjected to some degree of authorial revision—a process that might help "explain" the parallelism—the impressionism that characterizes his discourse ("curling flower spaces") seems

---

31. The terms are Ross's; see chapter 2 of *The Inexhaustible Voice* for further explication of them.

to mark them as more-direct emanations. Without overstating the importance of such parallels, then, it seems possible to suggest that Benjy's and Quentin's idioms have more in common than the novel's conventions—its careful sorting of "speakers" into distinct chapters, the implied privacy of characters' thoughts—would seem to allow. In fact, there is a surprising degree of sameness among the novel's ostensibly distinct speakers. When Benjy, for instance, reports that "we went through the rattling leaves" (6); or when he notices Caddy's "book-satchel swinging and jouncing behind her" (6); or, while watching a fire, observes "T. P. squatting in his shift tail in front of it, chunking it into a blaze," it is not necessarily easy to delineate the "idiot's" thoughts from his highly intelligent brother's (28). Conversely, some of Quentin's comments come surprisingly close, in spontaneity or naïveté, to Benjy's: "Her fingers closed about them, damp and hot, like worms" (127); "My nose could see gasoline" (173); "A sparrow slanted across the sunlight" (79). There are general differences: Quentin favors the past perfect; Benjy, the present or past progressive. But even this distinction doesn't hold up; thus Benjy can report "I leaned my face over where the supper was. It steamed up on my face"; and Quentin, "Then the curtains breathing out of the dark upon my face, leaving the breathing upon my face" (24, 174).

Perhaps most suggestive in this regard is the surprisingly wide circulation of a phrase that, within the diegesis, is consistently associated with and even in some sense "attributed" to Benjy. Early in the novel, Benjy learns of Damuddy's death by smell: "I could smell it," Benjy thinks, and he repeats the phrase twice for emphasis: "I could smell it"; "But I could smell it" (34). Intuiting what has happened, T. P. reports "He smell hit," just as Dilsey will recognize when "he smellin hit": phrases that, while reflective of the speakers' idiolects, come so close to Benjy's in their syntactical construction that they almost seem to qualify as jointly authored (34, 288). Later, Quentin recalls his brother' realization-by-smell, in T.P.'s words: "Benjy knew it when Damuddy died. He cried. *He smell hit. He smell hit*" (90). And Jason, too, eventually recalls the episode, reflecting that Benjy "cannot hear it unless he can smell it" (174). What is striking, though, is that only a page before, Jason has already adopted the phrase for himself: having filled his car with gasoline, a smell he loathes, he has washed his face and hands, "but even then I could smell it" (172). A short time later, he reports, "I turned out the light and went into my bedroom, out of the gasoline, but I could still smell it" (172). Though the phrase itself is unexceptional, and though its submersion into these longer lexical units dilutes it, there is no denying this unacknowledged instance of verbal symmetry between the two brothers. Nearly as striking is that Reverend Shegog, during his sermon, produces his own iteration on this formula:

"I sees hit, breddren! I sees hit!" (296). Indeed, one starts to find variations on this phrase surfacing inter-, as well as intratextually, as when Bayard Sartoris, near the beginning of *The Unvanquished,* reports, "Then I began to smell it again" (10).

There are differences, of course, between these instances of "smelling" and "seeing" it, or "hit." What is more interesting than any single instance of this expression, however, is the cumulative effect of its reiteration. For in distributing so widely a phrase generally associated with one character, Faulkner underscores the capacity for speech in the novel to index not just individual characters but the groups, regions, or cultures to which they belong. As a result, readers may find themselves struck not only by the truly singular examples of character speech but by the recurrence of more generic formulations—such as the similarly redundant interjections issued by Dilsey and Caroline, among others: "You, Luster!"; You, Jason!" Ross, noticing this pattern, has argued that "Faulkner seems more concerned with typical speech habits than with how a particular utterance sounds" (75). But this shift in focus from "particular" utterances to "typical" ones would seem to have even broader implications than he implies. In fact, this change in emphasis may necessitate a corollary change in critical approach, since the question becomes not just "who" is speaking in a fictional text, but whether it *matters* who is speaking. In a world where a white Harvard student "talks like a colored man" and a black preacher "sounds like a white man," and where an aging matriarch speaks like the household servant, how can speech, the novel implicitly asks, serve as a reliable mark of identity (120, 293)?

Even more suggestive may be the extent to which not just voices but qualities become progressively undifferentiated as the novel proceeds. With increasing frequency, Faulkner assigns the same, highly particularized epithets to at least two characters, often in what seems like meaningful proximity. At the start of the novel's fourth section, for instance, he describes Dilsey's paunch as "almost dropsical" (265) and then notes that Benjy's "skin was dead looking and hairless; dropsical too" (274). The Reverend Shegog's voice is described as "inflectionless," shortly after Caroline calls to Dilsey, "without inflection" (293, 267). Both the Reverend Shegog and Benjy are respectively "emptied" or "empty" (284, 294). And then there is Benjy's "gaze empty and untroubled," which mimics that of the statue of the Confederate soldier, which "gazed with empty eyes" (SF 320, 319).[32] Both descriptions, in turn, recall Jason's evocation of Caddy's gaze: "She looked at me then everything emptied out of her eyes

---

32. Singal also notes this doubling but reads it as proof of the significance of Confederate imagery (143).

and they looked like the eyes in statues blank and unseeing and serene" (163). Then there is the fact that several characters share the same names—Jason, Quentin, Maury—a practice that may be as much a gauge of intersubjectivity as it is of heredity.

Indeed, the attribution of a single characteristic or name to more than one fictional subject hints at the potentially disconcerting possibility that Sharon Cameron raises in *Impersonality*: namely, that especially in certain modern and modernist texts, literary "character does not seem to be an autonomous or independent entity. . . . Rather, [characters] share traits we might have thought exclusively the property of one or the other" (181). Considered in this light, Faulkner's decision to locate the same "traits" across different characters and contexts challenges the logic of containment that many of the novel's subjects insist upon. The Compsons' decision to change Benjy's name, for example, seems to stem from a superstition that negative qualities might be shared or somehow communicated between namesakes. Notably, it is Dilsey who rebuts this thinking most forcefully. When Luster tells her that the Compsons are "funny folks" and that he's "Glad [he] aint none of them," she corrects him: "Aint one of who?' Dilsey said. 'Lemme tell you somethin, nigger boy, you got jes es much Compson devilment in you es any of em'" (276).

The implication is not only that identity, like language, may be more "inherited" than "freely chosen," to return to Kenner's terms, but more specifically that identity is a product of proximity and familiarity, as much as the criteria of race and family. It is worth noting that this idea almost directly contradicts Benn Michael's thesis that American identity in the early twentieth century had become an "ambition," something to be invented, earned, and selectively bestowed (3). Here, the opposite seems true: Identity is revealed to be less a function either of "blood," as Jason and Caroline would have it, or of carefully policed nativist conventions, as Benn Michaels suggests. Instead, it is the almost involuntary result of shared experience, of something as banal as propinquity and routine. Thus, while the Easter Sermon is generally regarded as the apotheosis of intersubjective experience in the novel, the prevalence of both verbal and characterological sharing in the novel suggests that subjectivity isn't just something overcome in exceptional or utopian moments. In fact, its contravention may be the default state of affairs, despite the generalized resistance of the novels' subjects to accept that. In this sense, the novel may offer less a "critique of subjectivity itself," as Arnold Weinstein has suggested, than a critique of the personal or cultural attachment to an ideal of subjectivity in its most romantic and self-contained forms (343).

At the same time, however, Faulkner does not disavow the enduring power of this ideal. Like "The Dead," *The Sound* ends with a surprisingly monologic flourish: the return of "Faulkner's rhetoric," which "previously held in check ... bursts into full flower" (Bleikasten, *Ink* 132). If the first three sections, then, have historically been "cast as soliloquies," the fourth seems to represent a different, largely authorial order of subjectivity (Lester 143). In its emancipation from any particular character psychology, the section seems to reflect a fantasy of literary autonomy of the sort Faulkner claims to have achieved during the composition of the novel. As biographer Jay Blotner has noted, "the writing was apparently an experience of unparalleled intensity for him," as Faulkner would confirm in the introduction to the novel: "One day I seemed to shut a door ... between me and all publishers' addresses and book lists. I said to myself, Now I can write. Now I can make myself a vase like that which the old Roman kept at his bedside and wore the rim slowly away with kissing it" (212).

What Faulkner describes is the realization of those interrelated desires—for privacy, independence, autonomy—that he assigns to (but leaves unfulfilled in) his novel's characters. The image of the "shut a door" is particularly suggestive, since it in many ways bespeaks a Quentin-like desire to "isolate" himself and his creations from "the loud world." Practically speaking, this sort of isolation would become an increasingly elusive goal for Faulkner as he assumed the burden of caring for family members, "most of whom," as he put it, "I dont like and with none of whom I have anything in common" (Blotner 438). But by his account, Faulkner would always maintain that *The Sound* allowed him an unprecedented measure of artistic (if not personal) independence. The difference, he claimed, was that during the novel's composition, "I believed then that I would never be published again. . . . I had stopped thinking of myself in publishing terms" (220). He wrote the book, then, not only "with a sense of liberation from any practical constraints," but with a more general sense of liberation from any *response* (220). However accurate or apocryphal his assessment of the novel's production, what is most striking is Faulkner's insistence that he wrote the novel not with an eye to public reception but with a sense of indifference to it. Thus the "non-response" that was such a painful reality for James (and would be for Faulkner as well) may in the earlier stages of his career have also served as a salutary fiction (Edel 663). And thus Faulkner succeeded in constructing for himself the sort of expressive scenario of which Quentin, in particular, could only dream.

And yet it would be false to suggest an equivalence between Faulkner's fantasy of (creative) autonomy and his characters' attempts to preserve theirs—especially given the proximity of their efforts to a segregationist and supremacist ethos. In this sense, the discursive shift in the final section seems motivated less by a psychological need on Faulkner's part, as some of the commentary above seems to imply, than by a more targeted ideological agenda. It's no coincidence, in other words, that when the narration is finally decoupled from the Compsons, readers are most emphatically invited to pass judgment on them. At the same time, by redistributing narrative attention to Luster and Dilsey and assigning both textual priority and lexical particularity to *their* speech, the final section valorizes the experiences and language of not just the novel's principal black characters but, by extension, the African American community subjected to the family's all-too-typical brand of white exceptionalism. When asked, during a well-known interview at the University of Virginia, about the "trouble" with the Compsons, Faulkner's response was that "they are still living in the attitudes of 1859 or '60" (U 18). In other words, they are products of an ancient, if enduring, pre-bellum regime, whose values survive not only in the racist content of Jason's speech, say, but in the possessive and paranoid ways the Compsons think *about* speech. In this sense, the stakes of the fourth section's synthesis of lyrical and empirical tendencies could not be higher, inasmuch as it implies Faulkner's willingness to leverage his own rhetorical power to elevate (and, in the Easter Sermon scene, celebrate) the voices of historically disenfranchised speakers. In this sense, *The Sound and the Fury* ends by forcefully disallowing the kinds of readerly confusion Joyce seems to actively court. By first deploying and then dispensing with the cloak of character discourse, Faulkner detaches his voice from that of his compromised speakers so as to deliver—in a frankly authorial register—the kind of commentary that could not remain only indirectly said.

CHAPTER 4

# The Paradoxical Voice

*Faulkner's and Woolf's Implausible Speech*

NEAR THE BEGINNING of *Absalom, Absalom!,* as Mr. Compson recounts to Quentin the series of improbable events that culminated in Rosa Coldfield's engagement to Thomas Sutpen, he imagines the impression Sutpen must have made on the much younger Rosa. For her, he surmises, Sutpen must always have been

> that ogre-face . . . seen once and then repeated at intervals . . . like the mask in a Greek tragedy interchangeable not only from scene to scene but from actor to actor and behind which the events and occasions took place without chronology or sequence and leaving her actually incapable of saying how many separate times she had seen him for the reason that, waking or sleeping, the aunt had taught her to see nothing else. (AA 48–49)

The figure is in many ways an instructive one for readers of Faulkner's novel, whose multifarious speakers appear over the course of the narrative to adopt, if not an "interchangeable" mask, then an equally interchangeable or invariable voice. Not only do the novel's diegetic speakers and its extradiegetic one use nearly identical idiom; they also appear to draw from the same rhetorical inventory. Thus, for instance, the "ogre-face" surfaces both in Mr. Compson's imagination and in the minds of Quentin and Rosa, who allude on separate occasions to Sutpen as an "ogre-shape" and the subject of an "ogre-tale" (8, 15). In this sense, the excerpt above would seem to constitute what Paul de Man describes as an "allegory of reading": a trope *of* reading, and one that can also generate a reading (*Allegories*). In other words, Mr. Compson's metaphor might serve to illuminate not just the frightening physiognomy of a single character but the similarly monstrous (because monstrously similar) aspect of the entire novel. Like the actors in a "Greek tragedy," the narrators of Faulkner's novel share among themselves a single stylized prop: a voice that improbably remains the same "not only from scene to scene but from actor to actor."

This feature of the novel has hardly gone unremarked by commentators, for whom the undeviating sameness of character speech has become something of a commonplace. Gerald Langford provides an early and authoritative account of this phenomenon when he notes that "no matter which narrator is speaking the style throughout the book remains uniformly poetic and intricately structured" (21). Stephen Ross argues similarly that while many "have emphasized differences among the narrators, finding each discourse to be motivated by the psychic needs of the storyteller," any distinctions they may find are overshadowed by "the overwhelming consistency of an oratorical Overvoice" (*Inexhaustible Voice* 220). Along comparable lines, Peter Brooks speaks of the "transindividual voice" that pervades Faulkner's text, which he dubs a "duet for four voices" (294, 304). And John T. Matthews, further anatomizing the "collective voices" of the novel, confirms that they all display the same, highly unlikely combination of "baroque prolixity . . . nightmarish breathlessness, and . . . Latinate polysyllabism" (121).

Despite the widespread recognition of vocal homogeneity in *Absalom*, however, there have been surprisingly few attempts to consider its implications. Far more frequent have been attempts to rationalize it. In a recent article, for instance, Jeanne A. Follansbee suggests that Faulkner's use of "similar diction and syntax to represent each person's speech" may be less a deliberate aesthetic technique than at least partly a by-product of his compositional method: "the result of [his] practice while writing to move portions of the novel from one narrator to another" (84).[1] And Ross seems to similarly curtail the potential resonance of this narratological feature when he suggests—albeit persuasively—that the characters' monotonous and long-winded speeches might reflect the cadences of Southern oratory (*Inexhaustible Voice* 212). In so doing, Ross and Follansbee are representative of other critics who seem to delimit the significance of this textual phenomenon by situating it within what

---

1. Pamela Dalziel notes the similar critical tendency to "reconcile" perceived narrative contradictions, as well as stylistic ones, by "attributing 'inconsistencies' to the narrators' limited viewpoints or (usually as a last resort) to Faulkner's carelessness" (277).

Milan Kundera has referred to as the "*mini-mini-mini-context*" of an author's biography (269). By contrast, my goal in this chapter will be to explore what Faulkner's staging of character speech might tell us not just about this novel but about the modernist novel and its uses of dialogue more generally.

To this end, I'd like to consider the invariability of character voice in *Absalom* alongside a parallel instance of the phenomenon that arises in a roughly contemporaneous work: Virginia Woolf's 1931 novel, *The Waves*. Although there is no definitive evidence that Faulkner read the novel, Woolf herself, significantly, gives us some reason to believe that he had. As Mark Hussey reports, "Woolf . . . noted in her diary on June 1, 1937, that William Faulkner had 'most intelligently (& highly)' praised *The Waves*," even though "no mention by Faulkner of the novel has been traced" (*Virginia Woolf from A to Z* 356). It is therefore at least possible to speculate that Faulkner may have had Woolf's narrative in mind as he constructed his own, which, like *The Waves*, is organized around a series of putative (and putatively differentiated) speeches that not only don't seem to have been spoken but also convey the impression of having *not been spoken* by the same speaker. Such similarities are further reflected in critical assessments of Woolf's novel, which dovetail remarkably with those of Faulkner's. As Eric Warner puts it, the six characters in *The Waves*—like those in *Absalom*—"all speak the same language" and "all employ the same 'poetic' devices of parallelisms, repetitions, metaphorical passion, elisions, etc., often sharing the same key phrases or words"; in short, "an undifferentiated high style unites them all" (79–80). Like Faulkner, then, Woolf "makes no attempt to distinguish the style of one speaker from that of any other" and thus creates the similar impression that her novel's fictive speakers are less fully embodied subjects than "characters manqué" (Graham, "Point of View" 95; Naremore 164).

At first glance, then, these two texts might just appear to take to more radical extremes the tendency discerned in the previous chapter through an analysis of Faulkner's earlier novel, *The Sound and the Fury*, and Joyce's "The Dead": namely, the willingness of early twentieth-century authors to collapse distinctions among character idioms and, in so doing, to challenge the principles of linguistic differentiation that have been central to the novel's construction and reception. What further distinguishes *The Waves* and *Absalom*, however, is that the refusal to differentiate among figural voices is coupled, in each case, with an equally pronounced insistence on attributing them. In other words, both works present as textually distinct utterances that would otherwise, were it not for formatting and punctuation, read as indistinguishable. Indeed, there is very little talk in these novels that goes unattributed: Woolf presents the entirety of the novel's nine episodes as direct speech, allocated to one of six speakers, while Faulkner—though a larger portion of the text derives from an omniscient source—assigns the vast majority of it to one of four character narrators. This reliance on direct discourse is especially striking given how proportionately less it featured in the authors' previous works, which offer, by contrast, some of literature's best-known examples of free indirect or fully internalized discourse: Mrs. Dalloway's stream of consciousness, Benjy's interior monologue, Addy Bundren's posthumous soliloquy. And in each case, it is often only the presence of certain textual features—primarily the use of quotation marks and the regular occurrence of speech tags[2]—that recall attention to the allegedly "spoken" status of what might otherwise be received as interior discourse. There is, then, a curious paradox at the heart of these novels: If both convey the sense of having made "the demarcation between characters' voices . . . less rigid," in the manner of the texts discussed in the second chapter, structurally they still insist—conspicuously and continuously—on precisely this kind of demarcation (Thomas, "Dialogue" 82). In this sense, the novels might actually be seen to dramatize *two* paradoxes: by presenting as speech what is manifestly not spoken and by assigning to distinct speakers a voice that gives every sign of belonging to all.

The question is what to make of this paradoxical presentation of speech and the novels' oscillating investments in at once disambiguating and conflating character voice. In contrast to the proprietary attitudes toward speech discussed in the previous chapter, which emerged from a comparative analysis of *The Sound* and "The Dead," the interest in pairing voices with "owners" appears at times to originate less with fictional subjects than with the authors themselves. Thus, if the monological impulse evident in those earlier texts seem motivated by the "psychic needs" of their speakers—by characters like Gabriel, Quentin, or Jason, who sought to safeguard the illusion of their own verbal sanctity—here, the demarcation of characterological utterance becomes a far more obvious textual feature, making it difficult to read as anything other than the work of some supradiegetic agency (Ross, *Inexhaustible Voice* 220). No longer explainable with reference to character psychology alone, then, such a pattern presents itself as the work of some organizing intelligence, the product of deliberate authorial design.[3] Indeed, the prominence of this pattern

---

2. This practice is widely noted among Woolf's commentators. See Graham, who notes how "rigorously" Woolf "follows two conventions for rendering direct speech: the use of 'said' to indicate a speaker, and the use of quotation marks to set off the speech itself" ("Point of View" 95).

3. That this design can in turn be discerned in two texts has the effect of amplifying the significance of what, considered singly, might more readily be dismissed as idiosyncrasy: unfairly so, I would add, since even singular or unusual phenomena are exemplary of a broader

seems to raise questions for theorists of narrative, and modernist narrative in particular. Why, given the homogeneous quality of these figural utterances, go through the motions of differentiating them? And why represent as speech language so clearly coded, by its high degree of stylization, as nonspoken?

On the one hand, it would be possible to position the novels' highly stylized talk as the natural outcome of a larger literary historical trend: the telos of dialogue's antirealist trajectory during the nineteenth and twentieth centuries. While the Victorian novel evinced the "growing demand for realism" among contemporary audiences and placed an attendant pressure on writers to produce mimetic and "true-to-life" speech, the twentieth century witnessed significant changes in the literary representation of dialogue, as I discuss at greater length in the first chapter (Chapman 10, 3). Thus, if realist dialogue-writing reached its apex, as some have argued, in the work of Dickens, novelists of the early twentieth century, as Bronwen Thomas has demonstrated, not only "introduce[d] new speech varieties" but began to "experiment with dialogue in a more overtly self-conscious way" ("Dialogue" 81). Indeed, at the risk of overstating the modernists' "break" with narrative tradition, their construction of dialogue often seems less indebted to immediate fictional predecessors than to older and non-novelistic modes of representing speech. The structure of talk in *The Waves*, for instance, has frequently been compared to that of the chorus or soliloquy[4] (Woolf herself referred to her "dramatic soliloquies"), while James's and Hemingway's dialogues, discussed in the first chapter, appear at times to owe more to the classical dramatic technique of stichomythia than to recent literary custom (*A Writer's Diary* [hereafter WD] 156). Similarly, some have suggested that the expressive strategies on display in both *Absalom* and *The Waves* resemble those of mythical or biblical speakers more than novelistic ones because they display a similar proclivity for declamatory monologue: a tendency, like the one Lennard Davis ascribes to Job's comforters, to "break into speeches rather than engage in speech" (172).

By this logic, one could conclude that Faulkner and Woolf, in keeping with the familiar account of modernist practice, were intent on disrupting the mimetic presentation of character, which depends so crucially on the perceived verisimilitude and "appropriateness" of their speech.[5] In other words,

---

spectrum of modernist experimentation with dialogue, as described in the introduction and documented in chapter 1.

4. Critics have often resorted to generic reclassification to make sense of *The Waves*; see Mark Hussey, *Virginia Woolf*, pp. 348–62, for a summary of the ways the text has alternately been positioned as drama, lyric, and "anti-novel."

5. Ross cogently describes the mutually reinforcing role of speech and character in sustaining mimetic illusion: "Character governs appropriate speech, and character in turn devolves from speech" (*Inexhaustible Voice* 85).

by "breaking up . . . the connection between voice and presence"—as the texts, despite their meticulous habit of attribution, seem constantly to threaten to do—they could be seen to mount a critique of not just the realist project but the Western metaphysical one (O'Donnell 2).[6] If, as Ross has argued apropos of Faulkner's work, mimetic voice has traditionally served in fiction as "an index of personal identity," then a manifestly *un*mimetic voice of the sort on display in these texts would seem to function antithetically to abstract or occlude identity (*Inexhaustible Voice* 85). In this light, the novels' implausible or "unspeakable" discourse, to use Ann Banfield's term, could be seen as a corrective: a "remedy," as literary historian Jonathan Rée puts it, "for the maladies of ontology" (Banfield, *Unspeakable Sentences*; Rée 1049).

Rather than attempt to assign this feature of the novels such a diffuse and totalizing agenda, however, this chapter will argue that Faulkner's and Woolf's paradoxical deployments of character voice might in fact represent a more targeted critique of literary convention. My specific contention is that these novels, by so distorting the structure of novelistic conversation, call attention to its status *as* a structure—one that has a particular history and ideology and has served to reproduce the genre's preference for and orientation around the fully particularized subject.[7] In using those formal devices most commonly used to differentiate among characters—quotation marks, speech tags, proper names—even as they showcase their *failure* to differentiate, Faulkner and Woolf appear to at once vividly highlight and radically question the role of the individual as the organizing principle of the novel. But this technique also takes on a particular resonance in the worlds of each novel: reproducing, in *Absalom,* the futility of Sutpen's self-mythologizing "design" and, by extension, the white South's. Meanwhile, in *The Waves,* it serves a distinct yet similarly sociopolitical function, highlighting the bankruptcy of myths of heroic individualism so successfully mobilized by the imperialist status quo. Thus, if dialogue has most typically been made "to denote individuality or even eccentricity" in the novel, Faulkner and Woolf press it into more polemical service: calling attention, through their frankly implausible constructions, to the assumptions that inhere in one of the novel's most default forms (Fogel 56). In this sense, the presentation of character voice in *The Waves* and *Absalom* constitutes a commentary on the events of their novels, as well as a critique of conversation as it had been previously been practiced in *the* novel.

---

6. See Matthews for more on the ways in which Faulkner's work "challenges the consequences of the 'metaphysics of presence'" (30).

7. A long tradition of novel theory rests behind this assertion; see Watt for an authoritative account of the "primacy of individual experience in the novel" (11).

## I. QUOTATION AND ACCOUNTABILITY

In suggesting that these novels deploy dialogue for such pointed rhetorical purposes, I am diverging from existing theories of fictional speech, which, as discussed in the first chapter, have typically stressed its subordinate function: "to further plot, to develop character, to describe setting or atmosphere, to present a moral argument . . . or to perform any combination of these purposes" (Page 55). Among literary theorists, Bakhtin is one of the few who has recognized the capacity of quoted speech to express more nuanced authorial commentary or critique. In *Problems of Dostoevsky's Poetics* (which appeared shortly before the publication in 1936 of *Absalom*) he grants direct discourse a more variegated range of aesthetic and communicative functions. Even in texts where character speech—or "represented or objectified discourse"—appears more or less singular in intent, there is always, he notes, the possibility of a divergent voice, since "the author may . . . make use of someone else's discourse for his own purposes, by inserting a new semantic intention into a discourse which already has, and which retains, an intention of its own. . . . In one discourse, two semantic intentions appear, two voices" (PDP 189).

It has been a frequent practice, given the homogeneous texture of the talk in *Absalom* and *The Waves*, to read the discourse as each author's own rather than as "someone else's"—and as a result to elide its polysemic potential. As this chapter will demonstrate, however, Faulkner and Woolf not only exploited this potential—an unremarkable feat on its own—but did so with a degree of prominence, and for a set of purposes, that distinguishes them from their novelistic forerunners. Flaubert, for instance, though he may be remembered for his use of free indirect discourse, was similarly strategic in his deployment of direct discourse. Yet in his novels, it is generally the content rather than the form of a character's utterance that does the satirical work, and the object of fun is generally the speaker him- or herself. As Stirling Haig explains,

> citation was always one of Flaubert's satirical moves: he thereby displayed, "showcased" stupidity. The procedure is prophylactic. The quotation marks enclosing bits of Homais' speech are like forceps with which the narrator aseptically handles infectious asininities, the italics like a dye-stain identifying the diseased tissues of gangrenous speech. (18)

What is especially striking in Haig's account of Flaubertian style is his observation that the quotation marks in *Madame Bovary* function as "forceps," a means by which Flaubert safely "handles" character speech, so as to prevent its contamination with his (or his narrator's) own. Even more striking is the proximity of Haig's image to one Daniel Ferrer evokes in his study of *The Waves,* in which, he notes, quotation marks function as a "sanitary cordon," which may on occasion become permeable, with the result that "the interstitial narrative is no longer safe from contamination by the subjectivity of the monologues" (92). Like Haig, then, Ferrer presupposes both the prophylactic quality of quotation marks and, more suggestively, the *need* for such prophylaxis in the first place: the perceived necessity of preventing not only cross-character contamination but the spread of "asininity"—or even just "subjectivity"—from character to narrator. Rée expands on this line of thinking in his analysis of oral citation practices, when he compares "air quotes" to "warning signs" meant to alert auditors that "the speaker is alienated from the words in question and wishes it to be known that they are being used deprecatingly" (1042). It is for this reason, he adds, that "they are sometimes called 'scare quotes'": monitory signs, indicating the presence of dubious language ahead (1042).

"Forceps," "sanitary cordons," "warning signs": It is suggestive that these three commentators seem to have drawn from the same repertoire of imagery to describe quotation's role within nineteenth- and twentieth-century literary and verbal culture. That all three take for granted the need for "protection" is similarly telling, indicative both of how polluting a quantity we have come to consider the verbal output of another and of how precious a commodity, perhaps, we have come to regard our own. Indeed, as Thomas points out, it was during the Victorian period that the "notion of speech as private property" first emerged and, perhaps not coincidentally, the moment in which the use of quotation marks became, after a long period of lackadaisical and inconsistent punctuation, more assiduous (or what Rée calls "ludicrously fussy") (Thomas, "Dialogue" 81; Rée 1044).[8] Though Rée is more circumspect about the onset of this "quotation anxiety"—seeing it instead as a kind of existential condition—he agrees that its apotheosis coincides with the advent of modernity: "The age of the quotation mark," which, as he whimsically describes it, witnessed "a fall from a sunlit realm of joyous verbal freedom, into a squalid, loveless world where the poison of possessive individualism has spread even to people's relations to their own words" (Rée 1053). Contributing to this rise in verbal possessiveness might have been a heightened awareness of just how great a degree of linguistic variation was possible and of how radically the discourse of others might differ from one's "own" (which is to say, the discourse to which speakers not only laid claim but deemed superior to other, foreign variants). As Chapman has pointed out, the nineteenth century, at least in

---

8. See Elizabeth Bonapfel, pp. 69–73, for additional history of punctuation in the novel.

England, was "a time when people became increasingly aware of forms of speech different from those of their immediate circle":

> Greater mobility and the spread of communication brought more familiarity with other regional and social groups. The complexity of spoken English became apparent, at the same time that the importance of a certain type of pronunciation became more important for social prestige. The understanding between author and reader in the matter of dialogue became more discerning and more demanding. (9)

The implication, Chapman implies, was a heightened vigilance on the part of Victorian subjects: a new concern with the proper delineation and citation of speech both in conversation and in print. To recognize a socially "prestigious" type of speech, after all, is to recognize the existence of—and possible threat posed by—a type that is less so.

If quotation practices in nineteenth-century literature reflect these twinned impulses toward possession and protection, however, the use of quoted speech in Faulkner's and Woolf's novels suggests a self-conscious break from such traditions. Indeed, by putting up the "sanitary cordon of quotation marks" around discourse that is so obviously already "contaminated," *The Waves* and *Absalom* seem to short-circuit the kind of possessive function quotation had been made to serve (Ferrer 92). At the same time, by so meticulously citing—and thus appearing to ensure proper "possession" of—character speech, the texts seem to dramatize not just quotation's failure to "cordon" off but the persistence of the conviction that it *should*. In this sense, Woolf and Faulkner deliver a kind of facsimile of differentiation, designed less to "showcase" any particular character—as, say, Flaubert's quotations in *Madame Bovary* did Homais—than the kinds of compulsively atomistic conventions that have governed the presentation of speech and self within fiction.

In staging speech nonpossessively—that is, in such a way that the "ownership" of discrete language is obscured—these texts would seem to oppose not only linguistic tradition (in which speech is insolubly linked to subjectivity) but literary theoretical tradition, which has long relied upon a rhetoric of speakerly "responsibility." Epitomized by the question Genette poses in *Narrative Discourse*, "Who is speaking?," this line of thought presupposes a subject who originates or is "responsible" for any given utterance in a text. In *S/Z*, Barthes would make the degree of speech's attributability a primary criterion of textual plurality, a work's status as *writerly* as opposed to *readerly*. Thus, he explains, "the more indeterminate the origin of the statement, the more plural the text" (41). Such ambiguity assumes a more negative valence in the work of Peter Brooks, who in his analysis of Flaubert decries the *style indirect libre* as a "technique of irresponsibility," which is used to "avoid and prevent direct attribution of what is spoken and reported"—a suggestive formulation, but one that strikes me as somewhat paranoid in its presumption that Flaubert should be so intent on indemnification (Brooks, *Reading* 194). If free indirect discourse has been associated with ideologically dubious activity, however, direct discourse of the kind foregrounded in *Absalom* and *The Waves* would at least appear to qualify the novels as paragons of accountability. And yet both, in assigning the "same" speech to multiple speakers, seem more accurately to parody this logic and its usefulness in understanding discourse within a fictional (and thus not reality-bound) context. More than a prophylactic use of quotation, in which utterances are kept safely apart, one could say that Faulkner's and Woolf's texts model a more *parasitic* one, in which even carefully cordoned off utterances play host to other echoes and influences. Instead of a means of authorial distantiation, then, quotation in these texts only offers a further opportunity for the author's insinuation and inflection.

## II. "GRANDFATHER SAID": COMPULSORY ATTRIBUTION IN *ABSALOM, ABSALOM!*

Faulkner's own unabashedly "irresponsible" approach to quotation is perhaps best illustrated by one of the changes he made to *Absalom* during revision. In a draft of the manuscript, the omniscient narrator recounts the bulk of the second chapter before ceding narration to Mr. Compson near the end. In the published novel, by contrast, Mr. Compson commences narrating much sooner. To make this change, Langford reports, "Faulkner simply introduce[d] quotation marks five pages earlier in the book than he had done in the manuscript. In turning a passage of omniscient narration into oral discourse, he made no changes to give the telling a colloquial tone" (21). While one hesitates to read too much into this single act of revision, the casualness with which Faulkner seems to have reallocated discourse in the novel is telling. Indeed, it appears to epitomize a more diffuse unconcern with maintaining even the appearance of difference among novelistic speakers. It is not unusual, for instance, to find the same phrase verbalized by multiple characters, as evidenced by the opening example. Thus, for instance, the narrator alludes to Henry as "the son who widowed the daughter who had not yet been a bride," while just a few pages later Rosa Coldfield will speak similarly of Judith as "the daughter who was already the same as a widow without ever having been a bride" (7, 10). (Later, Mr. Compson refers yet again to Judith as "who had been widowed before she had been a bride" [167].) From the beginning, then, the novel underscores the continuity among its diegetic speakers and its omniscient speaker. When the narrator refers to "that air of children born too late into their parents' lives," Rosa seems to "overhear" the thought and repeat it in her own account just a few lines later: "Because I was born too late. I was born twenty-two years too late" (15). If *The Sound*, by contrast, minimized and submerged homologies among character speech—requiring that the overlap between Quentin's and Benjy's speech, or Benjy's and the Reverend Shegog's, be actively discerned by a reader—*Absalom* puts such synchrony fully on display. Moreover, *Absalom* permits Quentin an awareness of this phenomenon that he did not enjoy in the earlier novel, allowing him to register and repeatedly protest the resemblance between, say, Shreve's voice and Mr. Compson's: "*He sounds just like Father*, he thought [. . .] *Just exactly like Father if Father had known as much about it the night before I went out there as he did the day after I came back*" (AA 147–48). The implication is that such incidents of "likeness" are now sufficiently prominent to attract the attention of the novel's characters, as well as its commentators. And that what emerged as a latent feature in *The Sound* must here be reckoned as an undeniable part of the narrative reality.

As noted above, most critics have not hesitated to remark on this feature of Faulkner's novel. What is striking, however, is how frequently it has been seen as an insolubly negative symptom. Like Quentin, many have been similarly perturbed by the extent to which the characters sound "like" each other and, to paraphrase Phil Stone's complaint, like Faulkner himself (Blotner 465). For Ross, as mentioned above, the speakers' monolithic style reflects the excesses and pervasive influence of Southern oratory (*Inexhaustible Voice* 212). Follansbee goes further in suggesting that it qualifies the novel as a cautionary tale, a "fascist fable" about the "corrosive effects of monologism in the South" (86). As she sees it,

> this interchangeability of voices in *Absalom* underscores the novel's insistence on a single story, told from the point of view of the planter class and its descendants, while the totalizing aesthetic perspective works to neutralize the fragmentation of white elite power in the social sphere. (84)

In interpreting the speakers' "interchangeabilty" as evidence of their social and intellectual conformity, Follansbee frames the uniform texture of character voice as cause for lament. And in fact Faulkner's own commentary might seem to support such a desultory interpretation of the novel's style. Speaking to students at the University of Virginia, he noted the role of speech in catalyzing and consolidating social conformism:

> I think that there's too much pressure to make people conform and I think that one man may be first-rate but if you get one man and two second-rate men together, then he's not going to be first-rate any longer, because the voice of that majority will be a second-rate voice, the behavior of that majority will be second-rate. (qtd. in Gwynn and Blotner 269)

In light of Faulkner's observations, one could readily conclude that the speakers' homogeneity does indeed constitute an ominous sign: a case study of what occurs when individuals cannot withstand the "pressure to . . . conform" and when the "voice of [the] majority" (in this case, a white, landholding majority) successfully colonizes and monopolizes the voice of a "minority."

Yet a closer analysis of both the texture and the organization of discourse in the novel may not support such a singularly pessimistic reading and, in fact, suggests that Faulkner is dramatizing something more nuanced than the dangers of dogma. In particular, the novel's delineation of character utterances—through the use of textual practices like quotation and italicization—would appear to complicate interpretations that emphasize only their homogeneity (as does Bakhtin's insight that "monotony of language" does not preclude the presence of textual polyphony) (PDP 182).[9] Even more significant a complicating factor, however, may be the characters' own commitment to vocal disambiguation. This tendency manifests most visibly, perhaps, in the gestures of attribution that punctuate the speakers' accounts, and which are particularly concentrated in Quentin's narrative, in the seventh chapter:

> . . . and Grandfather said how he sat there with the firelight on his face and the beard and his eyes quiet and sort of bright, and said—and Grandfather said it was the only time he ever knew him to say anything quiet and simple . . . (AA 200)

> (he did not mean shrewdness, Grandfather said. What he meant was unscrupulousness only he didn't know that word because it would not have been

---

9. See *Problems of Dostoevsky's Poetics*, especially chapter 5, for further explanation of this counterintuitive point. Though "it might even seem that the heroes of Dostoevsky's novels all speak one and the same language, namely the language of their author," Bakhtin argues that superficial, linguistic differentiation is less significant than the "*dialogic angle*" from which discourse is presented (182).

in the book from which the school teacher read. Or maybe that was what he meant by courage, Grandfather said) . . . (201)

Grandfather said even he—all of them—could tell that the architect was not apologising; it was fine, Grandfather said, and he said how Sutpen turned toward him . . . (207)

What is noteworthy in these passages—which are representative of the chapter as a whole—is not just the high frequency of the speech tag, "Grandfather said." It's the impression that Quentin inserts this phrase *more* than is necessary merely to establish the speaker or source of narrative authority. Given its superfluity, the recurrence of this inquit suggests there is something compulsive, or even compulsory, about Quentin's gesture, which represents one manifestation of a larger attributing habit within the novel. For instance, this rhetorical tic recalls the similarly prominent trend toward what I would call *dual indexing*, which is characterized by the speaker's practice of including pronouns alongside—rather than instead of—their antecedents, which are featured in the following parentheses: "his (Quentin's) father's youth" (6); "it (the talking, the telling) seemed (to him, to Quentin)" (15); "She (Miss Rosa)" (39); "he (Henry)" (72); "she (Judith)" (99); "*it (my body)*" (111); "*her (Clytie)*" (126) "*her (Miss Coldfield)*" (138); "he (Sutpen)" (204); "he (Grandfather)" (207); "he (Wash)" (232); "he (Bon)" (265); "he (the lawyer)" (265). This kind of double appellation—the insertion of both the pronoun and the noun (often proper) that it renames—is practiced by all of the novels' speakers, including the omniscient one. In fact, the pattern is even present in less pronounced form in earlier novels, where characters are often doubly interpellated. Here, I am thinking of phrases like "You, Luster!" or "You, Marengo!"—typical constructions in *The Sound* and *The Unvanquished*, respectively (SF 269; UNV 27).

Of course, one could argue that this tendency is simply the product of necessity: In a story with so large a cast of characters and so byzantine and uncertain a plot, *not* clarifying one's referents, after all, runs the risk of rendering the narrative impenetrable. And yet as with Quentin's inquits, this redundancy does not seem designed exclusively or even primarily to clarify. At times, the noun is openly superfluous ("It (the wedding) was in the same Methodist Church") (AA 37). More generally, these instances of double indexing have the effect—much like the novel's broader pattern of parenthetical asides—of elevating the mechanics of telling to the same level of prominence as the story being told. That Faulkner significantly amplified this feature during revisions, as a survey of his changes to the manuscript reveals, suggests that he intended the apparent mannerism to be meaningful.[10] In practice, it telegraphs a certain ambivalence: a concern to preserve the kinds of distinctions between subjects that the novel pretends but ultimately fails to sustain. As in *The Ambassadors,* the widespread distribution of what appears to be a highly idiosyncratic discursive feature seems intended to convey a common attitude or set of priorities shared by multiple speakers. Indeed, it is possible to see this attributive habit as a corrective response to the loss of vocal originality registered by Quentin's earlier comment. In other words, when Quentin credits his grandfather for "saying," or when he or one of the other characters takes pains to name the sources or subjects of their discourse, one could argue that they are manifesting the kind of "quotation anxiety" that Rée identifies as a prototypically modern symptom (1054).

In this light, it seems especially significant that characters favor *quoting* the speech of others rather than paraphrasing it. The irony, of course, is that in most cases the speakers did not witness—and thus, have no knowledge of—the conversations they claim to recap. Yet the purely speculative status of these exchanges does not lessen the significance of the fact that they are ostensibly being presented verbatim. Despite the interchangeability of their own voices, then, when the characters themselves represent speech, they go out of their way to recreate verbal idiosyncrasy. Both Shreve and Quentin, for instance, seem to almost exaggerate the distinctiveness of Wash Jones's idiolect. "Well, Kernal, they mought have whupped us but they aint kilt us yit, air they?" Shreve imagines him saying, and Quentin similarly imbues Wash's granddaughter's speech with idiomatic difference ("Light the lamp, Grandpaw") (AA 225, 233). Even Sutpen, in their renderings, speaks in a manner distinct from the present-day narrators: "Ah, Clytie. Ah, Rosa.—Well, Wash. I was unable to penetrate far enough behind the Yankee lines to cut a piece from that coat tail as I promised you" (AA 223).

In the aggregate, what these speakerly habits demonstrate is how radically the characters' means of representing discourse diverge from and even oppose Faulkner's own. On the one hand, this propensity for differentiating speech might seem to merely continue certain of the trends documented in *The Sound*—say, Quentin's rehashed and fully tagged conversations or Jason's gestures of self-attribution ("like I say"; "what I say"). Yet the manifest status of these verbal tics seems to imply that they have an aesthetic, more than primarily "psychological," significance within the novel, revealing the presence

---

10. See Langford; a comparison of the manuscript copy with that of the published novel reveals that Faulkner systematically inserted these kinds of parentheticals into the text during revision.

*within* Faulkner's novel of narrative designs inimical to his own. Though their approach may seem no more than Faulkner's to be emblematic of what Watt calls *formal realism,* the character narrators lavish more attention on differentiating speech than the narrative that contains them. If the novel, as Ian Watt has argued, has been "distinguished from other genres . . . by the amount of attention it habitually accords both to the individualization of its characters and to the detailed presentation of their environment," then one could argue that it is the *speakers'* narratives, more than Faulkner's, that qualify as more traditionally "novelistic" (17–18). In this sense, Faulkner seems at once to dramatize and ironize one of the central conventions of the genre, assigning to his diegetic narrators the kind of individuating impulse he himself makes it a point to elide.

### III. "IT MIGHT HAVE BEEN EITHER OF THEM": QUENTIN AND SHREVE'S COMPOUND TELLING

If the novel at first glance could arguably be seen to endorse the characters' attributive tendencies—since, like Quentin, Rosa, Mr. Compson, and Shreve, Faulkner does allocate speech to precise speakers—a closer reading reveals the extent to which it casts doubt on the logic of individuation structuring their discourse. It does so most explicitly in the later portions of the narrative, which thematize the decreased salience of attribution as both a compositional paradigm and an interpretive one. This implication reaches its apotheosis in the concluding chapters, as Quentin and Shreve sit talking together in their dorm room:

> They stared—glared—at one another, their voices (it was Shreve speaking, though save for the slight difference which the intervening degrees of latitude had inculcated in them (differences not in tone or pitch but turns of phrase and usage of words), it might have been either of them and was in a sense both: both thinking as one, the voice which happened to be speaking the thought only the thinking become audible, vocal; the two of them creating between them, out of the rag-tag and bob-ends of old tales and talking, people who perhaps had never existed at all anywhere, who, shadows, were shadows not of flesh and blood which had lived and died but shadows in turn of what were (to one of them at least, to Shreve) shades too) quiet as the visible murmur of their vaporising breath. (AA 243)

Though Quentin and Shreve are often positioned in the novel as amateur historiographers, in this passage they seem to qualify less as writers of history than as writers of fiction, "creating between them . . . people who had perhaps never existed at all anywhere." And significantly, what their activity seems to allude to or enact is a mode of authorship so collaborative that it no longer makes sense to acknowledge individual contributions, since "it might have been either of them and was in a sense both." Framed in the terms Alan Palmer introduces in *Social Minds in the Novel,* Quentin and Shreve display a capacity for "intermental thought" that seems singular, inasmuch as it is not shared by the novel's other dyads (Quentin and this father; Quentin and Rosa) (41).[11] Together, then, they exemplify a paradigm in which voice is no longer valued for its "difference"—whether in "tone or pitch" or "turns of phrase and usage of words"—but for its combinatory potential, its capacity to merge with other discourses, the "rag-tag and bob-ends of old tales and talking." In this sense, the writer, at least as metaphorically incarnated by Quentin and Shreve, emerges less as an auteur than a bricoleur, less a "maker" of speech than a skillful recompositor of it. In this sense, *Absalom* seems to precipitate, through the mechanism of Quentin and Shreve's telling, a kind of shift in novelistic aesthetics. If discourse can no longer be understood as the product of a single author—or, in turn, if speech can no longer be seen as originating with a single speaker—then quotation as conventionally practiced in the novel is rendered moot.

In this way, one could say that *Absalom* narrates the obsolescence of its own narrative procedure. Of particular interest is the way Faulkner progressively stages the erosion of ontological and verbal distinctness. In *Absalom*'s later chapters, it becomes clear that the names and identities the speakers have made it such a point to cite are of diminishing value:

> where there were now not two of them but four, the two who breathed not individuals now yet something both more or less than twins . . . (AA 236)

> not two of them there and then either but four of them riding the two horses through the iron darkness and that not mattering either: what face and what names they called themselves and were called by so long as the blood coursed . . . (AA 237)

> Because now neither of them was there. They were both in Carolina and the time was forty-six years ago, and it was not even four now but *compounded still further,* since now both of them were Henry Sutpen and both of them

---

11. See Palmer for a more extended discussion of *"intermental thought,"* which he defines as "thinking [that is] joint, group, shared, or collective, as opposed to intramental, or individual or private thought. It is also known as *socially distributed, situated,* or *extended* cognition, and also as *intersubjectivity*" (41).

were Bon, *compounded each of both yet either neither* . . . (AA 280, italics mine)

By thus "compounding" identity—conflating "two" and "four," consubstantiating Quentin and Shreve with Henry and Bon—the novel indicates its refusal to recognize or valorize the kinds of distinctions (among "faces," "names," and especially "blood") that the Sutpen narrative is fundamentally about. If Shreve and Quentin, unlike Henry and Bon, are not linked by an actual instance of "miscegenation," the novel's emphasis on their "compound" or *mixed* status nonetheless assumes a distinct ideological valence within the novel, serving to repudiate the virulent logic of segregation that structures the drama within it.

Particularly illustrative of this compounding process is the sudden decline of the sorts of differentiating gestures catalogued in character speech above. In the eighth chapter, for instance, the incidence of indexical or deictic markers seems to drop significantly, as does the perceived need for them:

(neither of them said "Bon." Never at any time did there seem to be any confusion between them as to whom Shreve meant by "he") (AA 249)

it was not Bon he meant now, yet again Quentin seemed to comprehend without difficulty or effort whom he meant . . . (AA 251)

But he didn't need to say that either, any more than he had needed to specify which he he meant by he, since neither of them had been thinking about anything else . . . (AA 253)

The fact that Quentin and Shreve stop specifying "which he he meant by he" needn't suggest that they now enjoy a complete and perfect understanding of the Sutpen narrative. Rather, they believe themselves to enjoy a kind of intimacy that might be achieved only through the loss of a measure of singularity—the kind of ontological conflation documented above. However much Quentin, in particular, tries to retain a sense of his own discursive autonomy ("I'm telling," he asserts at one point), the novel itself repeatedly confirms that "it did not matter . . . which one did the talking, since it was not the talking alone which did it, performed and accomplished the overpassing, but some happy marriage of speaking and hearing" (253). In this sense, the novel reveals the dialogic ethos underlying its apparently monologic surface: wherein meaning obtains not from unilateral utterances but from the "marriage" or "coupling" of expression and reception. Rather than present verbal synchrony as a sign of conformity, then, Faulkner's novel at least entertains the idea—diffuse, as we have seen, in James's fiction—that it might stand as at least a fragile proof of intimacy.

Whether such intimacy is actually achievable or, as I suggested in the conclusion to the second chapter, ultimately untenable, *Absalom* reveals the benefits of approaching novelistic speech as a coproduction, rather than as something for which one can assign individual "responsibility." While Brooks has suggested that one of the defining features of Faulkner's novel is the difficulty of determining "who is speaking"—since, at any given moment, "Faulkner seems to call upon both the individual's voice and that transindividual voice that speaks through all of Faulkner's characters"—it's possible this is the wrong question to ask of *Absalom*, a novel in which it may not *matter* who is speaking (*Reading* 294). Instead, Faulkner presents readers with a radically de-particularized narrative situation in which anyone (or everyone) can tell, and anyone and everyone can listen; in which the hierarchy of narrator and auditor threatens to collapse. Again and again, the novel confronts readers with the fact that the identity of the speaker is of secondary or tertiary interest, compared to the contents of their speech. In place of a "possessive" model of discourse, then, *Absalom* seems to model instead a promiscuous one, in which language may mix or enjoy intimate ties with more than one speaker.

Indeed, one of the central revelations of *Absalom* is that narrative is taking place regardless of, even independently of, any particular narrator. Or better, it has already taken place, since as the narrator explains, "It has all been said before" (AA 283). In the second chapter, Quentin reflects on "the listening, the hearing in 1909 even yet mostly that which he already knew since he had been born in and still breathed the same air in which the church bells had rung on that Sunday morning in 1833" (23). The implication is not only that the story has already been told, but that its telling is the product not of a single individual but of the culture that has colluded in its circulation. Upon Sutpen's appearance in town, for instance, "the stranger's name went back and forth among the places of business and of idleness and among the residences in steady strophe and antistrophe: *Sutpen. Sutpen. Sutpen. Sutpen*" (24). By interpolating the terminology of Attic drama, Faulkner frames the story as a myth or "legend," with the townspeople as a Greek chorus. Like a myth, Sutpen's narrative is oral, not written; it does not originate with a single author; and its significance does not obtain from any one version or recital. Indeed, as we see, the story outstrips the capacities of any one narrator and proceeds according to a momentum of its own—a stark departure from conventionally novelistic ways of telling. It is Shreve, the one character who did *not* grow up with the story, who is repeatedly overwhelmed by what he perceives to be its ungovernable force: "'Wait then,'" Shreve will repeatedly plead with Quentin, "for God's sake wait'" (175).

Further attesting to the marginal status of the individual speaker are the proliferating instances in the novel of voices operating, if not exactly independently, then outside normal expressive or conversational constraints. Like the final portion of *The Sound*, which in referring to the Reverend Shegog's voice as "it," appears to emancipate it from its speaker, *Absalom* continually foregrounds instances of vocal behavior so extreme, or of such extreme duration, as to be uncanny. Indeed, the novel is rife with instances of vocal automatism: Mr. Compson's voice "speaking on while Quentin heard it without listening" (102); or Rosa Coldfield's, which "would not cease" (4); or the impression conveyed by Bon's letter, of "the dead tongue speaking after the four years and then after almost fifty more, gentle sardonic whimsical and incurably pessimistic, without date or salutation or signature" (203).

Perhaps even more substantive evidence of the vitiated status of the individual in the narrative economy, however, arrives on the level of imagery. De-individuating events pullulate throughout the novel, from the explicit conflations of character—of Quentin and Shreve, Henry and Bon—to the more submerged trend toward clustering subjects and objects. In the first chapter, for instance, we find people organized in a "clump," "crew," "crowd," "large following," and "mob" (28, 28, 36, 44). As the text proceeds, such instances of agglomeration become increasingly frequent:

> they (men) were all of a kind throughout all of earth which he knew ... (232)

> all the voices, the murmuring of tomorrow and tomorrow and tomorrow beyond the immediate fury ... (232)

> all boy flesh that walked and breathed stemming from that one ambiguous eluded dark fatherhead and so brothered and perennial and ubiquitous everywhere under the sun ... (240)

Of course, such totalizing gestures—the grouping together of "all" the men, or voices, or "boy flesh"—are hardly unique to Faulkner. Indeed, one could as readily trace this kind of "massifying" tactic through earlier modernist fiction like *Heart of Darkness*, which has a similar (if more ideologically charged) habit of agglomerating characters, generally to racist ends. Here, however, the phenomenon seems to be part of a more emphatic movement in the novel toward de-particularizing, spreading out experience over a larger group. Through such systematic acts of generalization, Faulkner's novel offers an alternative vision of the novel's organization, a schema in which occurrences and utterances are no longer necessarily subordinate to—experienced *by*, voiced *by*—a single fictional "subject." This may be powerfully illustrated by Faulkner's distribution of what seems like a characteristically "authorial" brand of omniscience among his characters, who all, despite a piecemeal and incomplete understanding of events, speak with what can only be described as gnomic tone.

In this light, Faulkner's novel becomes much less persuasive as a story about the dangers of forceful individualism than as an allegory of its insolvency. By enacting the failure of attribution as both a literary convention and an interpretive paradigm, *Absalom* seems also to enact the failure of the individualist logic that has shaped fictional narratives, as well as historical ones. Such a logic, significantly, finds its paradigmatic expression in Sutpen's "design," which is as relentlessly singular and self-oriented as Faulkner's is compound and pluralistic.[12] In seeking to "accomplish his allotted course to its violent . . . end," independent of others or external contingencies, Sutpen ascribes to the sort of "great man" theory of history that Faulkner's novel (like contemporaneous historians) would deem obsolete (7). Indeed, it may be the anachronistic status of Sutpen's scheme that make it such an enduring object of fascination within the narrative economy. If the ur-theme of Faulkner's fiction is the past's perverse survival in and incursion on the present, it makes sense that he should co-locate the aleatory and combinatory discourse of Quentin and Shreve within a narrative shaped by enduring beliefs in teleology and individual achievement. Thus, even as *Absalom* travesties narrative conventions, remarkably, it does so through the *telling* of a conventional narrative, the tale of a fiercely self-aggrandizing individual who "dream[s]s of grim and castle-like magnificence" (29). Though *Absalom* may gesture toward a less particularizing direction for the novel, it is also obligated to inscribe, in the shape of the Sutpen story, the persistent, centripetal tug of personality on and within it.

## IV. HE SAID, SHE SAID: THE PRETENSE OF SPEECH IN *THE WAVES*

If anything, *The Waves* is even more self-conscious about its de-particularizing tendencies, allowing several of the characters an expanded capacity to reflect on the kinds of ontological and vocal blurring that in *Absalom* go generally

---

12. See Ross Hamblin for more on this contrast.

unperceived by the novel's subjects.[13] Thus, for instance, Woolf's speakers routinely worry about their idiosyncrasy and singularity, on the one hand, and their sameness and lack of distinctness, on the other; in this way, Woolf effectively thematizes the paradox that her novel also performs. In so doing, she also foregrounds to a greater extent than Faulkner did the rhetorically complex and highly mediated quality of supposedly direct speech. Even as *The Waves* presents a larger percentage of its total discourse *as* speech, then, it also more radically diminishes its plausibility. Unlike Faulkner's novel, Woolf's doesn't provide what Dorrit Cohn calls a "moment of locution" or what Ross dubs a "narrating scene"—some context to help substantiate the sense that fictional speech is part of a communicative exchange (Cohn 13; Ross 169).[14] She also heightens the expressive impossibility of her characters' utterances, not only through her choice of tense, diction, and figuration but through the incidence of what I would call *shared locution*: those moments, more pronounced but otherwise similar to those instances in *Absalom* when multiple speakers can be "heard" to articulate an identical or a near-identical utterance. Thus, for instance, Neville can conclude that "it is the first day of the summer holidays," and within two pages, both Susan and Rhoda reiterate the phrase (W 43, 45). In general, if *Absalom* made some effort to support the illusion that its characters are actually speaking, to actual others, *The Waves* does not hesitate to disclose the ersatz quality of its talk—its status as pure pretense. Or, as Ferrer puts it, Woolf never allows us "to take the word *said* literally" but instead "places us from the start outside the conventions of realism" (66, 65).

Yet even as she discards so many of the "conventions of realism" in rendering character speech, Woolf conspicuously retains others—in particular, the speech tags, quotation marks, and proper names that are an even more regular feature of this novel than Faulkner's. Significantly, these are the very features that have historically been most fundamental to the rendering of fictional dialogue. As Lennard Davis, among others, has demonstrated, it was during the eighteenth century that novelists first developed a fairly conventional method of transcribing conversation, or what

> linguists call "direct discourse"—that is, a method to indicate the opening and closing of direct speech with quotation marks (or in the continental tradition only the opening of the conversation with a dash), and to indicate

---

13. For more on this distinction, see Ross, who argues that characters in *The Waves*, for instance, engage in "explicit introspection," whereas the Compson brothers in *The Sound* "express but do not analyze their own thoughts or emotions" (167, 168).

14. Here, I diverge from Ross, who argues that Woolf's novel *does* provide us with such a scene (in contrast to, say, *The Sound*) (*Inexhaustible Voice* 169).

the speaker by tagging or interrupting the speech with "he said" or "John replied." (172)

The question, of course, is why Woolf should choose to make use of such "conventions" in rendering speech when the speech itself is so unconventional—or, put another way, to retain in her conspicuously innovative text what Nathalie Sarraute refers to as "symbols of the old regime" (112). In short, why preserve the apparatus of the realist novel in a text so apparently uninterested in realism?

Though critics have frequently raised this question, most have tended to respond in one of two ways: either by recovering realist tendencies in the novel—including differentiated speakers—or by declaring their absence.[15] In the latter camp are those who claim that the novel's "undifferentiated style" is indicative of its "radically a-novelistic" agenda and hold up as proof Woolf's own comment that the "six characters were supposed to be one" (Graham 95, qtd. in Lee 612).[16] More intriguing, however, may be those who read the novel in the opposite direction, attempting to transmute Woolf's "torrent" of prose into a vocally individuated and character-driven fiction (WD 160). Hussey notes that Kathleen McCluskey has been particularly assiduous in "illuminating how Woolf associates particular devices and styles with individual characters" ("'I' Rejected" 357). More recently, Hild has argued along similar lines that "clear and highly differentiated characters do emerge" in *The Waves*, since "after all, Woolf carefully sets off passages with quotation marks, and labels each shift of speaker with an attached name" (70).[17] But perhaps most symptomatic of this critical desire to recover subjectivity may be the pedagogical experiment conducted by Renée Dickinson, who asked her class to read Woolf's novel aloud. The result, she reported in *Virginia Woolf Miscellany*, was that the students "were more able to distinguish clearly the six characters

---

15. As Allison Hild notes, critics have "frequently debated Woolf's mode of speech in the novel" (70). See Hussey, pp. 348–62, for a synoptic account of this debate.

16. Hussey points out that "the idea . . . that the six are aspects of a single being has been common in critical discussion of *The Waves* from early on" ("'I' Rejected" 358). Representative of this position is Naremore, who endorses the idea that the discrete soliloquies "often seem more like one pervasive voice with six personalities" (152). Many others have come out in support of this kind of "single character" or "single personality" theory, concluding, as Lee does, that the novel's "emphasis on rhythm overwhelms distinctions of character" (Hussey 359; Lee 164).

17. Ariane Mildenberg likewise takes Woolf at her word when she suggests that the novel be read as a "gigantic conversation" (72; Woolf, WD 153). Though Woolf herself entertained the possibility that *The Waves* could end in such a fashion, Graham notes that there is "no sign in the manuscript of any attempt at conversation in which every life has its voice," nor is there much evidence in the published novel ("Point of View" 109).

and to follow their development because the characters were separately and aurally determined for them" (31). As one student reported, "'I felt that reading it aloud, with varying readers assuming a character... [captured] the idiosyncrasies and distinctions of the individual voices of humans'" (31).

In general, these approaches are representative of the primary ways critics have worked to resolve the contradiction inherent in the novel's form: either by insisting on a single speaker or by recovering many speakers. As in the case of Faulkner's novel, however, what's striking is the near-unanimous insistence on treating voice's representation in the novel as a "problem" to be solved rather than a feature to be elaborated and explored. In fact, *The Waves* seems to reward neither compliance with Woolf's quotation marks (as Hild or Dickinson implies) nor readerly defiance of them, as required by the "single-character" hypothesis. What the novel does do, though, is require readers to *notice* these marks and to acknowledge their status as rhetorical structures capable of powerfully shaping reader response and experience.[18] It is in this sense, then, that I would suggest Woolf is interpolating into her text certain novelistic conventions for the sake of both publicizing and, to some extent, parodying them. Among Woolf's commentators, H. Porter Abbott comes closest to such a claim when he proposes that the "continuation" of character in *The Waves* might represent "a kind of nineteenth century baggage ... that she couldn't help but carry on even as she sought to jettison it" (397). Yet I would argue that the constructs that persist in *The Waves* seem less like accidental "baggage" than something deliberately "carried on" and indeed carried over from her extensive theorizing about fiction in the years preceding the text's publication.[19]

Particularly revealing, in this light, is Woolf's use of inquits, which despite the range of possible speech-tagging options remains doggedly invariant: The first line of every soliloquy is punctuated by the phrase, he or she "said."[20] While speech tags in fiction, as William Flesch has noted of their presence in poetry, are generally "unstressed," Woolf's repetitious use of them has the effect of stressing them and, in the process, of calling attention to their "subliminal assimilative power": their capacity to assimilate or render natural what literary historians maintain is a highly unnatural textual phenomenon

---

18. For a fascinating discussion of punctuation's signifying potential, specifically in the context of Joyce's *Dubliners*, see Bonapfel's "Marking Realism."

19. As Hussey notes, Woolf's "essays, together with [her] examination of women's writing in *A Room of One's Own*, indicate how profoundly she was considering the nature of fiction in the years immediately preceding the inception of *The Waves*" (353).

20. See Lambert, who in his study of quotation use in Victorian fiction attests to both the "variety of speech tags" and the "variety of possibilities of their deployment" (8).

(164, 163).²¹ In this sense, Woolf's refusal to "relieve the monotony of constant 'he-saids' by resorting to elegant variations"—and her insistence on using them to tag something that doesn't satisfy the criteria for novelistic speech—seems to qualify as an act of stylistic disobedience, a way of self-consciously opposing the novel's prodigious naturalizing apparatus (Page 27). More than "foregrounding and ridiculing the banality of the he-said she-said formula," as Bronwen Thomas suggests of later twentieth-century writers like Henry Green, she is highlighting the existence and covert *power* of this formula ("Dialogue" 84). Put another way, the prominence of such speech conventions in Woolf's novel could be seen to reflect their prominence in the novel genre and in turn the prominence of the individuating agenda they've served to promote. Following Fredric Jameson's conception of modernist fiction, *The Waves* might be seen as an attempt to elucidate the novel's "unconscious": its bias in favor of particularity and its reliance on structures that are at once omnipresent and overlooked.

## V. TOWARD A NONIDIOSYNCRATIC VOICE

The possibility that Woolf both perceived such a bias and chose to problematize it in her novel is supported not only by analyses of the text itself but also by surveys of her personal and critical writings. Both Woolf's diary and many of her essays reflect what biographer Hermione Lee called her "lifelong argument about egotism," as evidenced in frequent, deprecatory comments about the "damned egotistical self" (587; WD 22). Repeatedly, Woolf reproaches this tendency in herself ("For if one lets the mind run loose it becomes egotistic; personal, which I detest") and in the work of others—especially male others (WD 67). As she wrote in *A Room of One's Own* about the experience of "taking down a new novel" by the hypothetical author, Mr. A,

> after reading a chapter or two a shadow seemed to lie across the page. It was a dark, straight bar, a shadow shaped something like the letter "I." One began dodging this way and that to catch a glimpse of the landscape behind it. Whether that was indeed a tree or a woman walking I was not quite sure. Back one was always hailed to the letter "I." One began to be tired of "I." (103)

---

21. See especially Davis, who documents conversation's status as not just a historical but an ideological construct; in particular, he examines "how these sets of signs and arrangements on the page, which actually look and sound almost nothing like real conversations, got to be accepted as the rule for conversation rather than the exception" (163).

One finds similar riffs on the theme of first-person pronoun fatigue throughout Woolf's writing, as commentators note. Graham, for one, usefully summarizes Woolf's "growing dissatisfaction . . . with what she called 'psychology'; her desire to break free from 'personality' as the subject of her fiction; and her determination to achieve in her fiction the impersonality she associated with poetry" (Graham 105). (The fact that she would jettison the narrating "I" she initially developed in *The Waves* is particularly significant in this light.[22]) Like Faulkner, then, but in more explicit fashion, Woolf can be seen to use the novel to challenge a primary tenet *of* the novel: the idea it should be organized around individual experience; that it should by default privilege "psychology," "personality," or eccentricity.

At first glance, this may seem like a surprising assertion, given the association of modernist authors, and particularly Woolf, with the representation of subjective experience. Yet it is precisely in light of this reputation—the presumed focus of modernist fiction on the psyche—that the emphasis on *externalizing* discourse in the form of quotations assumes such significance. Not only does it imply some desire, on Woolf's part, to eschew the kind of interiority she had foregrounded in her previous work; it also disallows the kinds of ambiguity that other discursive techniques are designed to accommodate. As Hite has noted, one of the more surprising features of *The Waves* is that, when compared to "the subtleties of Woolf's free indirect discourse in *Jacob's Room*, *Mrs. Dalloway*, and *To the Lighthouse*, in *The Waves* there is no doubt about whose point of view is presented at a given point" (xxxvii). In *The Waves*, then, one could say that discourse is manifestly *un*free. It is as if, by so plainly answering the question of "who is speaking?," Woolf, like Faulkner, hoped to provoke in readers a different, less subject-oriented line of questioning.[23]

On the one hand, it would be possible to argue that Woolf's search for impersonal or a-psychological modes of representation culminated in the works she produced after *The Waves*—in *The Years*, for instance, in which as Lee points out, "There is no 'I,' no inward 'stream of consciousness'" and in which ideas found their "most generalised and de-centered" expression (627). Or perhaps in *Between the Acts*, the novel considered in the subsequent chapter, and whose composition would prompt a shift in pronominal allegiance:

---

22. See Hite, p. xli, and Graham, "Point of View," pp. 98–102, for accounts of Woolf's initial attempts to include a narrator in *The Waves*; see also The Waves: *Two Holograph Drafts*.

23. In this sense, I concur with David Herman's suggestion that "Woolf's representations of talk require a rethinking of modernist narrative construed as a foregrounding of inner experience ("Dialogue" 75–76).

... "I" rejected: "We" substituted: to whom at the end shall there be an invocation? "We" ... the composed of many different things ... we all life, all art, all waifs and strays—a rambling capricious but somehow unified whole—the present state of my mind? (WD 279)

Yet it is *The Waves*, precisely because it features multiple *I*'s, that represents the most intriguing (because apparently contradictory) instance of how the novel might render speech less beholden to particular speakers. During the writing of the novel, Graham notes, Woolf often felt her method "trapped her in the personality of her characters," since it meant that all feelings had to be "rendered as felt by a character ... rather than as a feeling generated in the reader by the narrator itself" (106). Yet the actual text implies the opposite: that feelings may be "felt," and speech spoken, by *more than one* character. Indeed, Woolf seems to have had precisely this kind of inter- or extrasubjective ambition in mind while composing the characters' discourse. The challenge in creating these "dramatic soliloquies" was to "keep them running homogeneously in and out, in the rhythm of the waves" (WD 156); elsewhere, she elaborates on this idea, noting that

> what it wants is presumably unity ... Suppose I could run all the scenes together more?—by rhythms, chiefly. So as to avoid those cuts; so as to make the blood run like a torrent from end to end ... that indeed is my achievement; if any, here; a saturated, unchopped completeness; changes of scene, of mind, of person, done without spilling a drop. (WD 160)

By at once creating "lonely soliloquies," and "keep[ing] them running homogeneously in and out," Woolf seems to be exaggerating the novel's anatomizing tendencies and demonstrating a way in which they might be surpassed (Lee 587). Like Rhoda, then, Woolf seems to believe she "must go through the antics of the individual" in order to expose them *as* antics, behaviors that might be variously exorcised or overcome (W 164).

In this sense, *The Waves* points the way toward a mode of representing speech non-pragmatically, as something other than a discrete performative act by a single speaker. Instead, perhaps drawing on her experience of talk within Bloomsbury, she presents discourse as a kind of communal practice or property.[24] It is an attitude that she seems similarly to impute to her characters, and particularly Bernard, who like Quentin is positioned as first among

---

24. See Lee, p. 265, who notes that Woolf prized Bloomsbury's lively and participatory conversations, which "were often compared to 'orchestral concerts,' with Virginia Woolf as conductor" (265).

characterological equals. Yet unlike Quentin, who is bothered by the possibility of such verbal sharing, Bernard is untroubled by it: by the notion that, as he puts it, "when we sit together, close . . . we melt into each other with phrases. We are edged with mist. We make an unsubstantial territory" (W 9). If anything, Woolf's characters seem to worry as much about their distance from others as their uncomfortable proximity. Thus Bernard, for instance, can avow the rather Woolfian mantra, "I do not believe in separation. We are not single" (W 48).

Yet if at first glance Bernard would seem to emerge as Woolf's likeliest spokesman, the character best able to conduct her "argument about egotism" or critique of "personality" through the text, he also emerges as her foil (Lee 587).[25] Indeed, it is noteworthy that he personifies some of the very tendencies Woolf most excoriated in the novel and documented, most famously, in her 1924 essay, "Character in Fiction" (later republished as "Mr. Bennett and Mrs. Brown"). Such tendencies surface in the episode in *The Waves* during which Bernard converses with an unnamed fellow traveler on the train. "As we exchange these few but amiable remarks, about country houses," Bernard explains, "I furbish him up and make him concrete":

> He wears a large ornament, like a double tooth torn up by the roots, made of coral, hanging at his watch-chain. Walter J. Trumble is the sort of name that would fit him. He has been in America, on a business trip with his wife, and a double room in a smallish hotel cost him a whole month's wages. His front tooth is stopped with gold. (W 48)

In isolation, this brief description might seem unexceptional. But to readers of Woolf's criticism, particularly "Mr. Bennett and Mrs. Brown," the episode is suggestive, since Bernard's method is strikingly similar to the one Woolf ascribes to Arnold Bennett and his fellow Edwardians, who "laid an enormous stress upon the fabric of things" (*The Essays of Virginia Woolf* 432). In his similar reliance on physical and material detail—his dwelling on "Walter J. Trumble's" clothes, physiognomy, and immediate environs—Bernard is guilty of the very literary crimes Woolf accuses Bennett of committing in *Hilda Lessaways*. (The analogy between Bernard and Bennett, as presented in Woolf's critique, is strengthened by the fact that both are "caught" in the act

---

25. Many readers have seen the writer Bernard as Woolf's textual surrogate, and indeed he espouses many of her ideas and even idioms. Asked about her current novel, for instance, Woolf once reported herself to have joked, "Oh, I put in my hand and rummage in the bran pie" (WD 33). In *The Waves*, this figure becomes Bernard's, when he reflects that "every hour something new is unburied in the great bran pie" (54).

of describing a stranger they encounter in railway carriage.) Even Bernard's term of art (*furbishing*) is unpromising, indicating, as it does, his position on the wrong side of literary history. If, as Erich Auerbach argues in *Mimesis*, this sort of demonstrable "harmony between . . . person and. . . . milieu" was a primary criterion of nineteenth-century European realism, modernist authors would champion opposing models of characterization (470). In 1922, Willa Cather put forth her call for the novel *demeublé*, which, as Elaine Showalter notes, advocated for "an *unfurnishing* and stripping down of the overstuffed house of fictional realism": "How wonderful it would be," Cather wrote, "if we could *throw all the furniture out the window,* and along with it, all the meaningless reiterations concerning physical sensations, all the tiresome old patterns, and leave the room as bare as the stage of a Greek theatre" (Cather qtd. in Showalter 293, emphasis mine). For Woolf, then, undue emphasis on material detail was a diagnostic: an acid test for the kind of formal realism that the Georgians, by her account, were committed to reject.

It is in this sense, then, that we might read *The Waves* as part of both Woolf's "comprehensive critique of character," as Abbott has argued, and her critique of the characteris*tic*: of the sort of highly particularized and idiosyncratic subject the novel has recognized and has taught readers to recognize *as* character (396). It is a possibility Hite hints at when she concedes that whether the novel's speakers qualify as "characters" depends on the (highly contingent) criteria used to define the term. As she explains:

> If the usual conventions of characterization applied, we would have to either hypothesize that Jinny had a secret life with many volumes of poetry and a thesaurus, or to conclude that her diction and phrasing fail to fit her character. The latter is closer to the case, of course . . . but only if to be a character, one must display "characteristic," individuated speech mannerisms. (xlvi)

By not displaying such "individuated speech mannerisms," then, Woolf's characters challenge the default understanding *of* character. It is yet another act of disobedience on Woolf's part, a way of realizing the ambition she describes in "Mr. Bennett and Mrs. Brown," to create characters less defined by their superficial qualities than by their immaterial ones.

Notwithstanding Woolf's ambitions, it seems difficult to conceive of character being portrayed noncharacteristically. But Woolf's own figurations of subjectivity shed light on how this apparent conflict might be resolved. On the one hand, Woolf had a habit of referring to identity as something fixed, solid, and above all "sharp": In her diary, she speaks deprecatingly of her "sharp absurd little personality," and longs for those moments when "one's angularities and obscurities are smoothed and lit" (WD 119, 132). In *The Waves* Bernard laments along similar lines, "There is always somebody, when we come together, and the edges of meeting are still sharp, who refuses to be submerged" (155). Significantly, however, she will also associate identity with images of fluidity rather than fixity. In "Mr. Bennett and Mrs. Brown," for instance, she describes the "impression" produced by her fictional subject as something diffuse: "It came pouring out like a draught, like a smell of burning" (*Essays* 425). In *The Waves*, Bernard will similarly liken identity to a "persistent smell," which instead of "pouring out" "steals in through some crack in the structure" (W 83). Far from being a sharp-edged solid, such images suggest that selfhood might be reimagined as effervescent, an element that could be combined or admixed, resulting in the alchemical production of something or someone else altogether. Woolf's characters at once shrink from and celebrate the possibility. "How painful to be recalled, to be mitigated, to have one's self adulterated, mixed up, become part of another," Neville reflects, while Bernard, by contrast, rejoices at the sensation of "admixture": "The entirely unexpected nature of this explosion—that is the joy of intercourse. I, mixed with an unknown Italian waiter—what am I? There is no stability in this world" (W 83, 85).

In short, if subjectivity was previously "solid" in fiction, *The Waves* suggests it has increasingly melted into air. But Woolf's real innovation was to demonstrate that speech must evolve to reflect that. Instead of a technique of individuation, Woolf manages to turn dialogue into a vehicle of amalgamation: a device used to "mix" selves—to reflect their admixture—rather than create the impression of their difference. In this way, she simultaneously challenges not only the presentation of characters per se but the relationship among them: the construction of what Alex Woloch, writing of the nineteenth-century European novel, calls "character space." If speech has historically been one of the many tools used to facilitate the "asymmetric structure of realist characterization," whereby characters are sorted into "major" and "minor," then Woolf's refusal to variegate speech, and in turn character, has the effect of obstructing the formation of such hierarchical relations (*The One* 31). The result is a startlingly even characterological field that is radical in its refusal to accommodate minor-ness. "The equal status of six major figures," Hite notes, "is a generally unregarded way that *The Waves* unsettles the familiar habits of reading" (xxxviii). Through the creation of an undifferentiated voice—and, as I'll suggest in the following chapter, an increasingly democratized one—Woolf supplants the competitive model of character relations Woloch claims for the nineteenth-century novel, offering in its place a more collective and symmetrical one. In so doing, she provides a definitive critique of the novel's default organizational logic, its orientation, as Woloch describes it, around the "one" at the expense of the "many."

At the same time, she also develops, through the discursive trajectory of *The Waves,* a more local but no less resonant critique of this logic's actual, destructive potential. Not only does the novel attest repeatedly to the "burden of individual life," how it conduces to "indifference" and "hate and rivalry," among other effects (81, 80). It also reveals, more implicitly, the mechanisms by which institutions of nation and Empire have co-opted the rhetoric of individualism for their own purposes. It is no coincidence, after all, that Percival, the novel's designated "hero," is also its main casualty, killed in the line of imperialist duty, and the one character who uncritically embodies rather than interrogates the conceptions of selfhood all the speakers are shown to have similarly inherited. In this way, Woolf, like Faulkner, insists on not only the persistence of myths of heroic individualism but on their more than merely literary consequences.

CHAPTER 5

# The Choral Voice

## Woolf's and Stein's Democratized Talk

EARLY IN WOOLF'S final novel, *Between the Acts*, several characters emerge simultaneously from the library of Pointz Hall, the country estate where the narrative unfolds. The moment is described as a kind of collaborative discursive event:

> Across the hall a door opened. One voice, another voice, a third voice came wimpling and warbling: gruff—Bart's voice; quavering—Lucy's voice; middle-toned—Isa's voice. Their voices impetuously, impatiently, protestingly came across the hall saying: "The train's late"; saying, "Keep it hot"; saying: "We won't, no, Candish, we won't wait." (*Between the Acts* [hereafter BTA] 26)

The episode is at once of no consequence and of maximum consequence; that is to say, it does little to advance readers' understanding of the novel's characters or plot while revealing much about the structure and status of dialogue within the text. Of particular note is the conspicuously "choral" organization of voices in this passage: the combination and coordination of "one voice, another voice, a third voice." It is just one manifestation of the sort of vocal pluralism that broadly characterizes *Between the Acts* and that constitutes one of the text's most distinctive and widely remarked-upon features. Indeed, Woolf herself identified the achievement of discursive collectivity as one of her chief ambitions for the novel, writing in her diary at the outset of its composition: "But 'I' rejected: 'We' substituted: to whom at the end there shall be an invocation? 'We' . . . the composed of many things . . . we all life, all art, all waifs and strays—a rambling and capricious but somehow unified whole—the present state of my mind?" (WD 279).

Historically, there has been little disagreement among critics as to whether *Between the Acts* succeeds in accomplishing the apparently paradoxical goal of creating a "rambling . . . but unified whole." Fortified, perhaps, by Woolf's private avowal, it has become almost canonical to refer to the novel's *communal* or *choral* qualities, terms also used (often interchangeably) to describe the text's disposition of discourse across a remarkably varied yet geographically proximate field of speakers. Melba Cuddy-Keane, for one, has written extensively about the "choral" or "choric" voices in *Between the Acts*,[1] noting that the novel "records a multiplicity of disparate, varying, and often contradictory voices, diffused through time and space yet sounding together" ("Virginia Woolf, Sound Technologies" 92). Jane Marcus similarly positions the chorus as a seminal influence on Woolf's work,[2] while Rachel Blau DuPlessis analyzes what she variously refers to as the "choral," "communal," or "group" protagonist of *Between the Acts* (among other of Woolf's later works) and the "collective" nature of discourse that results (Marcus, "Some Sources" 1–2; DuPlessis, *Writing beyond the Ending*). Indeed, given the central role of the chorus in Woolf's conception of *The Waves*, as discussed in the previous chapter, there has also been a tendency to see *Between the Acts* as a valedictory expression of dialogic tendencies already present in this and other earlier texts such that, as Cuddy-Keane has argued, "the chorus heard by Bernard . . . expands [in *Between the Acts*] to become a pluralistic soundscape" ("Virginia Woolf, Sound Technologies" 92).

Yet while there has been consensus about the chorality of Woolf's final novel, its ideological valence remains more contested, and its distinctness from the discursive attributes in her earlier fictions, somewhat underexplored. To date, scholarly accounts have been divided largely between those, like Susan Lanser's and Alex Zwerdling's, that see the utopian potential inherent in the

---

1. See, for instance, Cuddy-Keane, "The Politics of Comic Modes" (275–76), and "Virginia Woolf, Sound Technologies, and the New Aurality," as well as her introduction to the Harcourt edition of *Between the Acts*.

2. In "Some Sources for *Between the Acts*," Marcus observes that in *The Years*, Woolf "attempt[ed] to write a modern Greek drama with the chorus merging into individual heroes and heroines; she dissolves the individual and the authorial voice in a collective voice." In particular, Marcus sees the "collective voice of the chorus as a radical response to the aesthetic problem of writing an anti-heroic but deeply historic novel."

novel's collective vocal configurations as having dissipated by the novel's end;[3] and those such as Cuddy-Keane's and DuPlessis's, that position such configurations as viable (if aspirational) alternatives to the more patriarchal and univocal orientation that has characterized the novel form. Rather than attempt to arbitrate this particular debate or to offer a competing interpretation of the choral voice in the discrete context of Woolf's novel, this chapter, much like the previous ones, aims to theorize this discursive strategy by historicizing it and by considering it in relation to both contemporaneous deployments of "group speak," as well as a longer, premodernist tradition of chorality.

Before proceeding, however, a quick note to clarify terminology: When I describe the arrangement of voice in certain narratives as "choral," I do not mean to imply that characters are literally speaking in unison, in the manner of an Attic chorus (though they periodically do) or even necessarily in overlapping fashion, as in the quotation above. I also do not intend to denote the better-documented phenomenon of "we" narration, whether entailing an individual character speaking on behalf of a group or what Natalia Bekhta has recently advocated for as the "dominant" mode: "narration by a collective subjectivity" (165).[4] Rather, I use the term more figuratively, to describe the largely sequential and unusually symmetrical distribution of speech among a company of speakers; a crucial index of chorality, then, is that the status of any single speaker is subordinate to that of the group, which emerges, over and above the individual, as the primary unit of narrative interest. (In this sense, *The Waves* qualifies as at once similarly choral and less so, inasmuch as it manifests a more consistent commitment to single characters.) That the accumulated voices strike readers as more synchronic than divergent—whether because they emerge from a delimited diegetic space and time or because they share a set of thematic concerns—makes it difficult to characterize them as "polyphonic" in the Bakhtinian sense. For if polyphony entails many voices, sounding independently and seemingly at random (as in, say, the "Wandering Rocks" or "Circe" episodes of *Ulysses*), chorality, by contrast, implies a more coordinated vocal performance, one whose evident orchestration "outs" it as

---

3. See Lanser's chapter on Woolf in *Fictions of Authority*, which frames the novel's discursive strategies as a means of consolidating Woolf's own vocal authority rather than producing what (citing DuPlessis) she calls an "antiauthoritative 'communal' consciousness" (Lanser 110). Similarly, Zwerdling argues that it is a "great distortion to read *Between the Acts* as an essentially celebratory work affirming unity and continuity" given that the possibility of community is gradually undermined by the "forces of dispersal" (229).

4. See Bekhta, "We-Narratives," for an account of "we" narration as something carried out by a specifically plural, collective subject. See also Richardson's *Unnatural Voices* (141–42) and Fludernik's "The Category of 'Person' in Fiction" (pp. 100–41) for a catalogue of examples of "we" narration, as well as additional bibliography on this phenomenon.

the product of authorial design rather than characterological exertion.[5] In this sense, choral fiction could be seen as the inverse of the twentieth-century tradition which Kacandes terms "talk" fiction, which "promote[s] a sense of relationship and exchange in readers that we normally associate with face-to-face interaction" (1). By contrast, choral texts tend not to evince this quality of "addressivity," instead conveying the impression of talking not *to* readers but despite them—focused, as they so visibly are, on acts of intradiegetic address and the elaboration of a self-contained dialogic structure (Kacandes xiii).[6]

My particular focus in the chapter will be not just on Woolf's novel but also on the work of her contemporary, Gertrude Stein, whose *Three Lives* displays a comparable commitment to at once centering character speech as a narrative component and *de*centering its presentation with her texts. At a glance, Stein might seem like a counterintuitive choice of case study, given that she is better known for her idiosyncratic authorial voice than for her cultivation or curation of character voice. Yet that reputation obscures the degree to which her fiction at once dramatizes and frequently thematizes talk as a collective, broadly inclusive activity, one more conducive to the expression of communal than individual identity. Despite the putative status of *Three Lives* as a collection of "portraits," the sheer fact of their multiplicity, as well as the structure of the middle story, "Melanctha"—the longest and most experimental of the three—serves to exemplify the choral impetus of her fiction and its general movement away from what Fredric Jameson terms "protagonicity" and toward polycentricty.[7] Like *Between the Acts*, "Melanctha" entails the relatively proportionate distribution of speech among its multiple speakers[8] (an observation that recalls the compositional "symmetry" that Stein has Toklas ascribe to the story in *The Autobiography of Alice B. Toklas*, achieved "by exac-

---

5. What Richardson remarks of "we" narration might just as easily hold true of choral—or what he calls "multiperson"—fictions: that they stand out for their "relative rarity" and "continuously defamiliariz[e] the conventional nature of traditional narrative forms" (*Unnatural* 56).

6. See Kacandes, especially the preface and the first chapter, "Secondary Orality: Talk as Interaction."

7. In *The Antinomies of Realism*, Jameson discusses the "deterioration of protagonicity" as it manifests specifically in the context of the nineteenth-century Spanish novelist Benito Pérez Galdos (96). Yet the phenomenon as Jameson describes is also localizable in the twentieth-century texts considered here, which similarly entail the "movement of putative heroes and heroines to the background, whose foreground is increasingly occupied by minor or secondary characters whose stories . . . might once have been digressions but now colonize and appropriate the novel for themselves" (96). Where I diverge is in not framing this "movement" as an inherently aggressive and acquisitive one.

8. See Fogel for further discussion of what he calls the "abstract proportional model" of dialogue, which examines the "relative amount spoken" by different characters (6).

titude, austerity, absence of variety in light and shade, by refusal of the use of subconscious") (AABT 50).

More specifically, there are qualities of talk in both texts—its superficiality and fragmentation in Woolf's case; its convolution and redundancy in Stein's—that have the effect of flattening the speakers, with the result that no character is sufficiently "rounded," to use E. M. Forster's term, to qualify as the "main" one.[9] Not only, then, do Woolf's and Stein's texts serve to elaborate the narrative potentialities inherent in the unrounding of character; they also, as Fogel has suggested of Conrad's fiction, "as[k] the reader to think of dialogue as formal and proportional rather than simply expressive" (19). Framed in the terms Woloch introduces in his study of novelistic character, their work evinces a similar and surprising willingness to sacrifice "referentiality" for the sake of form—and in so doing propose a solution to what Woloch presents as an insoluble conflict within the novel, between "language *or* reference, structure *or* individuality" (*The One* 17). In using dialogue as a method of equilibrating rather than differentiating characters, then, Woolf and Stein present an alternative to what Woloch calls the "asymmetric structure of realist characterization," one "in which many are represented but attention flows toward a delimited center" (31). If, as Woloch has argued, speaking privileges in the realist novel were generally a mark of narrative prestige—making direct discourse among the determinants of a character's "major" or "minor" status[10]— the fact that both Woolf and Stein make a point of lowering the barrier to entry and extending those privileges more equitably or to a more diverse field of speakers suggests that they are assigning speech in such a way as to vitiate rather than sustain novelistic hierarchies.

In this sense, *Between the Acts* and "Melanctha" could readily be seen to extend the critique of literary conventions outlined in the previous chapter, with reference to the *The Waves* and *Absalom, Absalom!*—both of which, I argued, repurposed "default" forms of representation (such as speech tags and quotation marks) to call into question some of the novel's foundational assumptions and ideologies. Yet as I suggest, both Woolf's later novel and Stein's much earlier one provide an even more pointed sociopolitical critique: offering, in their emphatically democratic distribution of talk, a challenge to

---

9. Forster's *Aspects of the Novel* appeared in 1927: well after Stein's work appeared, but before Woolf's.

10. As I note in the introduction, one of the observations Woloch cites in support of his argument is Tony Tanner's insight regarding *Emma*: that Austen affords her protagonist a "a wider range of discourse than anyone else in the novel. She can out-talk, over-talk, everyone" (qtd. in Woloch, *The One* 87). By contrast, Woloch suggests that minor-ness is reflected in or can function to "catalyze . . . inadequate speech" (26).

the specifically patriarchal structures that have informed novelistic practice. If, as Adrienne Rich has argued, "feminism has always been shaped and fired by the question, *how can things be other than they are?*" it becomes possible to discern in Stein's and Woolf's commitment to elaborating new uses and arrangements for dialogue political as well as literary ambitions (190). The goal of this chapter, then, is to explore the philosophical and specifically feminist implications of this more diffuse, egalitarian, and intersubjective distribution of talk that emerges in *Between the Acts* and "Melanctha." In particular, it will suggest that Woolf and Stein dramatize through the discursive framework of their texts a paradigm of character relations that differs significantly from the one Woloch discerned in the nineteenth-century realist novel: one based on the democratic and seemingly "indiscriminate," rather than asymmetrical and preferential, allocation of narrative attention. In this sense, *Between the Acts* and "Melanctha"—however dissimilar in theme or style—enact in the very *structure* of character dialogue a similar system of values, one based around paradigms of collaboration and inclusion rather than competition and exclusion.

At a glance, the attribution of such overly democratic ambitions to Woolf, in particular, might appear to be in conflict with her reputation for elitism. Yet as Cuddy-Keane has argued, there is in fact abundant evidence that discredits both "the older image of Woolf as elitist or 'aloof' and more recent accusations that she was an aesthetic capitalist bent on acquiring cultural and economic power through self-commodification" (*Virginia Woolf* 2). Instead, she suggests, Woolf is more accurately understood as a "democratic highbrow"—a writer committed to using her own considerable knowledge for the public good and whose status as a high modernist should not militate against her identity as an "advocate for both democratic inclusiveness and intellectual education" (1).[11] Stein, meanwhile, despite her own reputation for a-politicism, consistently assumed in her writing what Ulla E. Dydo has described as implicitly antihierarchical and antiauthoritarian stances:

> Her rejection of the rigid conventions of language led her gradually to dissociate herself from all inflexible forms, including hierarchical thinking, authoritarian organization, prescriptive grammar, and chronological narrative—aspects of patriarchy. In a sense, all her work is a demonstration of

---

11. While Cuddy-Keane discerns this commitment largely within Woolf's nonfictional writing (and specifically her appeal to the "common reader" and "wide-ranging and catholic reading practice"), *Between the Acts* demonstrates that such concerns were enacted similarly in her fiction (*Virginia Woolf* 2).

the possibilities of grammar for democracy. She was interested in spacious, living sentences. (*Gertrude Stein: The Language That Rises* 17)

Indeed, it's a priority broadcast not only in the titles of Stein's major prose works—such as *Everybody's Autobiography* or *The Making of Americans,* which Stein described in *The Autobiography of Alice B. Toklas* (AABT) as "a history of all human beings, all who ever were or are or could be living" (56)—but also in her own self-mythologizing. In *Autobiography,* for instance, she has Toklas report that "she was democratic, one person was as good as another": "The important thing, she insists, is that you must have deep down as the deepest thing in you a sense of equality" (174).

Further substantiating this comparison is the historical evidence to suggest that Woolf was familiar with Stein's fiction and, just as importantly, her theoretical work.[12] Of particular note is Woolf's encounter with "Composition as Explanation," which Leonard Woolf solicited for publication by the Hogarth Press in 1926 and which represented Stein's most sustained work of self-exegesis. Whatever Woolf's assessment *of* the essay, it is suggestive that two of the compositional principles Stein expounds—"distribution" and "equilibration"—are useful heuristics for considering the structural nonconformity of Woolf's own novel (*A Stein Reader* [hereafter SR], 493–503). The relevance of Stein's theory to both *Between the Acts* and Stein's own work in *Three Lives* becomes especially clear when considered in light of DuPlessis's helpful gloss:

> By the term "equilibration"—the construction of a stable, balanced, or unchanging system, and by the term "distribution—apportioning or allotting or any spatial or temporal array," Stein suggests that her ideal is a form in which there is no torque or trajectory, where *everything is equal on all sides,* where all pushes and pulls cancel each other out—and where there is no change. ("Woolfenstein, the Sequel" 42, italics mine)

What DuPlessis's exposition helps to illustrate is that the notions of "equilibration" and "distribution" might be instrumental to understanding not just

---

12. DuPlessis has been especially instrumental in articulating what she calls a "Woolfensteinian critical narrative," which considers the two authors' work intertextually. See "Woolfenstein" and "Woolfenstein, the Sequel"; in the latter, she highlights a letter from Woolf to Roger Fry, written after having received a copy of *The Making of Americans*: "We are lying crushed under an immense manuscript of Gertrude Stein's. I cannot brisk myself up to deal with it— whether her contortions are genuine and fruitful, or only such spasms as we might all go through in sheer impatience at having to deal with English prose" (qtd. in DuPlessis 44; *Letters* 3:209). See also G. Johnston.

Stein's "anti-Aristotelian poetics" but Woolf's as well, reflected in her curation of character utterances (42).

But perhaps the most suggestive evidence in favor of seeing Woolf and Stein as uniquely invested in character speech as a vehicle for engineering inclusivity is the fact that both writers in their own lives had enjoyed such longstanding experience with conversation as a participatory and progressive exercise. It is not incidental, in other words, that Stein and Woolf helped to cultivate two of the twentieth century's most famous crucibles of conversation: the coterie of Bloomsbury, in Woolf's case, and the literary salon Stein convened in her Parisian residence at 27 Rue de Fleurus. As Woolf's biographer Hermione Lee notes, "When [Woolf] describes Bloomsbury, she very often refers to conversation," as did others: "Bloomsbury conversations were often compared to 'orchestral concerts,' with Virginia Woolf as conductor" (265). Indeed, so invested was the Bloomsbury group in the artistic and intellectual value of its members' talk that at one point they experimented with recording the voluble but otherwise unproductive Desmond McCarthy, "with the idea that . . . a literary work might be made out of his talk. But Virginia wrote to Vanessa that the stenographer reported, 'It is the dullest thing you can imagine to read,' and the project was abandoned" (Hite l; *Letters* 2: 471). Notwithstanding this setback, Woolf was consistent in her perception of conversation as a crucial (and crucially democratic) mode of generating and disseminating knowledge. Ann Banfield, for instance, argues that "the implicit *raison d'être* of Bloomsbury discussions" was not just the group's "liberation" but that of the broader public: namely, "the extension of knowledge beyond the confines of the university elite" (Banfield, *Phantom Table* 17).[13] That Stein, too, viewed conversation as a mode of intellectual production is reflected in her decision to structure "Melanctha" as an "extended dialogue" with what Linda Wagner-Martin suggests is a patently pedagogical agenda—to elaborate a "philosophical discourse between reason and emotion" (*Favored Strangers* 79). Then there is the fact that *The Autobiography of Alice B. Toklas*, Stein's own act of self-portraiture, is so substantially composed of recapped conversation and reported talk, including her own proclamations, aphorisms, and utterances.

Both authors, in other words, were invested in the notion of conversation as at once a uniquely expressive discursive modality and a maximally accom-

---

13. Further biographical proof that Woolf recognized conversation as an inherently inclusive and progressive enterprise was her stated belief that "the liberation of Bloomsbury dated from the moment when the word *semen* was said aloud, in mixed company" (Cuddy-Keane, "Introduction" 152n).

modating one.[14] What is significant, for the purposes of this project, are the ways in which the dialogic structure of Woolf's and Stein's texts can be seen to enact these stances. Far from being exempt from ideology, so-called direct discourse is once again revealed to be an important (if "indirect") vehicle for authorial commentary. In the case of both Woolf's and Stein's fiction, the sheer force of dialogue's structural idiosyncrasies is enough to draw attention to its status as form capable of signifying other than in relation to or as an emanation of character. There is no longer any pretense that fictional conversation, in other words, is anything other than "made" and, as a result, a refreshing lack of coyness on the part of both texts about the extent to which it manifests its authors' distinct—and distinctly disruptive—ideological convictions.

## I. THE HISTORY AND POLITICS OF CHORALITY: JEAN TOOMER'S *CANE*

Before considering the presence and ideological significance of choral structures in Woolf's and Stein's work, it is first instructive to acknowledge chorality's longer literary history and to locate the authors' work at the midpoint of that history; for in contrast to the forms of "consensual," "exceptional," and "paradoxical" talk documented in earlier chapters, the "choral" is a comparatively established category. In Italian literature, for instance, *coralità* has long been an important critical paradigm, one perhaps most strongly associated with the work of *veristi*, or realist, writers like Giovanni Verga, whose 1881 novel, *I malavoglia*, is noted for its "village-chorus narration" and use of a "choral narrative voice" (Wood 24; Parks 142).[15] Subsequently, postwar Italian writers—many of them influenced by Anglo-American modernists—used what were widely recognized by contemporary viewers and critics as "choral" configurations, as reflected in novels such as Elio Vittorini's *Conversations in Sicily* (1941) and Cesare Pavese's *The Moon and the Bonfire* (1949). Even more suggestive, however, may be Italian cinema of the period, including Vittorio de Sica's *Shoeshine* (1948), Giuseppe de Santis's *Bitter Rice* (1946), and especially Roberto Rossellini's *Rome, Open City* (1945), a film that since its debut

---

14. A notion that corresponds with Cuddy-Keane's discernment of a specifically feminist "rhetorical tradition in which 'conversation' is conscientious political action" ("The Rhetoric of Feminist Conversation" 137).

15. As Moretti notes, Leo Spitzer was also an influential theorist of the "noisy, *multi*-personal 'chorus'" (*Graphs, Maps, Trees* 86). See Spitzer's "L'originalità della narrazione nei *Malavoglia*," originally published in 1956 and reproduced in *Studi italiani* (pp. 293–316).

has been seen as a flashpoint for discussion of "choral" aesthetics.[16] In a well-known contemporary review, for instance, Carlo Trabuccò described the film's first half as "truly choral and . . . representative of the whole population," a comment Rossellini would himself later echo in an interview: "I have no formula or preconceptions. But if I look back on my films, undoubtedly I find elements in them that are constant and that are repeated not programmatically but, I repeat, naturally. In particular, a choral quality. The realistic film is intrinsically choral" (qtd. in Sitney 29; qtd. in Bondanella 37).[17]

These comments exemplify a broader critical tendency to treat choral mechanisms as almost necessarily mimetic—designed, to paraphrase Trabuccò, "to represent a whole population." Put another way, many readers have assumed that the choral voice functions to index a "real," preexisting group, which is, generally, an impoverished one. Thus, Brian Richardson, writing of Ignazio Silone's postwar novel, *La fontamara,* has described its "'we' voice" as a "naturalistic method of indicating a collective sensibility of the Fontamara peasants"; as he puts it, "their life is shared, and so is their story" (44). And the impulse persists outside the Italian tradition, where choral structures have often been seen as expedient and largely unproblematic means of representing the masses; writing of Thomas Hardy's *Far from the Madding Crowd,* for instance, Chapman alludes to the "powerful choric effect of Hardy's peasants" (242). That choral arrangements have so regularly been associated with characters of the lower class serves to remind us not only that, as Thomas has put it, "the very forms of representing speech in literature carry ideological meanings" but that they might also telegraph the biases of authors and readers, predisposed to see underclass characters as indistinguishable ("Multiparty Talk" 663).

One of the aims of this chapter, then, is to complicate this view of chorality as an uncritically reflective device. More specifically, it will suggest that the choral voice functions in the context of Woolf's and Stein's fiction less as a naturalistic strategy than as a theatrical one—used not to reproduce an existing community but to imaginatively project new modes of affiliation and organization.[18] In so doing, I draw on an equally established tradition of critical response that has recognized the rhetorical and even polemical potential of collective discursive forms. Particularly significant in this regard is the work of

---

16. See Alsop, "The Imaginary Crowd," for more on the function of choral structures in neorealist cinema.

17. Trabuccò's comment appeared in his review "Il festival cinematografico," published in *Il popolo,* and is excerpted and translated by P. Adams Sitney.

18. An argument I've previously developed in relation to postwar Italian cinema and its strategic use of choral aesthetics. See Alsop, "Imaginary Crowd."

Sandra Zagarell, Sue Lanser, and, more recently, Monika Fludernik, who have all sought to theorize the phenomenon of *communal voice* (their preferred term) in Western literature—which Fludernik identifies as the single most "under-researched aspect of collective narrative" ("The Many in Action and Thought" 143). Even more recently, Natalia Bekhta has argued persuasively for the recognition of specifically "plural, collective characters and narrators in fiction" as a way of developing a more rigorous account of "we" narration (165).

Lanser and Zagarell have been particularly attuned to the ideological resonance of collective narrative strategies, which they agree have been at once underutilized and underexamined.[19] As a result, these theorists imply, the very decision to represent groups in Western literature qualifies as a provocation. Zagarell, for one, notes that "narratives of community" have been almost inevitably framed as subversive in the context of a genre that has historically privileged the "heroic" individual over the "collective life of the community" (503).[20] Lanser concurs in seeing communal forms as inherently political and goes even further in arguing that the communal voice has been specifically congenial to female writers and other members of "marginal or suppressed communities; I have not observed it in fiction by white, ruling-class men perhaps because such an 'I' is already in some sense speaking with the authority of a hegemonic 'we'" (21). Implicit in Lanser's argument is the idea that only communities that have in some way been marginalized (whether as a result of gender, sexuality, race, or class) are motivated to dramatize themselves *as* communities; to insist upon the numeracy and solidarity of their voices.[21] Conversely, groups that enjoy default status have little need for such unusual forms (though presumably even artists with more privileged status might be

---

19. As Lanser notes, "Because the dominant culture has not employed communal voice to any perceptible degree, and because distinctions about voice have been based primarily on the features of this dominant literature, there has been no narratological terminology for communal voice or for its various technical possibilities" (21). Fludernik similarly identifies the historic inattention within narratology to the "study of groups in their functions as agents, narrators, and focalizers" ("Many" 140).

20. Per canonical accounts of the novel, as exemplified by Ian Watt's influential "triple rise" thesis. As Zagarell notes, "As Watt established it, the rise of the novel keeps pace with the rise of the individual; and the rise, or fall, of individuals—or, as critics of nineteenth-century fiction often put it, the interaction between the individual and society—is what novels are about" (504).

21. See also Richardson, who similarly addresses the political expediency and activist potential of "we" narration for historically marginalized groups, though in perhaps unnecessarily proscriptive terms: "For socialists, feminists, and Third World intellectuals who denounce the extremes of bourgeois egoism and the poverty of an isolated subjectivity, 'we' narration must seem a prefiguration of the new, more communal, and more egalitarian society they are working to promote" (*Unnatural Voices* 56).

moved to use them). In short, only those who cannot take their representation for granted—who require "invention" in fiction—are driven to go to such narrative extremes.[22]

It's a notion that tallies with the assessments of other scholars, including Richardson and Cuddy-Keane, both of whom align choral structures with progressive political agendas, including anti-imperial and antipatriarchal ones. As Cuddy-Keane writes, specifically about Woolf's discursive procedures in *Between the Acts*, "The narrative act of transforming all voices into a chorus is unavoidably political," inasmuch as "it subverts the habitual dominance of the leader figure and introduces a new concept of community" ("Politics" 275). Even more interesting, however, may be DuPlessis's suggestion that there is something essentially feminist—and especially *modernist*—about this discursive modality. For her,

> the choral or group protagonist is . . . another major strategy of female modernism, a means of empowering narrative if one chooses to depend neither upon the romance and personal *Bildungs* plots nor upon some of the assumptions (beginning with gender polarization and the dichotomy of male and female, public and private spheres, and moving to hero and heroine and the "hard visible horizon" of the isolated individual) underlying those plots. (DuPlessis, *Writing* 162)

In this passage, DuPlessis usefully positions chorality as a strategy of modernism rather than as a tool of social realism. And by further linking it to the work of female writers, she also provides an impetus for considering not only the inherently "political" but also the specifically feminist potential of this particular dialogic convention. Without endorsing the notion that choral structures are perforce gendered—which seems to encourage an overly essentialist reading of narrative form—I'd like to broaden this claim by suggesting that the engineering of discursive collectivity might qualify as a "major strategy" not just of female modernism but of other traditions, including queer and African American modernisms, similarly committed to disrupting inherited plots and procedures[23] (while noting, of course, that it

---

22. There are notable exceptions to Lanser's generalization, including such modernist examples as *The Nigger of the 'Narcissus,'* "A Rose for Emily," and, in more recent years, Joshua Ferris's *Then We Came to the End*. By and large, however, they are exceptions that prove the rule.

23. Supporting such a hypothesis is Richardson's suggestion that "we" narration frequently serves "as a vehicle for representations of intersubjective feminist, agrarian, revolutionary, and postcolonial consciousnesses" (*Unnatural Voices* x).

might easily not qualify as such a strategy—or, alternatively, that it might be employed by writers with a less progressive agendas; the techniques themselves are agnostic).

Stein's and Woolf's work provides opportunities to consider the feminist and queer potential of communal modes. But by way of more fully testing the extent to which the choral voice might be understood as a critical strategy, I want to first consider Toomer's *Cane* as a case study both for assessing chorality as a tool for advancing an African American critique of the novel and for imagining new and more inclusive narrative arrangements. Without collapsing the historically specific circumstances of these different authors, it nonetheless seems useful to examine how a similar representational strategy might variously function across the fiction of three writers positioned outside the mainstream of "white, ruling class men."

*Cane* proves an especially useful site for theorizing the "choral" as a narratological and literary historical category, in part because it represents one of modernism's most sustained attempts to organize a fictional text around a community. At the same time, on a thematic level *Cane* also usefully complicates the generally romantic associations with communal or "folk" speech. Beginning with the earliest stories, collectively generated talk functions less as proof of the text's progressive bona fides than a source of dubious and potentially destructive hearsay—a type of speech that, in Richardson's words, can "vary in its reliability" (*Unnatural Voices* 46). In one of the early stories, "Carma," the narrator indirectly reports what amounts to town gossip under the guise of relaying fact: "Her husband's in the gang. And it's her fault he got there. Working with a contractor, he was away most of the time. She had others. No one blames her for that" (11). In this way, "Carma" seems to anticipate Faulkner's own famous "narrative of community," "A Rose for Emily," in which prurience is a prime motive behind the town's talk. The more relevant analogue, however, may be Zora Neale Hurston's *Their Eyes Were Watching God*, which opens with an indelible scene of verbal excoriation, attributed only vaguely to "they," an anonymous group of the town's women who "made burning statements with questions, and killing tools out of laughs. It was mass cruelty. A mood come alive. Words walking without masters, walking together like harmony in a song" (2). In Toomer's text, as in Hurston's, community provides cover for speakers, ensuring a kind of verbal anonymity—"words walking without masters"—that licenses, if not "cruelty," then an overreliance on group think. In this way, Toomer's stories evoke what Karen Lawrence has described, apropos of the "Eumaeus" chapter of *Ulysses*, as the "public, anonymous 'voice of culture' . . . a transpersonal repository of received ideas" (168). That both Toomer and Hurston—two canonical African American modernists—associate this "public" voice with social judgment, however, implies the potentially different stakes for black characters (and authors) confronted with an anonymous vocal majority.

What makes the collective voice problematic in the context of *Cane*, however, is not only the degree of anonymity it affords speakers but its tendency to occlude their diversity. In other words, readers are reminded that truly "communal" vocalization would necessarily encompass *all* the voices in a community—as does not appear to be the case. For example, in *Cane*'s second story, "Becky," the narrator makes clear that the reported talk of the town breaks down along racial lines: The story opens with one qualifying phrase, "said the white folks' mouths," repeated twice within the first five lines, and another, "said the black folks' mouths," reiterated just below. In neither instance is what is being "said" of any clear value within the narrative economy; the purpose of these reports, then, seems to reveal the community in question to be bifurcated and unsettled, as is the narration generally, which oscillates between "I" and "we," sometimes even within the space of several sentences ("Through the dust we saw the bricks in a mound on the floor . . . I thought I heard a groan . . . somehow we got away" [7]). In contrast to many other famous instantiations of the "we" voice—in Faulkner's story, for instance, or even in more generic form in "Eumaeus"—Toomer's disallows the presumption of discursive unity. In the subsequent story, "Fern," the narrator concludes his recap of popular wisdom about the title character with a brief but crucial qualification: "And it is only black folks whom I have been talking about thus far. What white men thought of Fern I can arrive at only by analogy. They let her alone" (15). In these lines, Toomer exposes the lie of omission that has underwritten so many fictional communities, whose cohesion presumes and relies on (often invisible) forms of racial exclusion. In revealing the racial fault lines with which a truly inclusive community would have to contend, Toomer's work gestures toward the politics inherent in the ideal of "consensual" speech, at least as imagined by a white author like James. By electing to write large portions of his text in dialect, as Hurston would do, and insisting on categorical differences between groups of speakers, Toomer draws attention to the tensions inherent in "collective" narration—a mode that may aspire to pluralism while achieving its opposite.

It does not seem coincidental, then, that as *Cane* proceeds, there is a distinct shift in the strategies Toomer uses to represent characters' discourse: away from individual narrators speaking on behalf of a group, often using the first-person plural, and toward group members deputized to speak on their own behalf. Framed in terms of Lanser's taxonomy, *Cane* moves from employing the "*singular*" form of the communal voice—which entails "one narrator speak[ing] for a collective"—and toward the "*sequential*" form, "in which individual members of a group narrate in turn" (21). In the context of *Cane,* and for the purposes of my project, it is important to further clarify that Toomer specifically enables those group members to *speak* in turn and that he amplifies their contributions by turning to theatrical conventions for representing talk rather than novelistic ones. At the same time, the distinctly *lyrical* narrative voice in the earlier stories increasingly gives way to what, in the first chapter, I called the *empirical* voice of characters, with the narrator's discourse sounding more like stage directions.

Thus, for instance, starting in the story appropriately titled "Theater," Toomer begins using a character's name, followed by a colon, to offset dialogue, rather than the more typical quotation marks and speech tags. Initially, this "theatrical" framing is used to designate interior monologue, rather than spoken dialogue, but that distinction dissipates by the time we reach "Kabnis." On the one hand, this technique amplifies the "staged" and notably stylized quality of the speakers' utterances. In "Box Seat," for instance, one character asks another, "But Murial, life is full of things like that. One grows strong and beautiful in facing them. What else is life?" (58). Even more significant, perhaps, is that Toomer also imbues the characters of "Kabnis" with a measure of self-consciousness about the real-world standing of their cumulative talk (or lack thereof): that is, an awareness of the relative inconsequence of "black" talk in a white world. Relaying the circumstances of a recent lynching, for instance, Layman tells Kabnis, "White folks know that niggers talk, an they don't mind jes so long as nothing comes of it" (90).

By delegating the responsibility for their own self-representation *to* the community, and simultaneously imbuing characters with some awareness of the stakes of that representation, *Cane* dramatizes the politics inherent in the rendering of "groups," while implying that the novel, despite the Bakhtinian argument to the contrary, has not been completely up to the job: thus the increasing adoption of dramatic conventions, which are implicitly positioned as better suited to accommodating (without editorial commentary) a plurality of voices rather than a nucleus of "heroic" or more privileged ones. The result is that by the time Toomer concludes *Cane,* there seems to have been an almost total disinvestment in the novel at the level of form. In this sense, *Cane* provides readers and theorists of narrative with an opportunity for thinking through the relationship between inclusivity and the novel—and specifically the degree to which the latter, notwithstanding its vaunted elasticity and pluralism, has been inhospitable to the former. It's no coincidence, after all, that the three primary texts considered in this chapter incorporate elements of (and, in the case of Woolf's and Toomer's work, *make explicit reference to*) other genres, including poetry, theater, and melodrama[24] Neither is it accidental that Woolf's and Stein's corpora incite a certain amount of "genre" trouble; as Dydo asks of Stein, "What does [she] write? Novels? Plays? Poetry?" (*Gertrude Stein* 11). Indeed, it's possible to suggest that in mobilizing so many characters to contribute equally to the creation of extensible narrative universes, *Cane*, "Melanctha," and *Between the Acts* are no more closely aligned to the novel than the soap opera, a "textual system," as Robert C. Allen notes, that "remains . . . dependent upon not individual characters but an entire community of characters for its aesthetic effect and popular appeal" (57).[25]

These lessons—that novels may not naturally accommodate chorality, Bakhtin notwithstanding; and that having historically evolved to represent individuals rather than groups they might require deliberate infusion with other generic techniques—have important bearing on our understanding of Woolf's text, in particular. A survey of her writing suggests that she was always looking to other genres in her above-mentioned pursuit of a more "rambling" and accommodating narrative form; and it showed her increasingly willing in her later work to delegate dialogue more "directly," and in a sense theatrically, to characters.[26] If *Cane*'s decentralized structure seems designed, in part, to dramatize the kind of discursive plurality that has not typically been registered in the novel, *Between the Acts* could be seen as a similarly deliberate and artful act of protest: in this case, against the exclusion of those many (female) voices that have been continually preempted by the "shadow" of the masculine "I" (*A Room of One's Own* [hereafter AROO] 103).

## II. WOOLF'S VOCAL PROMISCUITY: INCLUSION AS ETHOS IN *BETWEEN THE ACTS*

For a novel that, I've suggested, is unabashed about its dialogic experimentalism, *Between the Acts* starts inauspiciously. A character named Mrs. Haines interrupts conversation about the village cesspool to offer reflexive commen-

---

24. Writing in her diary, for instance, Woolf referred to writing "*P. H.* poetry" when composing the novel, while in *Cane* the narrator suggests "Carma's tale is the crudest melodrama" (WD 331; Toomer 11).

25. In so doing, these authors provide support for the argument advanced by Kurnick that theater and the novel were not "forms . . . produced in isolation from each other" (6). Like Kurnick, then, this chapter has as an underlying goal to "complicate the antagonistic model of generic evolution that has shaped critical accounts of theater and the novel" (*Empty Houses* 6).

26. See Kurnick's *Empty Houses* for a broader account of the way the failed theatrical ambitions of many late nineteenth- and early twentieth-century writers informed the novel's aesthetics.

tary on the topic: "What a subject to talk about on a night like this!" (3). After this interjection, the narrator proceeds to describe the sequence of discursive events that follow:

> Then there was silence; and a cow coughed; and that led [Mrs. Haines] to say how odd it was, as a child, she had never feared cows, only horses. But, then, as a small child in a perambulator, a great cart-horse had brushed within an inch of her face. Her family, she told the old man in the arm-chair, had lived near Liskeard for many centuries. There were the graves in the churchyard to prove it.
>
> A bird chuckled outside. "A nightingale?" asked Mrs. Haines. No, nightingales didn't come so far north. It was a daylight bird, chuckling over the substance and succulence of the day, over worms, snails, grit, even in sleep. (3)

At a glance, these passages, with the narrator's dutiful recapping of the conversation's drift from municipal sanitation to birdsong, wouldn't seem to provide a particularly good illustration of either the novel's dialogic capacities or its specifically choral ambitions. If anything, the desultory, sub-Bloomsbury content of the conversation, combined with the choice to indirectly report the characters' comments rather than reproduce them directly, might send the first-time reader the message that Woolf was striving either to downplay dialogue as an expressive modality, or to consolidate it by filtering characters' discourse through the sensibility of the narrator rather than disseminating it among fictional subjects.

Yet in fact, these passages telegraph the unusually diffuse nature of talk in the novel: Woolf's tendency to distribute utterances to an exceptionally diverse and often underidentified field of speakers. Within the space of this brief excerpt, for instance, readers hear from a cow, Mrs. Haines, the old man (Mr. Oliver), a bird, and finally the narrator, whose voice conspicuously emerges at the end to editorialize about the "substance and succulence of the day." That Woolf intends readers to understand animals as contributors to the conversation is underscored by the fact that she attributes to them the distinctly human activities of "coughing" and "chuckling"; though these may be purely acoustic rather than strictly verbal ejaculations, they are, significantly, folded into the conversation, placed on the same level as the characters' sallies. The effect, significantly, is less to anthropomorphize the animals than to transmute the talk: to expand the parameters of fictional conversation to encompass sounds both verbal and non-, contributed by subjects both human and non-, using diction both pedestrian (those cesspools!) and elevated (a

Keatsian "nightingale"). In so doing, Woolf signals from the very start the text's refusal of central conventions regarding fictional conversation—and the installation, in their place, of a radically inclusive model for allocating speech, one that takes the egalitarianism incipient in *The Waves* and makes it at once the impetus and the ethos of the novel.

My specific contention is that the resulting discursive structure reflects Woolf's sustained critique of institutions to which, by the end of her career, she had developed demonstrable antipathy. Writing in her diary in 1940, for instance, Woolf reported that "the idea came to me that why I dislike, and like, so many things idiosyncratically now, is because of my growing detachment from the hierarchy, the patriarchy" (WD 347). And this "detachment" is evident, I'd argue, not only in the themes of this novel, which has been broadly construed as antiwar, but at the level of discourse, whose arrangement, as exemplified in the passage above and throughout the text, seems designed to redress the consolidation of power in the hands of a privileged (male) few. One consequence of such deliberate polycentrism is that the word *protagonist* loses much of its force; instead, readers are confronted with something closer to a kind of ensemble structure, one more closely associated, as noted above, with melodrama than the novel. In this sense, Woolf's final novel seems oddly anticipatory of more-contemporary narrative forms, including serial television, which as the critic Lili Loufbourow has noted, is frequently characterized by what she calls "promiscuous protagonism." One could say something similar of *Between the Acts,* a narrative whose central event—the performance of a highly participatory village pageant—dramatizes its commitment to both characterological and vocal promiscuity, a rebuke to a genre that theorists since Watt have portrayed as largely monogamous in its narrative commitments. Thus, if implausibility was Woolf's chief method of disruption in *The Waves,* inclusivity—or the distribution of speech to a potentially infinite and nonselective group of speakers—becomes her primary method of critique in *Between the Acts.*[27]

At the most basic level, Woolf's inclusive mandate is evident in her assignation of speech to a greater quantity and variety of characters, which effec-

---

27. Scholars have offered adjacent interpretations of the novel, with Cuddy-Keane suggesting, for instance, that Woolf's "revolutions in narrative form demonstrate a continuing protest against hierarchical power structures," with *Between the Acts* marking her attempt "to subvert and overthrow prevailing assumptions about the role of leaders and the nature of groups" (*Politics* 273). But while she locates the novel's subversive potential in Woolf's use of *generic* forms, I suggest that it is through discursive forms—especially the prominent and peculiar arrangement of dialogue in the text—that this potential is most fully realized.

tively inhibits the development of (or readerly exposure to) any one.[28] In other words, the sheer number of speakers featured in the novel tends to diminish the individuation of their speech. Far from a means of expressing a character's personality, then, talk in *Between the Acts* is often perversely unrevealing: superficial, nonspecific, or too fragmentary or brief in duration to allow readers to glean much about the subject doing the talking—if the speaker is even identified in the first place. Indeed, it's not unusual for characters' comments to be purely "reactive," which is to say motivated, as in the case of Mrs. Haines, not by any aspect of their psychology but by the behavior or offhand remark of another character or by a contingent event. This emphasis on speech as reaction rather than emanation corresponds with the novel's apparent preference for characterological breadth over depth. Indeed, Woolf's willingness to take what, following Alan Palmer, we might call a "social" rather than psychological approach to dialogue is part of what makes *Between the Acts* feel like such an unfamiliar experience for readers of the novel—a genre, after all, that in the modernist period (indeed, under Woolf herself) had evolved to become ever more adept at the rendering of the individual mind.[29] Instead, direct discourse in Woolf's novel departs from this depth psychology tradition and often seems to have as its goal the elaboration of social dynamics rather than the disclosure of self.

Take the speech of the novel's lower-class characters, the presence of which, in the context of Woolf's corpus, is a remarkable enough feature in its own right. Heightening its interest, however, is the fact that such discourse is generally catalyzed by encounters with other, more educated characters. Early in the novel, for instance, these encounters prompt the staff to disclose their private nicknames for Pointz Hall denizens: "'Batty,' Grace called her" (7); "'Old Flimsy on the hop,' said David" (20); "'Bossy' they called [Miss LaTrobe] privately, just as they called Mrs. Swithin 'Flimsey'" (44). Yet such disclosures don't deepen readers' understanding of Grace or David; unlike, say, the case of Lily in "The Dead," hearing from the servants doesn't offer greater insight into their private lives or thoughts. What it does do, however, is illustrate the hierarchical relationship, and attendant resentments, between the novels' social groups and the degree to which the lower class is inescapably "respon-

---

28. See Palmer, especially pp. 24–26, for a discussion of characterization that implies such curtailed exposure to characters might constrain the cognitive process by which readers construct them.

29. Not only was Woolf instrumental in such developments; she actively championed them in essays such as "Mr. Bennett and Mr. Brown," where she celebrates the Georgians' less materialist and more psychologically nuanced approach to character, and in her reading notes, where despite her reservations about *Ulysses*, she praised Joyce's attempt "to get thinking into literature" ("Modern Novels (Joyce)" 642).

sive" to the upper. The same holds true of even a more extended passage of free indirect discourse:

> The old girl with a wisp of white hair flying, knobbed shoes as if she had claws corned like a canary's, and black stockings wrinkled over the ankles, naturally made David cock his eye and Jessica wink back, as she handed him a length of paper roses. Snobs they were; long enough stationed that is in that one corner of the world to have taken indelibly the print of some three hundred years of customary behaviour. So they laughed; but respected. If she wore pearls, pearls they were. (19)

While portions of the passage clearly bear Woolf's authorial imprint, it also contains phrases ("The old girl"; "snobs they were"; "if she wore pearls, pearls they were") that appear to originate with the novel's various working-class characters. Because cross-class FID is not an inevitable feature of the modernist novel—as Genette notes, Proust, for one, "does not dare to take on the servant's lexicon without quotation marks: a sign of great timidity in the use of free indirect style" (182)—Woolf's greater if still mitigated degree of boldness is therefore of interest. It is especially notable given that unlike other authors famous for creating what Genette calls fully "objectivized language" for their characters—that is, language clearly delineated from the author's and linked meaningfully to the speaking character—neither the goal nor the primary effect of the servants' directly or indirectly rendered discourse appears to be verisimilitude (183).[30] Instead, it as if she commandeers these characters' idioms for the purposes of advancing a recognizably Woolfian class critique.

The impression that dialogue may be more revealing of Woolf's commitments than of those of her characters has the additional effect of discouraging readers from considering any single utterance synchronically, as meaningful *in itself,* rather than in relation to the network of utterances present within the novel. Indeed, *Between the Acts* continually preempts individual speaking at any length, often by using strategies of authorial interruption or redirection to curtail attention to a single character, and thereby reemphasizes their subordinate position within the group. Unlike *The Waves,* in which the characters generally soliloquize at length, speakers in *Between the Acts* generally don't hold the floor for long; instead, their exchanges are almost inevitably truncated, with the result that few succeed in gaining narrative traction. Early in the novel, for instance, Isa finds it difficult to sustain the thread of her

---

30. See Genette, p. 183, who suggests that the more "objectivized" the language, the more "mimetic" the narrative effects.

own discourse, and instead pivots from ordering fish for lunch to composing poetry sotto voce:

> "Mrs. Oliver speaking . . . What fish have you this morning? Cod Halibut? Sole? Plaice?"
> 
> "There to lose what binds us here," she murmured. "Soles. Filleted. In time for lunch please," she said aloud. "With a feather, a blue feather . . . flying mounting through the air . . . there to lose what binds us here." (BTA 11)

In this passage, Isa not only ricochets between topics and distinct vocal channels (the public and the private; the audible and the inaudible) but in the process illuminates a primary operating procedure of the novel: namely, its habit of digression over strict progression on the level of both sentence and plot. Of course, the play itself is the most notable example of this tendency, given the continual pauses, disruptions, and omissions that punctuate Miss LaTrobe's production, and it metonymically reproduces those in Woolf's own. When readers encounter, just after Isa's comments above, this oddly phrased question—"'Am I,' Isa apologized, 'interrupting?'"—they may recognize in the odd placement of the predicate not only the kind of slightly alienating technique that typifies Jamesian conversation but also an illustration of the principle of radical contingency continually thematized in the novel (BTA 13).

It's a lesson reinforced not just in monologue but in dialogue, which tends toward free association and irresolution. One example can be found in this early exchange, which, like the passage that opens the novel, swerves from one topic to the next:

> "He ate his breakfast?" Mrs. Swithin asked.
> 
> "Every scrap," said Isa.
> 
> "And baby? No sign of measles?"
> 
> Isa shook her head. "Touch wood," she added, tapping the table.
> 
> "Tell me, Bart," said Mrs. Swithin, turning to her brother, "what's the origin of that? Touch wood . . . Antaeus, didn't he touch earth?" (BTA 17)

Whether Woolf was attempting here to reproduce the divagatory quality of "real" talk, there also seems to be some other-than-mimetic design at work. Instead, the conversation seems to provide Woolf with an opportunity to stage a type of discourse—nonconsecutive, narrowly concerned with domestic matters, and unlike, say, Leopold Bloom's stream of consciousness, deliberately externalized—that has been relatively rare in the history of the novel. And, perhaps more interesting, the conversation seems to expose the gendered assumptions attached to such discourse. It is particularly suggestive that Woolf has the patriarch, Bart Oliver, issue the judgment, spurred by his sister's free association, that "she would have been, he thought, a very clever woman, had she fixed her gaze" (17); for it seems at once to represent Woolf's attempt to rebut criticisms she herself has received[31] and to indict a tradition of male novelists who have normalized the belief that the writer's "gaze" must remain "fixed" on heroic individuals rather than on the network of relations and social contexts to which they belong. The extent to which this preference for the "fixed" versus the wandering or aleatory is gendered is further underscored by Isa's own negative self-assessment: that her "words weren't worth writing in the book bound like an account book in case Giles suspected. 'Abortive,' was the word that expressed her" (11). The implications, of course, are not only that Isa's "abortive" qualities militate against the quality of her writing but that they are inimical to the values of men like Giles and the tradition of "bound books."

Far from reproducing these outmoded value systems, however, *Between the Acts* will continually center in its own construction the logics of divagation and association that Bart disparages—which is to say that it risks noncohesion for the sake of inclusion. Indeed, Woolf makes a point to assign to her female characters, in particular, a heightened awareness of and tolerance for the expansive quality of talk. Take, for instance, Mrs. Swithin's reflections on her own discourse: "'How did we begin this talk?' She counted on her fingers. 'The Pharaohs. Dentists. Fish . . . Oh yes, you were saying, Isa, you'd ordered fish; and you were afraid it wouldn't be fresh. And I said, 'That's the problem'" (22). What Mrs. Swithin's reconstruction of her earlier conversation with Isa underscores is that no utterance in *Between the Acts* exists in isolation. Or, as Isa herself later puts it, "But none speaks with a single voice. None with a voice free from the old vibrations" (106). It as if the Bakhtinian lessons Joyce and Faulkner insinuated in their fictions have become in *Between the Acts* Woolf's point of departure. Nowhere is that made clearer than in the staging of Miss LaTrobe's play, which is not only figuratively but also literally choral, inasmuch as it features a "chorus" of villagers whose presence (due to their frequent inaudibility) has symbolic as much as semantic value.

Further revealing of the novel's commitment to deprioritizing the individual utterance is the narrator's tendency to intercede in what begin as character-driven exchanges. Often, this sort of visibly authorial insertion manifests in the form of figurative language whose conspicuous artistry prevents it from

---

31. Indeed, Bart's comment is reminiscent of Arnold Bennett's suggestion that Woolf lacked "that 'reality' gift": the capacity necessary to create "characters that survive" (WD 56).

being feasibly attributed to the diegetic subjects. In the excerpt that begins this section, for instance, there is a shift from Mrs. Haines's comment ("A nightingale?"), to Mr. Oliver's indirectly reported response ("No, nightingales didn't come so far north"), to a statement whose stylization necessarily links it to a more authorially derived voice: "It was a daylight bird, chuckling over the substance and succulence of the day, over worms, snails, grit, even in sleep" (3). Similarly wrought and conspicuously figurative language repeatedly intrudes upon free indirect discourse linked to characters, often in the form of metaphors or similes. In subsequent passages, then, readers find that Mrs. Haines's interior reflections on her place in the social hierarchy, and the chauffer's report on the Oliver family, are eventually preempted by authorial "conclusions":

> Mrs. Haines was aware of the emotion circling them, excluding her. She waited, *as one waits for the strain of an organ to die out before leaving church.* In the car going home to the red villa in the cornfields, she would destroy it, *as a thrush pecks the wings off a butterfly.* (BTA 5, italics mine)

> The chauffeur didn't know. The Olivers, who had brought the place something over a century ago, had no connection with the Warings, the Elveys, the Mannerings or the Burnets; the old families who had all intermarried, and *lay in their deaths intertwisted, like the ivy roots, beneath the churchyard wall.* (BTA 5, italics mine)

The italicized phrases above reveal reflect the degree to which seemingly characterological discourse is intercalated with authorial asides rather than deliberately set apart and annexed (as they are in *The Waves*, for instance).

In this sense, *Between the Acts* showcases a mode of *less*-free indirect discourse, entailing a greater degree of entanglement with the narrator's language than prevailing accounts generally allow.[32] Thus, while Genette conceives of FID and interior monologue, in particular, as fully "emancipated right away ... from all narrative patronage," the recurrence of Woolf's voice in apparently character-inflected passages seems designed to signal the incompleteness of the liberation (174). In this sense, Woolf's approach seems less analogous to the one Genette discerns in Proust than to the one Gunn identifies in Austen's *Emma*, in which instances of FID "rather than operating autonomously or *freeing* themselves from narratorial discourse . . . are *embedded* in this dis-

---

32. See Daniel Gunn's "FID and Narrative Authority in *Emma*" for an overview of the dominant, Genettian account of free indirect discourse and his own alternative one ("FID").

course" (Gunn 43). But Woolf, through her curation of high discursive contrast—juxtaposing standard thought reports with artful simile—makes the fact of her authorial intrusion more overt. In *Between the Acts,* FID's value to Woolf seems to lie in its permeability. It's just one manifestation of the duality inherent in choral structures, which entail both the widespread designation of speech *to* characters and the continual inscription of an authorial presence *doing* the designating (a paradox that, as Gunn reminds us, Bakhtin sees as central to the novel, in which "artistic control [is] the context within which heteroglossia operates" [42]).

Perhaps particularly expressive of this tension is Woolf's emphasis on anonymizing voice. Throughout the text, but particularly in its later half, it is common to encounter "stray voices, voices without bodies, symbolical voices . . . bodiless voices" (BTA 103). Indeed, one of the most distinctive aspects of *Between the Acts* is how regularly it fails to connect voices with particular bodies or to provide answers to the classic Genettian question of "who speaks?" If classical narrative traditions (including cinematic as well as literary ones) have often treated this situation as a source of consternation, in Woolf's novel it reads as a more positive (if still puzzling) reflection of voice's power.[33] Indeed, it is not unusual for these newly empowered voices to act independently—at various points, we learn, they have "stopped" (26), "chattered" (82), "interrupted" (106), "sounded" (107), and "passed the bushes" (103). Once again, the novel's policy of underidentification precludes readers from evaluating voice in relation to character. Instead, utterances are more or less explicitly positioned as abstract components in what Cuddy-Keane calls a "free-floating aural 'composition,'" one with an "experimental, aleatoric quality" that includes "ambient noise and environmental sound," alongside verbal language ("Virginia Woolf, Sound Technologies" 85). In this way, *Between the Acts* proffers a kind of posthumanist vision in which speech shares the floor with any number of other nonverbal sonic components.

In so doing, Woolf enacts a novelistic system of values in which the sonic competes with the semantic and in which a broader and more variable range of acoustic events are celebrated. The result is a leveling of the discursive field; while certain characters still enjoy a greater capacity to hold forth, or verbalize poetically—as in the case of Isa—the abundant attention paid to animal sounds, ambient noise, and unheard or overheard language makes it clear that

---

33. See film scholar Michel Chion, who notes that "when a voice is not localized, it tends to suffuse the whole filmic space, and to take on terrifying powers" (63); see also pp. 24–27 for a full catalogue of the "powers" inherent in what Chion called the "acousmatic" voice. At the 2017 International Narrative Conference, Elicia Clements delivered a paper, "Acousmatic Sound and Virginia Woolf's Critique of War," whose title also evokes this relation.

less semantically meaningful sounds are also crucial, constitutive elements of the narrative space. A voice need not be, narratively speaking, "important"—or even "comprehensible"—for it to qualify for inclusion (129).[34] Thus, "the random ribbons of birds' voices" can achieve more volume than those of the "pilgrims singing," which "could be heard; but the words were inaudible" (BTA 139, 111); or that of the Reverend Streatfield, whose "first words . . . were lost," in part due to the competing noise of breeze and "leaves . . . rustling" (129). In this way, *Between the Acts* seems to imagine a narrative world in which particular voices, or voices at all, don't predominate; in which taxonomies are insufficient; in which forces environmental, natural, and animal complicate those human designs and hierarchies that have historically been maximized for exclusion.

## III. CONVERSATION AS EXPLANATION: "MELANCTHA'S" DECONSTRUCTIVE DIALOGUE

At a glance, "Melanctha" would seem to be a less demonstrably "choral" text than *Between the Acts*. After all, there are far fewer speakers in Stein's text compared to the indeterminate number that populate Woolf's; proportionately, it also has a significantly higher ratio of indirect to direct discourse, and it "delays" the introduction of dialogue until nearly a fifth of the way into the novella. Notwithstanding the less overt display of chorality, however, "Melanctha" is, like *Between the Acts,* similarly committed to the performative redistribution of dialogue as a means of redressing the fundamental disparities that have undergirded the presentation of speech in the novel. In particular, this section will suggest that what manifests as "dialogue" in "Melanctha" simultaneously announces itself as a single, highly engineered monologue, which Stein—in a theatrical manner not unlike Toomer's—has simply "assigned" to her story's players. In this way, talk contributes less to the mimetic development and "rounding" of characters than to their continual reinscription in what, readers are never allowed to forget, is a synthetic framework. If in *Between the Acts* it was often the number and variety of speakers that worked against the mimesis of particular characters and utterances, in "Melanctha," one could say, it is the *volume* of speech—coupled with its inefficiency and redundancy—that undermines its characterizing potential and gestures instead toward its more polemical agenda. Similarly, the fact that dialogue

---

34. As Cuddy-Keane notes, "Since many words cannot be heard, suggestion predominates over specific reference, and sound over signification" ("Politics" 281).

never occurs in proximity to the major story events—the births and deaths that occur disproportionately in the story's first and last pages—suggests that it has little bearing on narrative progression. In this way, not only does Stein, like Woolf, emphasize that the direct discourse in her text will fail to function in the usual ways: to either develop character or advance plot. She also, by ensuring that readers are made to contend with this oddly ineffectual dialogue at such length, carries out a deconstruction of discursive convention at once more exhaustive and more exhaust*ing* than similarly subversive attempts by contemporaries.

On the one hand, the notion that Stein has co-opted character discourse for her own purposes is in line with much existing commentary on the novella, which has understandably focused on the politics of Stein's act of transracial representation: her decision, in other words, to "put on" black speech for her own personal ends. Janet Malcolm offers a representative synopsis of the dominant view—one supported by Stein's own account in *The Autobiography of Alice B. Toklas*—that the decision reflects a self-serving desire to retell the story of her doomed romance with May Bookstaver, as she had tried and failed to do in *Q.E.D*, and thus to replay the story of her unhappy love affair in a different, and distancing, racial key (Malcolm 36–38).[35] Michael North, meanwhile, argues persuasively that such acts of "linguistic imitation and racial masquerade" had more far-reaching professional as well as personal benefits for Stein, allowing her, along with fellow modernists, to perform her liberation from bourgeois culture and literary convention (11). In his view, such acts represented a form of "rebellion through racial ventriloquism" (9), a strategy that "allow[ed] the writer to play at self-fashioning" (11).

Yet the controversy surrounding the referential dimension of "Melanctha's" dialogue—Stein's decision to explicitly designate its speakers as African American and her inclusion of certain bowdlerized elements of African American Vernacular English—have understandably distracted attention away from some of the highly idiosyncratic (and less stereotypic) aspects of its form and what they might function to accomplish. Perhaps contributing to this oversight is the surprising tendency among commentators to assume the characters' talk is still substantially mimetic. Thus, despite the fact that, as North rightly notes, "the speech in 'Melanctha' is so clearly inauthentic," a number

---

35. Malcolm provides a useful synopsis of the novella's genesis in Stein's private life, and its evolving reception by the public, noting that the story "which for many years was celebrated as some sort of wonderfully advanced study of black life by a white writer (and by today's less innocent standard . . . can only be called patronizing and uncomprehending), is based, not on Stein's experience of black life in America, but on a romance between herself and a woman named May Bookstaver . . ."(36).

of recent commentators have helped perpetuate the text's original reputation for realism (76).[36] John Carlos Rowe, for instance, refers to the way Stein's style "imitates African-American vernacular speech patterns, even though it cannot be said to specify a regional or otherwise identifiable African-American dialect" (228). Despite this concession, Rowe's assertion suggests the persuasive staying power of the "mimetic" hypothesis and the persistence of the belief that Stein had as her goal the imitation of black speech. Even North himself, in his influential reading of "Melanctha" as an expression of modernism's obsession with "racial masquerade," ultimately relies on the notion that Stein's ambitions are best understood as an ethically dubious but creatively advantageous form of "ventriloquism"—as an attempt at mimesis, however poorly executed or problematic (11, 9).

Moving beyond this assumption, however, opens up a number of other interpretive possibilities, as well as new problems and dilemmas. It's true, of course, that the characters' diction and phraseology do feature certain stereotypical markers of "black" orality, including the use of vernacular contractions ("ain't" [61]; "I'se" [61]); double negatives ("I don't say never Melanctha it don't hurt me" [144]); and other "folksy" omissions ("you know well as I do Miss Melanctha") (90). Notwithstanding these apparent attempts at verisimilitude, however, the dialogue on balance tilts heavily toward something far more stylized—or, to use the terms introduced in the first chapter, less *empirical* and more *mannerist* in construction. Put another way, it is evident almost immediately that what is most interesting about the dialogue is not the degree to which it is mimetic but the degree to which it is *not*. However reflective the characters' diction and repetitive cadence may be of "real" conversation, their syntax is more suggestive of an invented dialect than any naturally occurring one. Take a cross section of Melanctha's and Jeff's speech: "I certainly, Melanctha, never can tell just how it is that it comes so lovely" (97); "You certainly didn't anyway trust me now no more, did you, when you just acted so bad to me" (111); "Oh Jeff, you so stupid always to me and always just bothering with your always asking to me" (121); "Seems to me it certainly ain't only what comes right away when one is hit, that counts to be brave to be bearing" (127). Such excerpts suggest less African American Vernacular English than Stein's *idea* of that vernacular (any vernacular?) run through a kind of cubist abstracting machine.

---

36. A reputation, it should be noted, perpetuated both by Stein's publishers, who—perhaps for marketing purposes—had a played up the text's language as "photographically exact" (qtd. in North 72) and by Stein's own claim that she was writing a "negro story," which some commentators seem to have construed as an indication that she was working in a documentary and social realist mode (AABT 48).

On the one hand, it's possible to argue that Stein has jettisoned realist convention for the sake of assigning to her characters the same, similarly improbable, speech. As North notes, Jeff and Melanctha (not to mention Rose Johnson and Jane Herbert) use essentially "the same words" to the extent that "only tiny differences of arrangement separate what Jeff wants so badly 'just to say' from what Melanctha is 'just saying'" (75)—a conclusion that would seem to render Stein's insistent use of quotation marks and proper names as "paradoxical" as Faulkner's and Woolf's, as discussed in the preceding chapter. The fact that Stein foregoes paragraph breaks, placing the characters' utterances into sequential arrangement such that dialogue appears on the page as monolithic blocks of text, takes the experiment one step further: amplifying the idea that not only is one person's speech *like* another's but that one person's speech is *as good as* another's: or in this case as "bad," given that all the characters' discourse is equally inefficient, disordered, and hard to follow. The result is a discursive flattening both among the characters (who, as noted above, are assigned a single "peculiar dialect") and, as has been less widely remarked, between the voices of the characters and the narrator, who has been so readily conflated with Stein herself (North 74). It is not only, then, that these voices are qualitatively the same; it's that from an evaluative standpoint Stein seems to be textually engineering them to be equal.

And yet, this apparent equality of the text's talk does not prevent some characters, notably, from assigning their own discourse greater priority or prestige. From the beginning of their relationship, after all, it is established that "Jefferson still always liked to talk along about the things he believed in" (88), and Melanctha "mostly . . . listened to his talking" (88): a dynamic that sets Jeff up as a mansplainer, avant la lettre. When Melanctha, early in their acquaintance, challenges the quality of Jeff's talk ("it certainly does seem to me you don't know very well yourself, what you mean, when you are talking"), he "laugh[s]" at her comment and remains undeterred ("Melanctha's answer only made him talk a little harder") (82). As their relationship progresses, this dynamic only intensifies; as the narrator informs us, "Jeff Campbell had not got over his way of talking to her all the time about *all the things he was always thinking*. Melanctha never talked much, now, when they were together" (94, italics mine). In this way, it becomes clear that the stylistic parallelism of Jeff's and Melanctha's speech disguises what are in fact meaningful disparities between each character's discourse and the attitudes they evince toward it. In effect, Stein thematizes their rhetorical power differential, implying that such discursive asymmetries are predicated upon and sustained by class and gender hierarchies—according to which a male doctor can feel safe in assuming unconditional speaking rights in relation to a less educated woman.

Melanctha, significantly, is not unaware of the imbalance and the extent to which it reflects Jeff's sense of entitlement. As she comments shortly after their acquaintance, "You certainly do know very well Jeff, you don't think really much, of my talking" (94). And later she remarks, "I certainly never did see no man like you, Jeff. You always wanting to have it all out in words always, what everybody is always feeling" (121). Here, it seems significant that what Jeff "wants"—"to have it all out in words always, what everybody is always feeling"—is what readers have historically "wanted" of the novel as well. In a sense, then, Stein aligns herself with Melanctha, not as a wronged romantic partner, as biographically inflected readings would have it, but as a female subject resistant to fulfilling or measuring her own discursive behavior against a normative code of conduct, which, in the case of the novel, has often privileged a degree of "self-expressivity" and the disclosure of "feelings"—the production of characterological depth and roundedness—that Stein, as an author, was not inclined to provide. In this sense, much as Woolf uses the exchanges between Isa, Lucy Swithin, and Bart Oliver, Stein mobilizes the dialogue between Jeff and Melanctha at least partly for the purposes of surfacing a gendered system of values that has disproportionately informed the novel's modes of characterization and speech representation. That "Melanctha" will ultimately refuse to endorse the presumption—textually linked to the story's main male character—that talk be used to clarify "thinking" and "feeling" suggests that Stein intends the story's dialogue to function as a rebuke to these default narrative preferences. Indeed, the cumulative result of Stein's denaturalizing strategies (the nonselectivity and redundancy of the story's dialogue; the collapse of difference between "he said" and "she said") is not simply to thwart or even queer the heterosexual romance plot but to stage the progressive devolution of those assumptions about gender, discourse, and power that have played such a crucial role in sustaining it.

The result, then, is that "Melanctha" features conversations every bit as unnatural and oddly concatenated as those in *The Ambassadors*—significant, given Stein's belated recognition of her own debts to James.[37] The difference is that here, as in *Between the Acts*, the engineering of intersubjectivity manifests as authorial rather than characterological in origin, with the dialogue conveying the impression of deriving from an extradiegetic rather than a diegetic source. Put another way, unlike the deliberately consensual speech

---

37. In *The Autobiography of Alice B. Toklas*, Toklas notes of Stein, "It is rather strange that she was not then at all interested in the work of Henry James for whom she now has a very great admiration and whom she considers quite definitely as her forerunner, he being the only nineteenth century writer who being an american felt the method of the twentieth century" (78).

of James's and Hemingway's fiction, for instance, the sameness of the talk in "Melanctha" doesn't give the impression of having been motivated by character psychology. Instead, this feature of Stein's discourse—much like Woolf's—seems designed to reflect a radically decentered approach to narrative, in which the "flattening" of individuals is not a flaw so much as a prerequisite for reimagining new forms of interrelation: the necessary price for achieving in fiction the kinds of parity that in social and political life remained deprioritized.

It is the frankly democratic impetus behind Stein's deliberate "equilibration" of dialogue that distinguishes the synchronies of speakers in "Melanctha" from, say, those on display in the fiction of male contemporaries like James and Hemingway. If, in the case of their novels, talking "like" becomes a means of furnishing proof of belonging to an exclusive group or coterie, in Stein's, by contrast, it isn't a self-conscious act—deliberately cultivated by the speakers—so much as the textual expression of the belief that Stein attributed to herself in *The Autobiography of Alice B. Toklas*: that "one person was as good as another" (AABT 174). Indeed, a useful intertext for making sense of Stein's method in "Melanctha" may be the anecdote she has Toklas relay in *Autobiography* about the admission procedures for newcomers to the salon at 27 Rue de Fleurus: "The idea was that anybody could come but for form's sake and in Paris you have to have a formula, everybody was supposed to be able to mention the name of somebody who had told them about it. It was mere form, really everybody could come in" (AABT 13).[38] In short, one must still go through the *rituals* of admission, but ultimately all are admitted. It seems particularly significant, in this light, that Stein elected to assign to the story's African American characters an only lightly modified version of her own writerly voice; for in doing so, one could see "Melanctha" as interested less in staging the "difference" of black speech from white than in staging its core of sameness. (Indeed, in this way, it is interesting to consider whether "Melanctha" might serve as a distant and much less self-aware antecedent of Toni Morrison's "Recitatif," which so deftly undermines readers' reliance on racial signifiers.) Malcolm hints at Stein's own linguistic neutrality when she describes "Melanctha" as "Stein's second stab at coming to terms with her heartbreak in a piece of writing," noting that "the fake black talk between Melanctha and her lover Jeff is a new version of the talk between the white women lovers of *Q.E.D*" (Malcolm 36–38). Without insisting on a false equivalency—

---

38. Jonathan Goldman reads this line as proof of the "exclusionary principle shaping this coterie," since the "name-dropping here is ritualistic, but also compulsory" (88–89). Yet in fact it seems to reinforce the underlying *democratic* principle at work: the idea that, formalities notwithstanding, "anybody" and "everybody" could come.

impossible, given the historical ramifications of white artists "using" black speech—it's nonetheless worth considering whether Stein sought to position them as functionally on par, an expedient (if problematic) way of expressing the idea that one "version" of talk was "as good as another."

The possibility that Stein would have perceived character discourse to be a fictional device well-suited to advancing her democratizing agenda is further substantiated by the dialogic evidence of *The Autobiography of Alice B. Toklas*—a surprising claim, given the text's apparent monologism. Yet despite the fact that *Autobiography* is narrated by and focalized through a single persona, it is ultimately composed of (and centrally concerned with) other people's voices. "Before I tell about the guests," Toklas reports, "I must tell about what I saw": a statement that frames the character's primary role as that of recapper (8). Thus, if Sarah Wilson has seen *Autobiography* as democratic insofar as it employs a "down-home, intimate voice that would have broad appeal and thus engineer far-reaching social connection," its pluralism might be better reflected by the quantity of voices it includes rather than by the perceived quality of the one Stein assigns Toklas (268). Indeed, considered from this angle, Toklas's putative monologue is in fact the perfect pretense for the aggregation and dissemination of dialogue: allowing Stein to engineer through her fiction what Woolf and her Bloomsbury compatriots sought to achieve via recording technology—a rendering of her own discourse community, a collective portrait in talk.

Further, *Autobiography*'s structure functions to "equilibrate" that talk, just as Jonathan Goldman suggests it strives to achieve parity among its many players. As he argues, Stein's text makes a point to "democratize" the featured characters—for instance, "by . . . throwing out names that are part of Stein's household without differentiating them from the more auratic names" (94). He cites Hélène as an example of one "familiar" character who "is given treatment resembling that of the more incandescent names," noting that "Stein presents the name of her domestic no differently" than any of the more "illustrious" figures named in the text (95). *Autobiography* thus positions the represented subjects on a continuum of narrative significance rather than within a hierarchy. In so doing, Stein, like Woolf, posits a reconception of the novel as an extensible discursive spectrum, a space in which all voices have the potential to be included and in which everyone qualifies as a subject of portraiture—or not. Fiction, thusly conceived, is not unlike Stein's literary salon: a place where, to paraphrase Toklas's assessment, everybody can come, and nobody makes any difference (AABT 123–24).

The evidence of "Melanctha" and *Between the Acts*, then, implies that Stein and Woolf were intent on reengineering the novel in such a way as to disrupt the compulsory individuation and hierarchization of characters by continually emphasizing their narrative and locutionary interdependence (a priority underscored in the very title of *Three Lives*). As Goldman notes of *The Autobiography*, the continual introduction of new characters "convey[s] the sense of an infinite chain of names, the aura of each adding its value to the whole" (89–90). Likewise, the continual emergence of new voices in *Between the Acts* conveys a sense of an infinitely accommodating fictional space; like a Whitman-esque catalogue,[39] Stein and Woolf suggest that the novel might similarly possess room for "everybody"—a word that occupies a central place in Stein's corpus—and not just particular, privileged somebodies.

Considered side by side, *Between the Acts* and *Three Lives*, as I've presented them here—and Woolf and Stein more generally—are instrumental to the larger project of rethinking assumptions about modernism as primarily concerned with the private individual. In addition to the textual evidence presented here, it is worth noting those paratextual phenomena that support a reading of Stein and Woolf as emblematic of a modernist interest in imagining collectivity, including the fact that both were so committed throughout their careers to the construction of *real* as well as fictional collectives and to domestic arrangements that resisted nuclearity and proscribed heterosexual frameworks. With this in mind, it is perhaps not surprising to find their fictions experimenting with ways of formally representing nonhierarchical relations or to recall that both authors were similarly willing to envision large-scale sociocultural change: Woolf, of course, in her famous, half-facetious aside in "Mr. Bennett and Mrs. Brown," that "on or about December 1910 human character changed," and Stein, in her aphoristic comments about the "lost generation" she discerned in the wake of the World War I, and "the great change in the Americans" she observed after the second ("Character in Fiction" 421; *Wars I Have Seen* 252). Such commentary reflects an overlapping interest in recalibrating narrative's ambitions and inherited techniques so as to be able to tell stories less of isolated individuals than the social matrix of the group.

---

39. Cuddy-Keane describes Woolf's "surprising affinity" for Whitman, noting that her "aims of peace and democracy . . . were realized in Whitman's democratic vision and his democratic relation to his common readers" (*Virginia Woolf* 41, 44–45).

CONCLUSION

# What Is the Dialogue Doing Now?

AT THE HEART of this project has been a central thesis regarding the rhetorical capacities of conversation in the novel and the ability of character dialogue to function as a vector of authorial expression—and thus as a narrative structure capable of signifying independently of fictional character or the mechanisms of plot. To this end, the book has sought to advance two interrelated claims. The first is a historical claim about modernism's contribution to the development of the novel and the role played by certain early twentieth-century American and British writers both in surfacing dialogue's poetic dimensions and in exploiting the indirect communicative possibilities inherent in so-called direct discourse. The second, a theoretical claim, concerns readers: in particular, the persistence of default modes of interpreting dialogue and their insufficiency when applied to texts not especially invested in the mimetic presentation of speech or speakers. Instead, the preceding chapters have modeled an alternative approach to construing character talk that is more attentive to its polysemy and poetic status—the fact, in other words, that even the most seemingly transparent of character utterances is only ever a stylization.

While dialogue may present itself as a hiatus in the narrating instance, then, this project has sought to elaborate the extent to which such putatively direct reporting, or "showing," is inevitably another form of "telling," albeit one with distinct shadings and capabilities. That such a truism needs elaborating reflects the power of both assumptions about the limited functionality of character speech and the long-standing conventions that insist on its innocence of authorial design. Yet as the previous chapters have demonstrated, dialogue, whether despite or because of its perceived exceptionalism, is often a particularly revealing site of ideological commitments, whether they are attributed primarily to characters (as in the case of the texts considered in chapters 2 and 3) or more openly claimed by the authors themselves (as in chapters 4 and 5). By identifying (without overstating) a tendency toward uncritical reading when it comes to character dialogue, this study has sought to affirm the premise with which Bakhtin begins "Discourse and the Novel": that critics "must overcome the divorce between an abstract 'formal' approach and an equally abstract 'ideological' approach" (DI 259). But it has also suggested that dialogue—precisely because it has often escaped either of these approaches—is especially in need of analyses that combine both.

This is not to suggest that naïveté has no place in reading or to imply, as de Man has, that readers of fiction must choose between being "rhetorically aware" and "aesthetically responsive"—a false dichotomy that presumes entry into the fictional story world can only come at the price of mystification (*Allegories* 72). Rather, the goal of this study has been to demonstrate the critical payoffs of reading fictional talk less, or less exclusively, as a mimetic product; of paying attention to how characters say, as well as what they say; and of attending to structures of fictional talk as well as its semantic contents. Shifting the angle of interpretive approach in this way not only makes evident the expressive potential inherent in one of the novel's more invisible and taken-for-granted features. It also highlights the necessity of reappraising the stories we tell about modernist style and of questioning whether early twentieth-century authors most regularly celebrated for their experiments in thought representation are due similar credit for refurbishing the novelistic presentation of speech. Of course, the fact that certain authors have *always* been associated with their dialogue—to the extent that their names are used to designate the conversation that takes place in their novels as recognizably "Dickensian" or "Jamesian"—means that the awareness of fictional talk's authorial origins and expressivity is always there at some level. What this study has sought to demonstrate is that features manifest in the utterances of the modernist canon—the superfluities of *Absalom, Absalom!* and "Melanctha"; the speakerly self-consciousness of "The Dead"; and the echolalia of *The Ambassadors*—functioned to make the suppression of such awareness less complete or easily sustained than it had been (and would continue to be) in other narrative contexts.

Significantly, however, strategies for responding to dialogue have not generally kept pace with changing methods for deploying it. Richardson, in

*Unnatural Voices,* hints at the extent to which interpretive paradigms derived largely from realist fiction might inadvertently constrain our modalities of response. Writing of *The Nigger of the 'Narcissus,'* for instance, he notes that "Conrad is doing something . . . radical here, something that transcends the mimetic poetics that . . . criticism implicitly presupposes" (42). Such antimimetic moves, he argues, necessitate a correspondingly "radical" shift in critical approach: Specifically, he writes, "We need to ask 'What is the narration doing now?' rather than 'Who is speaking here?'" (42).

Indeed, one of the central lessons to have emerged from the preceding analyses of modernist dialogue is that the Genettian question "Who speaks?" might yield a wider range of answers than has been implied by what Barthes calls the *classic text,* one in which "the majority of the utterances are assigned an origin" (41). In other words, if historically the question has been asked of utterances with the expectation that "we can identify their parentage, who is speaking," it's clear from the case studies considered here that some texts significantly complicate that identification process, if they don't obstruct it altogether (Barthes 41). It is not, then, that we *shouldn't* ask the question but that audiences should recalibrate their expectations about the range and definitiveness of possible responses. When readers of *The Waves,* for instance, insist on the distinctness and spoken-ness of the characters' "monologues," despite the indications to the contrary, it seems clear that practices of interpreting fictional speech remain prescribed by *readerly* investments in the prospect of attribution; or, conversely, that they are colored by an attendant fear of absenteeism: the threat posed by what Chion describes, apropos of cinema, as an *acousmatic* voice, which is "heard without its cause or source being seen" and derives from "an immaterial and non-localized body" (18, 24). Neither expression of this expectation, however—that fictional voices should be readily identifiable and traceable to a single origin—is especially useful when confronted with a text like *Between the Acts,* which, by scuttling such auratic conceptions of character speech from the start, simultaneously prompts inquiries into how *else* it might be deployed and received. In this sense, Woolf's later novel just manifests more overtly, through its pluralism and propensity for anonymization, the challenges to ready attribution raised by earlier texts: by the consensual speech of James's and Hemingway's characters and the contamination of Joyce's and Faulkner's; by the implausibility of talk in *The Waves* and its choral diffusion in "Melanctha" and *Cane.*

Equally important, however, is to recognize that "who speaks?" is just *one* of the questions readers might ask. At least as generative, I'd argue, is a variation on the query Richardson proposes: not "what is the narration doing now?" but, more specifically, "what is the *dialogue* doing now?" It is a question that catalyzes a movement away from a hermeneutic mode of reading and toward a rhetorically inclined one, which attends more closely to how authors use dialogue to produce aesthetic affects and convey ideological commitments. Employing less character-dependent paradigms of dialogue interpretation becomes even more crucial when confronting late modernist fiction—and, contemporaneously, modernist film—in which voices' relationships to bodies may undergo even more extreme attenuation. From the intermittently or minimally embodied talk of Beckett's trilogy, to the acousmatic sounds that surface in much of Godard's cinema,[1] both media have gone on to witness the more radical decoupling of speech from diegetic bodies. A novel like *Molloy*, for instance, frequently confuses the question not only of "who speaks?"—or, as Simon Critchley puts it, "Who is the indefatigable 'I' who always seems to say the same thing?" (125)—but even *whether* someone speaks, given that, as Cay Eileen Kelly observes, the "illusion of narrator-as-speaker" is compromised by "the psychologically dissociated state of Molloy as speaker," which "makes it difficult for the reader . . . to establish a consistent frame of interaction with any interlocutor other than perhaps Molloy himself" (2–3). Along related lines, Joshua Landy suggests of Beckett's fiction that the salient question is not "what Beckett's words *mean*, but what they are *for*," and he argues that this "what-for question" must be "answered . . . with relation to the reader," not just the author, such that it becomes a more personalized line of inquiry: "What do Beckett's texts do for *us*?" (125).

Indeed, *Molloy* seems to at once witness and periodically narrate the dissolution of dialogue as a tool for characterological expression. Even as the text indulges in what might be called *fantasies of centrifugality*—with Molloy recounting attempts to reach out to an unnamed stranger "so as to know him better, be myself less lonely"—he finds himself thwarted by centripetal forces: "But in spite of my soul's leap out to him, at the end of its elastic, I saw him only darkly" (11). And even attempts at dialogue devolve to monologue, as when Molloy attempts conversation with the ambiguously named interlocutor, "Mrs. Loy . . . or Lousse, I forget" (33):

> But either because she did not understand me, or because she preferred to leave me in ignorance, she did not reply to my question, but went on with her soliloquy, reiterating tirelessly each new proposition, then expounding

---

1. By 1982, Chion was able to assert that "the richest of voice-image relations, of course, isn't the arrangement that shows the person speaking, but rather the situation in which we don't see the person we hear, as his voice comes from the center of the image, the same source of all the film's other sounds" (9). Though Chion claims this "invention" for cinema (9), this study has sought to establish its significant precedents in fiction.

further, slowly, gently, the benefits for both of us if I would make my home with her. (47)

And all the time she never stopped talking, whereas I only opened my mouth to ask, at long intervals, more and more feebly, what town we were in. (48)

Even as the narrator of *Molloy* seems to engage in an analogous act of soliloquy—he "reiterate[s] tirelessly" and "never stop[s] talking"—he also recognizes the futility of all this locutionary activity, as when he describes "this trouble I had in understanding not only what others said to me but also what I said to them" (50). It's a conflict paradigmatic of Beckett's work: He can't go on talking; he'll go on talking. In this way *Molloy* dramatizes the failure of novelistic formula for representing speech at the same time that it constitutes an extended effort in this direction. As Critchley puts it, Beckett's novels are about both "the impossibility of narration or representation, and its necessity" (115).

Take the fact that Molloy and Moran evince outsized frustration with even (or especially) the most seemingly benign of representational strategies. Near the novel's beginning, Molloy reports an overheard conversation with neither speech tags nor quotation marks before giving up altogether: "Is this the man who ran over your dog, Madam? He is, sergeant, and what of it? No, I can't record this fatuous colloquy. So I will merely observe that finally in his turn the constable too dispersed, the word is not too strong, grumbling and growling" (33). Here, Molloy makes a point of repudiating *mimesis*—by refusing to record the "fatuous colloquy" between the lady and sergeant—in favor of more explicit *diegesis* ("so I will merely observe"). It is worth noting, of course, that he will subsequently express equal frustration with modes of indirect report. "Must I describe it?" he asks of Lousse's house, while later, Moran confesses, "I have no intention of relating the various adventures which befell us" (35, 131). But it is dialogue for which Molloy appears to reserve the most hostility:

And when I say I said, etc., all I mean is that I knew confusedly things were so, without knowing exactly what it was all about. And every time I say, I said this, or I said that, or speak of a voice saying, far away inside me, Molloy, and then a fine phrase more or less clear and simple, or find myself compelled to attribute to others intelligible words, or hear my own voice uttering to others more or less articulate sounds, *I am merely complying with the convention that demands you either lie or hold your peace.* (88, italics mine)

Here, Molloy essentially calls the novel's bluff by positioning fictional speech as a form of carefully orchestrated and artful "lying." Beckett goes even further in his 1961 prose work, *How It Is,* which opens with the even more brazen disclosure (and effective disavowal) of such formulas: "How it was I quote before Pim with Pim after Pim how it is three parts I say it as I hear it" (7). This repeated phrase ("I quote") is part of a larger repertoire of self-reflexive gestures—such as the narrator's habitual delineation of the text's construction ("here then part one") (7)—that cumulatively function to imply the impossibility of narrative business as usual.

What makes Beckett's deprecation of traditional discursive tactics so notable is its disclosure of how deeply entrenched mimetic bias has been. By conflating dialogue—the act of "attribut[ing] to others intelligible words"—with "lying," Beckett effectively *outs* what Genette describes as a long-standing cultural preference for directly "reported" (as opposed to "transposed" or "narrated") character speech (171–72). Genette traces these categories back to their Classical origins, juxtaposing Plato's predilection for narrative "distance" and the "reduction of speech to event" (170) with Aristotle's endorsement of the "dramatic" approach popularized by Homer. But these tendencies, he further explains, have exerted a notably lopsided influence on (Western) literary history. Speaking of Aristotle's "success" in "upholding . . . the superiority of the purely mimetic," he notes,

> We should not fail to appreciate the influence that this prerogative, massively granted to dramatic style, exerted for centuries on the evolution of narrative genres. It is expressed not only by the canonization of tragedy as the supreme genre in the entire classical tradition, but also, more subtly and well beyond classicism, in that sort of tutelage exercised over narrative by the dramatic model, expressed so well by the use of the word "scene" to designate the basic form of novelistic narration. Up to the end of the nineteenth century, the novelistic scene is conceived, fairly piteously, as a pale copy of the dramatic scene: mimesis at two degrees, imitation of imitation. (173)

The challenge, Genette's comments suggest, is to consider the impact this partiality for the "mimetic" over the "diegetic"—the "dramatic" over the "narrative"; the scene over the summary—has had on critical practice. Here, Genette implies that the signal achievement of the modern novel has been to double-down on this "dramatic" model, "obliterating the last traces of the narrating instance and giving the floor to the character right away" (173). Yet the previous chapters have sought to introduce an additional possibility: that modernism's specific accomplishments may lie in the opposite direction, not just in the facility with which its authors created the impression of vocal "emancipation" but in the artfulness with which they curtailed it: reinstating, through the structure of dialogue, the narrational aspect even as they often produced the sensation of having "obliterated" it. That is not to say that such authorial interference is necessarily visible in discrete utterances. Often, it is only when considering the dialogic evidence at scale that the "narrated" quality of "reported" speech, and the rhetorical motivations for it, fully emerge.

We must just as easily frame this argument in Bakhtin's terms rather than Genette's—which is to say, using the conceptual framework and critical vocabulary associated with theories of the novel rather than narratology. In "Discourse and the Novel," Bakhtin refers to the novel's capacity to include a "double-accented, double-styled *hybrid construction*": that is, "an utterance that belongs, by its grammatical (syntactic) and compositional markers, to a single speaker, but that actually contains mixed within it two utterances, two speech manners, two styles, two 'languages,' two semantic and axiological belief systems" (DI 304). Though Bakhtin's focus is on narration, we might also productively apply this insight to dialogue and thus recover for direct discourse the kind of complexity and "hybridity" indirect discourse has long enjoyed. As the previous analyses have helped to illustrate, dialogue, like narration, encompasses a similar spectrum, from the apparently *homoglossic* to the emphatically *heteroglossic*. Moreover, however seemingly unhybrid a single instance of character discourse might be, in the aggregate it is hard not to discern signs of an authorial "accent" or "style," of an additional, extracharacterological "manner" or "belief system." Dialogue, at the level of the individual utterance, may not as readily disclose the presence of discursive mixing, but that does not mean it is not similarly "mixed."

By way of concluding, I'd like to put forward one final, perhaps surprising, suggestion: that the possibilities inherent in such theoretical reframing might be best illuminated by examples drawn from modernist *filmmaking*, a tradition which has important parallels to modernist fiction but which necessarily falls outside the scope of this study. Nonetheless, I wish to end by offering brief observations on two filmmakers, Jean-Luc Godard and Michelangelo Antonioni, students of Anglo-American modernist fiction whose unapologetic presentation of voice as a poetic element (often more than an emanation of character) helps illustrate both the unrecognized affordances of direct speech and the benefits for viewers, or readers, willing to embrace what Phelan might describe as a new "ethics of the telling" (*Experiencing Fiction* 11). To a degree perhaps possible only in a medium where voice is an empirical reality, Godard made its autonomy from characters and diegetic events so central a feature of his cinema that viewers' expectations are preempted from the start. Thus, it's not uncommon for diegetic sound (for instance, a character's comments during a therapy session in *Weekend*) to be overwhelmed by the sudden amplification of the extradiegetic score—as if to expose, in a manner analogous to Beckett's *Molloy*, talk as a series of "fatuous" rituals. It's also not uncommon for lines of dialogue to plainly contradict the images seen on-screen—as when a character in *Pierrot le fou* (1965) reports, "I am kissing you all over," when she is doing no such thing. Liberated in this way from the burdens of exposition or accurate narration, voice is then freed for a host of *other* expressive purposes: to sing; to recite (poems, impromptu lists); to soliloquize; or to simply intone, in the manner of Anna Karina, who in *Pierrot le fou* walks the beach lamenting, "Qu'est ce que je peux faire, je sais pas quoi faire" ["What can I do, I don't know what to do"]. (Similarly, in Antonioni's *L'avventura* (1960), Anna's repetition of the word *perché?* [why?] functions not as an interrogative but as a monosyllabic declaration performed to the point of meaning fatigue.) In this way, Godard seems to share with Chion an interest in documenting "all that the cinema can do structurally with the voice": exploring the "syntax of possible relations between the film image and the voice" (9).

Antonioni's films are similarly experimental in their use of speech and sound. Near the end of *Red Desert* (1964), for example, there is a scene in which the protagonist, Giuliana, recounts a story to her young son about a girl who frequents a pink-sand beach—a scene dramatized as an interpolated episode accompanied by Giuliana's voiceover. One day, the story goes, while the girl is swimming, an apparently unmanned ship appears and then disappears; shortly after, she hears a woman's voice singing, but she cannot identify its source. Viewers will recognize the song from the opening credits and will register its acoustic difference from the mechanized din that pervades the film's score. "Ma chi cantava?" her son asks: Who was singing? "Everything," Giuliana replies, suggesting a kind of manifest or ambient origin for the song rather than a single vocalist. It's an illuminating parable both within the context of Antonioni's work—which is known for its willingness to decenter human figures and concerns—and the broader ambit of modernist prose, which perhaps as early as *Between the Acts* was not afraid to evince, as Beckett later would, a distinctly posthumanist sensibility.

In this way, speech in Godard's or Antonioni's film regularly fails to deepen our understanding of character or plot—and at times might even seem to impede it. Often, the emphasis is on its sonic as much as its semantic properties. My goal in pointing out this tendency within a few examples of 1960s art cinema is not simply to note the antecedence of some of its key narrative strategies in earlier twentieth-century fiction. Rather, I want to suggest more broadly that these examples—which are in many ways more didactic in their disruption of dialogic protocols—could serve as useful heuristics, provocations in one medium that might spur thinking about more easily overlooked forms of experimentation in another. Not only do the modernist novels considered in this study anticipate the incompletely ambiguated voices and frankly *made* conversations that would surface in later modernist fiction and filmmaking. They also attest fully and in their own right to the rich rhetorical and aesthetic potential inherent in less compulsory forms of speech representation. They remind us, in short, that the job of readers is to appreciate what dialogue *is* doing, rather than preempt it with preconceptions about what it should do.

# WORKS CITED

Abbott, H. Porter. "Character and Modernism: Reading Woolf Writing Woolf." *New Literary History,* vol. 24, 1993, pp. 393–405.

Allen, Richard. *Speaking of Soap Operas.* U of North Carolina P, 1985.

Alsop, Elizabeth. "The Imaginary Crowd: Neorealism and the Uses of *Coralità.*" *The Velvet Light Trap,* vol. 74, Fall 2014, pp. 27–41.

———. "Refusal to Tell: Withholding Heroines in Hawthorne, Wharton, and Coetzee." *College Literature,* vol. 39, no. 3, Summer 2012, pp. 104–5.

Antonioni, Michelangelo, director. *L'avventura.* Cino del Duca, 1960.

———, director. *Red Desert.* Rizzoli, 1964.

Armstrong, Nancy. *How Novels Think: The Limits of Individualism from 1719–1900.* Columbia UP, 2005.

Auerbach, Erich. *Mimesis.* Princeton UP, 1953.

Bakhtin, Mikhail. *The Dialogic Imagination.* Edited by Michael Holquist. U of Texas P, 1981. (DI)

———. *Problems of Dostoevsky's Poetics.* Edited and translated by Caryl Emerson with an introduction by Wayne C. Booth, U of Minnesota P, 1984. (PDP)

———. *Speech Genres.* U of Texas P, 1986.

Banfield, Ann. *The Phantom Table: Woolf, Fry, Russell and the Epistemology of Modernism.* Cambridge UP, 2007.

———. *Unspeakable Sentences: Narration and Representation in the Language of Fiction.* Routledge & Kegan Paul, 1982.

Barthes, Roland. *S/Z.* Hill & Wang, 1974.

Beach, Richard. "Discourse Conventions and Researching Response to Literary Dialogue." *Research Response to Literature and the Teaching of Literature,* edited by Charles Cooper, Praeger, 1985, pp. 103–27.

Beckett, Samuel. *How It Is.* Grove Press, 1994.

———. *Three Novels.* Grove Press, 1958.

Bekhta, Natalia. "We-Narratives: The Distinctiveness of Collective Narration." *Narrative,* vol. 25, no. 2, May 2017, pp. 164–81.

Benn Michaels, Walter. *Our America: Nativism, Modernism, and Pluralism*. Duke UP, 1995.

Berman, Jessica. *Modernist Fiction, Cosmopolitanism, and the Politics of Community*. Cambridge UP, 2001.

Berman, Marshall. *All That Is Solid Melts into Air: The Experience of Modernity*. Verso, 1983.

Bersani, Leo. *A Future for Astyanax: Character and Desire in Fiction*. Columbia UP, 1984.

Bishop, Ryan. "There's Nothing Natural about Natural Conversation: A Look at Dialogue in Fiction and Drama." *Oral Tradition*, vol. 6, no. 1, 1991, pp. 58–78.

Bleikasten, André. "Faulkner from a European Perspective." *The Cambridge Companion to William Faulkner*, edited by Philip Weinstein, Cambridge UP, 1995, pp. 75–94.

———. *The Ink of Melancholy: Faulkner's Novels from* The Sound and the Fury *to* Light in August. Indiana UP, 1990.

Blotner, Jay. *Faulkner: A Biography*. U of Mississippi P, 2005.

———, editor. *Selected Letters of William Faulkner*. Random House, 1977.

Bonapfel, Elizabeth. "Marking Realism in *Dubliners*." *Doubtful Points: Joyce and Punctuation*, edited by Elizabeth M. Bonapfel and Tim Conley, Brill, 2014, pp. 67–86.

Bondanella, Peter. *The Films of Roberto Rossellini*. Cambridge UP, 1993.

Bordwell, David. "The Art Cinema as a Mode of Film Practice." *The European Cinema Reader*, edited by Catherine Fowler, Routledge, 2002, pp. 94–102.

Brooks, Peter. *Body Work: Objects of Desire in Modern Narrative*. Harvard UP, 1993.

———. *Reading for the Plot*. Harvard UP, 1984.

Brooks, Van Wyck. *Van Wyck Brooks, the Early Years: A Selection from His Works, 1908–1925*. Edited by Christine Sprague, Northeastern UP, 1993.

Brown, Rita Mae. *Starting from Scratch: A Different Kind of Writers' Manual*. Bantam, 1989.

Bunselmeyer, J. E. "Faulkner's Narrative Styles." *William Faulkner: Six Decades of Criticism*, edited by Linda Wagner-Martin, Michigan State UP, 2002, pp. 313–31.

Burgess, Anthony. "A Paralysed City." Dubliners *and* A Portrait of the Artist as a Young Man: *A Casebook*, edited by Morris Beja, Macmillan, 1973, pp. 224–40.

Burton, Deirdre. *Dialogue and Discourse: A Sociolinguistic Approach to Modern Drama Dialogue and Naturally Occurring Conversation*. Routledge and Kegan Paul, 1980.

Butte, George. "Henry James and Deep Intersubjectivity." *The Henry James Review*, vol. 30, 2009, pp. 129–43.

Cameron, Sharon. *Impersonality: Seven Essays*. U of Chicago P, 2007.

———. *Thinking in Henry James*. U of Chicago P, 1989.

Campbell, Sarah. *The Turn of the Ear: Reading for Speech in Henry James*. 2008. State University of New York at Buffalo, PhD Dissertation.

Cheng, Vincent J. "Empire and Patriarchy in 'The Dead.'" *Joyce Studies Annual* vol. 4, 2003, pp. 16–42.

Chapman, Raymond. *Forms of Speech in Victorian Speech*. Longman, 1994.

Chion, Michel. *The Voice in the Cinema*. Columbia UP, 1999.

Clark, Katerina, and Michel Holquist. *Mikhail Bakhtin*. Harvard UP, 1984.

Clements, Elicia. "Acousmatic Sound and Virginia Woolf's Critique of War." Narrative Conference, 25 March, 2017, Hilton Lexington/Downtown, Lexington, KY.

Cohn, Dorrit. *Transparent Minds: Narrative Modes for Presenting Speech in Fiction.* Princeton UP, 1978.

Coleman, Dan. "Tuning in to Conversation in the Novel: *Gatsby* and the Dynamics of Dialogue." *Style,* vol. 34, no. 1, Summer 2000, pp. 52–77.

Conrad, Barnaby, and the Staff of the Santa Barbara Writers' Conference. *The Complete Guide to Writing Fiction,* Writer's Digest Books, 1990.

Conrad, James. *Lord Jim.* W. W. Norton, 1996.

Critchley, Simon. "Who Speaks in the Work of Samuel Beckett?" *Yale French Studies,* vol. 93, 1998, pp. 114–30.

Cuddy-Keane, Melba. Introduction. *Between the Acts,* by Virginia Woolf. New York: Harcourt, 2008.

———. "The Politics of Comic Modes in Virginia Woolf's *Between the Acts.*" *PMLA,* vo. 105, no. 2, March 1990, pp. 273–85.

———. "The Rhetoric of Feminist Conversation: Virginia Woolf and the Trope of the Twist." *Ambiguous Discourse: Feminist Narratology and British Women Writers,* edited by Kathy Mezei, U of North Carolina P, 1996, pp. 137–61.

———. "Virginia Woolf, Sound Technologies, and the New Aurality." *Virginia Woolf in the Age of Mechanical Reproduction,* edited by Pamela L. Caughie, Garland, 2000, pp. 69–96.

———. *Virginia Woolf, the Intellectual, and the Public Sphere.* Cambridge UP, 2003.

Cuddy-Keane, Melba, Adam Hammond, and Alexandra Peat. *Modernism: Keywords.* Wiley-Blackwell, 2014.

Dalziel, Pamela. "*Absalom, Absalom!* The Extension of Dialogic Form." *The Mississippi Quarterly,* vol. 45, no. 3, Summer 1992.

Davidson, Cathy, and Arnold Davidson. "Decoding the Hemingway Hero." *New Essays in* The Sun Also Rises, edited by Linda Wagner-Martin, Cambridge UP, 1987.

Davis, Fred. *Fashion, Culture, and Identity.* U of Chicago P, 1994.

Davis, Lennard J. *Resisting Novels: Ideology and Fiction.* Methuen, 1987.

Dawes, James. *A Language of War.* Harvard UP, 2002.

De Man, Paul. *Allegories of Reading: Figural Language in Rousseau, Nietzsche, Rilke, and Proust.* Yale UP, 1979.

Derrida, Jacques. *Of Grammatology.* Translated by Gayatri Chakravorty Spivak, Johns Hopkins UP, 1997.

Dickinson, Renée. "Pedagogical Performance: Reading *The Waves.*" *Virginia Woolf Miscellany,* no. 78, Spring/Summer 2008, pp. 30–31.

Dolar, Mladen. *A Voice and Nothing More.* MIT Press, 2006.

Doody, Terrence. *Confession and Community in the Novel.* Louisiana State UP, 1980.

DuPlessis, Rachel Blau. "Woolfenstein." *Breaking the Sequence: Women's Experimental Fiction,* edited by Ellen G. Friedman and Miriam Fuchs, Princeton UP, 1989, pp. 99–115.

———. "Woolfenstein, the Sequel." *Primary Stein: Returning to the Writing of Gertrude Stein,* edited by Janet Boyd and Sharon J. Kirsh, Lexington, 2014, pp. 37–56.

———. *Writing beyond the Ending: Narrative Strategies of Twentieth-Century Women Writers*. Indiana UP, 1985.

Dydo, Ulla E. *Gertrude Stein: The Language That Rises: 1923–1934*. Northwestern UP, 2008.

———, editor. *A Stein Reader*. Northwestern UP, 1993.

Edel, Leon. *Henry James: A Life*. New York: Harper & Row, 1977.

Ellmann, Richard. "The Backgrounds of 'The Dead.'" *Dubliners and A Portrait of the Artist as a Young Man: A Casebook,* edited by Morris Beja, Macmillan, 1973, pp. 172–87.

———. *James Joyce*. Oxford UP, 1982. (JJ)

Faulkner, William. *Absalom, Absalom!* New York: Vintage, 1991. (AA)

———. *As I Lay Dying*. New York: Vintage, 1985. (AILD)

———. "The Bear." *Go Down Moses*. Vintage, 1970.

———. *Requiem for a Nun*. New York, Vintage, 2012.

———. *The Sound and the Fury*. New York, Vintage, 1990. (SF)

———. *The Unvanquished*. New York, Vintage, 1991. (UNV)

Ferrer, Daniel. *Virginia Woolf and the Madness of Language*. Translated by Goeffrey Bennington and Rachel Bowlby, Routledge, 1990.

Flesch, William. "The Poetics of Speech Tags." *Renaissance Literature and Its Formal Engagements,* edited by Mark David Rasmussen, Palgrave Macmillan, 2002, pp. 159–84.

Fludernik, Monika. "The Category of 'Person' in Fiction: You and We Narrative—Multiplicity and Indeterminacy of Reference." *Current Trends in Narratology,* edited by Greta Olson, De Gruyter, 2011, pp. 100–141.

———. *The Fictions of Language and the Languages of Fiction*. Taylor and Francis, 1993.

———. "The Many in Action and Thought: Towards a Poetics of the Collective in Narrative." *Narrative*, vol. 25, no. 2, May 2017, pp. 139–63.

Fogel, Aaron. *Coercion to Speak: Conrad's Poetics of Dialogue*. Harvard UP, 1985.

Follansbee, Jeanne A. "'Sweet Fascism in the Piney Woods': *Absalom, Absalom!* as Fascist Fable." *Modernism/modernity*, vol. 18, no. 1, 2011, pp. 67–94.

Forster, E. M. *Aspects of the Novel*. Harcourt Brace, 1927.

Free, Melissa. "'Who is G. C.?': Misprizing Gabriel Conroy in Joyce's 'The Dead.'" *Joyce Studies Annual,* 2009, pp. 277–303.

Fulton, Lori Watkins. "Reading around Jake's Narration: Brett Ashley and *The Sun Also Rises.*" *The Hemingway Review*, vol. 24, no. 1, Fall 2004, pp. 61–80.

Fussell, Paul. *The Great War and the Language of Modernism*. Oxford UP, 2000.

Garber, Marjorie. *Quotation Marks*. Routledge, 2002.

Genette, Gérard. *Narrative Discourse*. Cornell UP, 1979.

Girard, René. *Deceit, Desire, and the Novel: Self and Other in Literary Structure*. Johns Hopkins UP, 1976.

Godard, Jean-Luc, director. *Pierrot le Fou*. Société Nouvelle de Cinématographie, 1965.

———, director. *Weekend*. Athos Films, 1967.

Godden, Richard. *William Faulkner: An Economy of Complex Words*. Princeton UP, 2007.

Goldman, Jonathan. *Modernism Is the Literature of Celebrity*. U of Texas P, 2012.

Graham, J. W. "Point of View in *The Waves*: Some Services of the Style." *Virginia Woolf: A Collection of Criticism,* edited by Thomas S. W. Lewis, McGraw-Hill, 1975.

———, editor. *The Waves: Two Holograph Drafts.* U of Toronto P, 1976.

Grice, Paul. *Studies in the Way of Words.* Harvard UP, 1991.

Gunn, Daniel. "Free Indirect Discourse and Narrative Authority in *Emma*." *Narrative,* vol. 12, no. 1, January 2004, pp. 35–54.

Gwynn, Frederick L., and Joseph L. Blotner. *Faulkner in the University.* UP of Virginia, 1995.

Haig, Stirling. *Flaubert and the Gift of Speech.* Cambridge UP, 1986.

Hale, Dorothy. "Henry James and the Invention of Novel Theory." *Cambridge Companion to Henry James,* edited by Jonathan Freedman, Cambridge UP, 1998, pp. 79–101.

Halliday, Sam. *Sonic Modernity: Representation Sound in Literature, Culture, and the Arts.* Edinburgh UP, 2013.

Hamblin, Ross. "'Longer than Anything': *Absalom, Absalom!* and Faulkner's Grand Design." *Faulkner and the Artist,* edited by Donald Kartiganer and Ann J. Abadie, UP of Mississippi, 1993, pp. 269–93.

Hannon, Charles. *Faulkner and the Discourses of Culture.* Louisiana State UP, 2005.

Hare, William. *Early Film Noir: Greed, Lust, and Murder Hollywood Style.* McFarland, 2003.

Hays, Peter L. "Hemingway's *The Sun Also Rises* and James's *The Ambassadors*." *The Hemingway Review,* vol. 20, no. 2, Spring 2001, pp. 90–98.

Helbig, Doris A. "Confession, Clarity, and Community in *The Sun Also Rises*." *The South Atlantic Review,* vol. 58, no. 2, 1993, pp. 85–110.

Hemingway, Ernest. *Ernest Hemingway: Selected Letters, 1917–1961.* Edited by Carlos Baker, Scribner, 1981. (EHSL)

———. *A Farewell to Arms.* Scribner, 1957. (AFTA)

———. *A Moveable Feast.* Scribner, 1961. (MF)

———. *The Sun Also Rises.* Scribner, 1926. (SAR)

Herman, David. "Dialogue in a Discourse Context: Scenes of Talk in Fictional Narrative." *Narrative Inquiry,* vol. 16, no. 1, 2006, pp. 75–84.

———. "The Mutt and Jute Dialogue in Joyce's *Finnegans Wake*: Some Gricean Perspectives." *Style,* vol. 28, no. 2, 1994, pp. 219–41.

Herman, David, John Manfred, and Marie-Laure Ryan, editors. *Routledge Encyclopedia of Narrative Theory.* Routledge, 2005.

Hild, Allison. "Community/Communication in Woolf's *The Waves*: Language as Motion." *The Journal of Narrative Technique,* vol. 24, no. 1, Winter 1994, pp. 69–79.

Hite, Molly. Introduction. *The Waves,* by Virginia Woolf. Harcourt, 2006, pp. xv–lxvii.

Houston, Neal B. "Hemingway: The Obsession with Henry James, 1924–1954." *Rocky Mountain Review of Language and Literature,* vol. 39, no. 1, 1985, pp. 33–46.

Humphries, David. *Different Dispatches: Journalism in Modern American Prose.* Routledge, 2006.

Hurston, Zora Neale. *Their Eyes Were Watching God.* Perennial, 1990.

Hussey, Mark. "'I' Rejected; 'We' Substituted: Self and Society in *Between the Acts*." *Reading and Writing Women's Lives: A Study of the Novel of Manners,* edited by Bege K. Bowers and Barbara Brothers, UMI Research Press, 1990, pp. 141–52.

———. *Virginia Woolf from A to Z: A Comprehensive Reference for Students, Teachers, and Common Readers to Her Life, Work, and Critical Reception.* Oxford UP, 1996.

Huyssen, Andreas. *Across the Great Divide: Modernism, Mass Culture, Postmodernism.* Indiana UP, 1987.

James, Henry. *The Ambassadors.* W. W. Norton, 1994. (A)

———. *The Awkward Age.* Everyman's Library, 1993. (AA)

———. *Collected Short Stories: Volume 2.* Everyman's Library, 1999. (CS)

———. *The Complete Notebooks of Henry James: The Authoritative and Definitive Edition.* Edited by Leon Edel and Lyall H. Powers, Oxford UP, 1987. (CN)

———. *The Golden Bowl.* Penguin, 2009. (GB)

———. *The Portrait of a Lady.* Penguin, 1986. (PL)

———. *The Question of Our Speech; The Lesson of Balzac: Two Lectures.* Houghton Mifflin & Co, 1905. (QS)

———. *The Turn of the Screw.* W. W. Norton, 1999. (TS)

———. *The Wings of the Dove.* Penguin, 1986. (WD)

Jameson, Fredric. *The Antinomies of Realism.* Verso, 2015.

———. *The Political Unconscious: Narrative as a Socially Symbolic Act.* Cornell UP, 1981.

Johnson, Samuel. *Johnson's Dictionary: A Modern Selection.* Edited by E. L. McAdam, Jr., & George Milne. Pantheon, 1963.

Johnston, G. "After the Invention of the Gramophone: Hearing the Woman in Stein's *Autobiography* and Woolf's *Three Guineas*." *Virginia Woolf Miscellany: Proceedings of the First Annual Conference on Virginia Woolf,* edited by Mark Hussey and Vara Neverow-Turk, Pace UP, 1992, pp. 88–96.

Jones, Gavin. *Strange Talk: The Politics of Dialect Literature in Gilded Age America.* U of California P, 1999.

Joyce, James. "The Dead." *Dubliners.* Penguin, 1993.

———. *Ulysses.* Edited by Hans Walter Gabler, Vintage, 1986. (U)

Kacandes, Irene. *Talk Fiction.* U of Nebraska P, 2001.

Kafka, Franz. *The Castle.* Schocken, 1998.

Kaplan, Carla. *The Erotics of Talk: Women's Writing and Feminist Paradigms.* Oxford UP, 1996.

Kelly, Cay Eileen. *Conversational Narrative: Functions and Forms of Talk in Samuel Beckett, Raymond Queneau, and Romain Gary (Emile Ajar).* 2000. University of California, Santa Barbara, PhD Dissertation.

Kenner, Hugh. *Joyce's Voices.* U of California P, 1978.

———. "The Last Novelist." *A Homemade World: The American Modernist Writers,* by Hugh Kenner, Knopf, 1975, pp. 194–222.

Kershner, R. B. *Joyce, Bakhtin, and Popular Literature: Chronicles of Disorder.* U of North Carolina P, 1989.

Kozloff, Sarah. *Overhearing Film Dialogue.* U of California Press, 2000.

Kreilkamp, Ivan. *Voice and the Victorian Storyteller.* Cambridge UP, 2005.

Kundera, Milan. *Testaments Betrayed.* HarperCollins, 1995.

Kurnick, David. *Empty Houses: Theatrical Failure and the Novel.* Princeton UP, 2011.

———. "What Does Jamesian Style Want?" *The Henry James Review,* vol. 28, 2007, pp. 213–22.

Lacan, Jacques. *Écrits: A Selection.* Translated by Alan Sheridan, W. W. Norton, 1977.

Lamb, Robert Paul. "Hemingway and the Creation of Twentieth-Century Dialogue." *Twentieth Century Literature,* vol. 42, no. 4, 1996, pp. 453–80.

Lambert, Mark. *Dickens and the Suspended Quotation.* Yale UP, 1981.

Landy, Joshua. *How to Do Things with Fictions.* Oxford, 2012.

Langford, Gerald. *Faulkner's Revision of* Absalom, Absalom! U of Texas P, 1971.

Lanser, Susan. *Fictions of Authority: Women Writers and Narrative Authority.* Cornell UP, 1992.

Lawrence, Karen. *The Odyssey of Style in* Ulysses. Princeton UP, 1982.

Lee, Hermione. *Virginia Woolf.* Vintage, 1999.

Lester, Cheryl. "From Place to Place in *The Sound and the Fury*: The Syntax of Interrogation." *Modern Fiction Studies,* vol. 34, no. 2, Summer 1988, pp. 141–55.

Levenson, Michael. *Modernism and the Fate of Individuality.* Cambridge UP, 1991.

Lockwood, Preston. "Henry James's First Interview." *The New York Times,* 21 March 1915.

Lodge, David. *After Bakhtin: Essays on Fiction and Criticism.* Routledge, 1990.

Loofbourow, Lili. "TV's New Girl's Club." *The New York Times Magazine,* 16 January 2015.

Lukács, Georg. *The Theory of the Novel.* MIT UP, 1974.

Malcolm, Janet. *Two Lives: Gertrude and Alice.* Yale UP, 2008.

Malinowski, Branisláw. "On Phatic Communion." *The Discourse Reader.* 3rd ed., edited by Adam Jaworski and Nikolas Coupland, Routledge, 2014, pp. 284–86.

Marcus, Jane. "Some Sources for *Between the Acts.*" *Virginia Woolf Miscellany,* vol. 6, 1977, pp. 1–3.

———. *Virginia Woolf and the Languages of Patriarchy.* Indiana UP, 1987.

Matthews, John T. *The Play of Faulkner's Language.* Cornell UP, 1982.

McCluskey, Kathleen. *Reverberations: Sound and Structure in the Novels of Virginia Woolf.* UMI Research Press, 1986.

McHale, Brian. "Speech Representation." *The Handbook of Narratology,* edited by Peter Hühn, et al., De Gruyter, 2009, pp. 434–46.

Melville, Herman. *Melville's Short Novels.* W. W. Norton, 2002.

Mepham, John. "Novelistic Dialogue: Some Recent Developments." *New Developments in English and American Studies,* edited by Zygmunt Mazur and Teresa Bela. *Proceedings of the Seventh International Conference of English and American Literature,* 1997, pp. 411–31.

———. "Psychoanalysis, Modernism, and the Defamiliarisation of Talk." *HJEAS: The Hungarian Journal of English and American Studies,* vol. 4, no. 1–2, 1998, pp. 105–19.

Middleton, Peter. "The Burden of Intersubjectivity: Dialogue as Communicative Ideal in Postmodern Fiction and Theory." *New Formations,* vol. 41, 2000, pp. 31–56.

Mildenberg, Ariane L. "Am I all of them? Am I one and distinct?": Woolf's 'Gigantic Conversation.'" *Etudes britanniques contemporaines (Revue de la Société d'Etudes Anglaises Contemporaines),* edited by Christine Reynier, Fall 2004, pp. 69–80.

Miller, J. Hillis. "Three Problems of Fictional Form." *Experience in the Novel.* Columbia UP, 1968.

Moglen, Seth. *Mourning Modernity: Literary Modernism and the Injuries of American Capitalism.* Stanford UP, 2007.

Moretti, Franco. *Distant Reading.* Verso, 2013.

———. *Graphs, Maps, Trees: Abstract Models for a Literary History.* Verso, 2005.

———. "Hamlet and the Region of Death." Interview by Richard Beck. *The Boston Globe.* 29 May, 2011. http://archive.boston.com/bostonglobe/ideas/articles/2011/05/29/hamlet_and_the_region_of_death. Accessed 2 February 2019.

———. *The Modern Epic: The World System from Goethe to García Márquez.* Verso, 1996.

Naremore, James. *The World without a Self: Virginia Woolf and the Novel.* Yale UP, 1973.

Nicholls, Peter. *Modernisms: A Literary Guide.* U of California P, 1995.

Norris, Margot. *Suspicious Readings of Joyce's Dubliners.* U of Pennsylvania P, 2003.

North, Michael. *The Dialect of Modernism: Race, Language, and Twentieth-Century Literature.* Oxford UP, 1998.

O'Donnell, Patrick. *Echo Chambers: Figuring Voice in Modern Narrative.* U of Iowa P, 1992.

Ozick, Cynthia. Introduction. *The Awkward Age,* by Henry James, Everyman's Library, 1993, pp. xi–xxxv.

Page, Norman. *Speech in the English Novel.* Palgrave Macmillan, 1988.

Palmer, Alan. *Social Minds in the Novel.* The Ohio State UP, 2010.

Parkes, M.B. *Pause and Effect: An Introduction to the History of Punctuation in the West.* U of California P, 1993.

Parks, Tim. *Hell and Back: Reflections on Writers and Writing from Dante to Rushdie.* Arcade, 2002.

Pasley, Malcolm. Afterword. *The Castle,* by Franz Kafka. Schocken, 1998.

Pecora, Vincent P. "'The Dead' and the Generosity of the Word." *PMLA,* vol. 101, no. 2, March 1986, pp. 233–45.

Phelan, James. "Charlie Marlow, Narrative Theorist, Discourses on 'Youth.'" *College English,* vol. 59, no. 5, September 1997, pp. 569–75.

———. "Conversational and Authorial Disclosure in the Dialogue Novel: The Case of *The Friends of Eddie Coyle.*" *Narrative, Interrupted: The Plotless, the Disturbing, and the Trivial in Literature,* edited by Markku Lehtimäki, et al., De Gruyter, 2012, pp. 3–23.

———. "Dialogue, Voice, and Tone; Or, Exploring a Neglected Channel of Narrative Communication," MLA Convention, 6 January, 2012, Seattle, WA. Unpublished conference paper.

———. *Experiencing Fiction: Judgments, Progressions, and the Rhetorical Theory of Narrative.* The Ohio State UP, 2007.

———. "Imagining a Sequel to *The Rhetoric of Fiction*; Or A Dialogue on Dialogue." *Comparative Critical Studies,* vol. 7, 2010, pp. 243–55.

———. *Living to Tell about It.* Cornell UP, 2005.

———. *Narrative as Rhetoric.* The Ohio State UP, 1996.

———. *Reading People, Reading Plots: Character, Progression, and the Interpretation of Narrative.* U of Chicago P, 1989.

———. "Rhetoric, Ethics, and Narrative Communication: Or, from Story and Discourse to Authors, Resources, and Audiences." *Soundings*, vol. 94, no. 1–2, Spring/Summer 2011, pp. 55–75.

———. *Somebody Telling Somebody Else*. The Ohio State UP, 2017.

———. "Voice, Tone, and the Rhetoric of Narrative Communication." *Language and Literature*, vol. 23, no. 1, February 2014, pp. 49–60.

Phelan, James, et al. *Narrative Theory: Core Concepts and Critical Debates*. The Ohio State UP, 2012.

Phillips, Gene. *Creatures of Darkness: Raymond Chandler, Detective Fiction, and Film Noir*. UP of Kentucky, 2003.

Pippin, Robert B. *Henry James and the Modern Moral Life*. Cambridge UP, 2000.

Proust, Marcel. *Du côté de chez Swann*. Gallimard, 1988.

———. *Swann's Way*. Modern Library, 2003.

Rauma, Sara I. *Cinematic Dialogue, Literary Dialogue, and the Art of Adaptation: Dialogue Metamorphosis in the Film Adaptation of* The Green Mile. 2004. University of Jyväskylä, PhD Dissertation.

Rée, Jonathan. "Funny Voices: Stories, Punctuation, and Personal Identity." *New Literary History*, vol. 21, no. 4, Autumn 1990, pp. 1039–58.

Rich, Adrienne. *Blood, Bread, and Poetry: Selected Prose 1979–1985*. W. W. Norton, 1994.

Richardson, Brian. "Commentary: Inhuman Voices." *New Literary History*, vol. 32, no. 3, Summer 2001, pp. 699–701.

———. *Unnatural Voices: Extreme Narration and Contemporary Fiction*. The Ohio State UP, 2006.

Riquelme, John Paul. "Joyce's 'The Dead': The Dissolution of Self and the Police." *Rejoycing: New Readings of Dubliners*, edited by Rosa M. Bollettieri Bossinelli and Harold F. Mosher, Jr., UP of Kentucky, 1998, pp. 123–41.

Rosenthal, Debra. *Performatively Speaking: Speech and Action in Antebellum American Literature*. U of Virginia P, 2015.

Ross, Stephen. *The Inexhaustible Voice: Speech and Writing in Faulkner*. U of Georgia P, 1989.

———. "The 'Loud World' of Quentin Compson." *Studies in the Novel*, vol. 7, no. 2, Summer 1975, pp. 245–57.

———. "'Voice' in Narrative Texts: The Example of *As I Lay Dying*." *PMLA*, vol. 94, no. 2, March 1979, pp. 300–310.

Roth, Henry. *Call It Sleep*. New York: Picador, 2005.

Rowe, James Carlos. "Naming What Is Inside: Gertrude Stein's Use of Names in *Three Lives*." *Novel*, vol. 36, no. 2, Spring 2003, pp. 219–43.

———. *The Other Henry James*. Duke UP, 1998.

Sabin, Margery. *The Dialect of the Tribe: Speech and Community in Modern Fiction*. Oxford UP, 1987.

Sarraute, Nathalie. *Tropisms and the Age of Suspicion*. Translated by Maria Jolas, John Calder, 1963.

Schneider, Karen. *Loving Arms: British Women Writing the Second World War*. U of Kentucky P, 1997.

Sherry, Vincent. *The Great War and the Language of Modernism*. Oxford UP, 2004.

Showalter, Elaine. *A Jury of Her Peers: Celebrating American Women Writers from Anne Bradstreet to Annie Proulx*. Vintage, 2009.

Singal, Daniel. *William Faulkner: The Making of a Modernist*. U of North Carolina P, 1997.

Sitney, P. Adams. *Vital Crises in Italian Cinema: Iconography, Stylistics, Politics*. U of Texas P, 1995.

Smith, Logan Pearsall. *Words and Idioms: Studies in the English Language*. Houghton Mifflin, 1925.

Smith, Zadie. *Changing My Mind: Occasional Essays*. Penguin, 2009.

Sorkin, Aaron. "Aaron Sorkin: The Writer behind *The Newsroom*." *NPR.org*. 16 July 2002. https://www.npr.org/2012/07/16/156841165/aaron-sorkin-the-writer-behind-the-newsroom. Accessed 2 November 2016.

Spilka, Mark. "The Death of Love in *The Sun Also Rises*." *Modern Critical Views: Ernest Hemingway*, edited by Harold Bloom, Chelsea House, 1985, pp. 107–18.

Spitzer, Leo. "L'originalità della narrazione nei *Malavoglia*." *Studi italiani* (Milan: Vita e Pensiero, 1976), pp. 293–316.

Stein, Gertrude. *The Autobiography of Alice B. Toklas*. Vintage, 1990. (AABT)

———. "Composition as Explanation." *A Stein Reader,* edited by Ulla S. Dydo, Northwestern UP, 1993. (SR)

———. *Everybody's Autobiography*. Random House, 2003.

———. "The Gradual Making of *The Making of Americans*." *Lectures in America*, Beacon, 1985.

———. *The Making of Americans*. Dalkey Archive Press, 1995.

———. "Melanctha." *Three Lives,* Penguin, 1990.

———. *Wars I Have Seen*. Random House, 1945.

Sternberg, Meir. "Point of View and the Indirectness of Direct Speech." *Language and Style,* vol. 15, 1982, pp. 67–117.

———. "Proteus in Quotation-Land: Mimesis and the Forms of Reported Discourse." *Poetics Today*, vol. 3, no. 2, Spring 1982, pp. 107–56.

Svoboda, Frederic. *Hemingway and* The Sun Also Rises: *The Crafting of a Style*. UP of Kansas, 1983.

Tanner, Tony. *Jane Austen*. Cambridge, 1986.

Thomas, Bronwen E. "Dialogue." *The Cambridge Companion to Narrative Theory*, edited by David Herman, Cambridge UP, 2007.

———. *Fictional Dialogue: Speech and Conversation in the Modern and Postmodern Novel*. U of Nebraska P, 2012.

———. "Multiparty Talk in the Novel: The Distribution of Tea and Talk in a Scene from Evelyn Waugh's *Black Mischief*." *Poetics Today*, vol. 23, no. 4, Winter 2002, pp. 657–84.

Thompson, Jon. "Joyce and Dialogism: Politics of Style in *Dubliners*." *Works and Days*, vol. 5, no. 2, 1987, pp. 79–95.

Todorov, Tzvetan. *Mikhail Bakhtin: The Dialogical Principle*. Translated by Wlad Godzich, U of Minnesota P, 1984.

Tomkins, David. "The 'Lost Generation' and the Generation of Loss: Ernest Hemingway's Materiality of Absence and *The Sun Also Rises*." *Modern Fiction Studies*, vol. 54, no. 4, Winter 2008, pp. 744–65.

Toolan, Michael J. "Analysing Conversation in Fiction: The Christmas Dinner Scene in Joyce's *Portrait of the Artist as a Young Man*. *Poetics Today*, vol. 8, no. 2, 1987, pp. 393–416.

———. "Analysing Fictional Dialogue." *Language and Communication*, vol. 5, no. 3, 1985, pp. 193–206.

———. *The Stylistics of Fiction: A Literary-Linguistic Approach*. Routledge, 1990.

Toomer, Jean. *Cane*. Liveright, 1975.

Trodd, Zoe. "Hemingway's Camera Eye: The Problem of Language and an Interwar Politics of Form." *The Hemingway Review*, vol. 26, no. 2, Spring 2007, pp. 7–21.

Vertov, Dziga, director. *Man with a Movie Camera*. Kino Lorber, 1929.

Wagner-Martin, Linda. *Favored Strangers: Gertrude Stein and Her Family*. Rutgers UP, 1995.

———. *The Modern American Novel, 1914–1945*. Twayne, 1990.

Warner, Eric. *Virginia Woolf:* The Waves. Cambridge UP, 1987.

Watt, Ian. *The Rise of the Novel*. U of California P, 2001.

Weinstein, Arnold. *Recovering Your Story: Proust, Joyce, Woolf, Faulkner, Morrison*. Random House, 2006.

Weinstein, Philip. "Strether's Curious 'Second Wind': Imagination and Experience in *The Ambassadors*." *Modern Critical Interpretations of Henry James's* The Ambassadors, edited by Harold Bloom, Chelsea House, 1988, pp. 47–81.

Williams, Raymond. *Keywords: A Vocabulary of Culture and Society*. Oxford UP, 1985.

Wilson, Sarah. "Gertrude Stein and the Radio." *Modernism/modernity*, vol. 11, no. 2, April 2004, pp. 261–78.

Woloch, Alex. "Minor Characters." *The Novel, Volume 2: Forms and Themes*, edited by Franco Moretti, Princeton UP, 2006, pp. 295–324.

———. *The One vs. the Many: Minor Characters and the Space of the Protagonist in the Novel*. Princeton UP, 2003.

Wood, James. *How Fiction Works*. Farrar, Straus and Giroux, 2008.

Woodward, C. Vann. *The Burden of Southern History*. Louisiana State UP, 1993.

Woolf, Virginia. *Between the Acts*. Harvest Books, 2008. (BTA)

———. "Character in Fiction." *The Essays of Virginia Woolf*. Vol. 3, edited by Andrew McNeillie, Harcourt, 1998.

———. *The Essays of Virginia Woolf*. Vol. 3, edited by Andrew McNeillie, Harcourt, 1998.

———. *The Letters of Virginia Woolf*. Vol. 3, edited by Nigel Nicolson and Joanne Trautmann, Houghton Mifflin, 1980.

———. "Modern Novels (Joyce)." Transcribed by Suzette Henke. *The Gender of Modernism: A Critical Anthology*, edited by Bonnie Kime Scott, Indiana UP, 1990, pp. 642–45.

———. *Mrs. Dalloway*. Harcourt, 1953.

———. *A Room of One's Own*. Harcourt, 1995. (AROO)

———. *The Waves*. Harcourt, 2006. (W)

———. *A Writer's Diary*. Harcourt, 2003. (WD)

———. *The Years*. Harcourt, 2008.

Yeazell, Ruth. *Language and Knowledge in the Late Novels of Henry James*. U Chicago P, 1976.

———. "Talking in James." *PMLA*, vol. 91, no. 1, 1976, pp. 66–77.

Zagarell, Sandra. "Narrative of Community: Identification of a Genre." *Signs*, vol. 13, no. 3, 1988, pp. 498–527.

Zwerdling, Alex. "*Between the Acts* and the Coming of War." *Novel: A Forum on Fiction*, vol. 10, 1977, pp. 220–36.

# INDEX

Abbott, H. Porter, 120, 125
*Absalom, Absalom!* (Faulkner), 13, 98–101, 103–4, 107–17, 161
Aciman, André, 82n23
acousmatic voice, 151n33, 162–63
African American Vernacular English, 153
Allen, Robert C., 143
*Ambassadors, The* (James), 39–41, 44–55, 59–61, 66, 70, 111, 161
*Antinomies of Realism, The* (Jameson), 131n7
Antonioni, Michelangelo, 166–68
"apperceptive background," 76
Aristotle, 165
Armstrong, Nancy, 37, 37n44
*As I Lay Dying* (Faulkner), 84
attribution, 11–12, 15, 52, 85, 91, 95, 103, 107–12, 162
Austen, Jane, 36, 132n10, 150–51, 150n32
authorial labor, dialogue as, 22–24
authorization, 28–29
*Autobiography of Alice B. Toklas, The* (Stein), 131–32, 134–35, 153, 156n37, 157–58
*Avventura, La* (Antonioni), 167
*Awkward Age, The* (James), 43, 45n10, 46n12, 48

Bakhtin, Mikhail, 2, 9, 15–16, 16n13, 36, 50, 70, 74, 76, 78, 82, 104, 109, 109n9, 130, 161, 166
Banfield, Ann, 19, 103, 135
Barnes, Jake, 31
Barthes, Roland, 11–12, 15, 106, 162
"Bartleby, the Scrivener" (Melville), 1–2, 12
"Beast in the Jungle, The" (James), 48, 49n16
Beckett, Samuel, 163–65, 167
Bekhta, Natalia, 130, 130n3, 138
Benjamin, Walter, 43
Bennett, Arnold, 29, 29n25, 149n31
Berman, Jessica, 43, 43n5
Berman, Marshall, 17, 17n15
*Between the Acts* (Woolf), 122, 128–30, 132–34, 133n11, 134–35, 139, 143–52, 145n27, 158–59
*Billy Budd* (Melville), 16–17
Bishop, Ryan, 14
*Bitter Rice* (de Santis), 136
Bleikasten, André, 37, 73n8, 84, 85n25
Blotner, Jay, 96
Bonapfel, Elizabeth, 49n16, 81n21, 105n8
Bookstaver, May, 153n35
Booth, Wayne, 16n13
Bridgman, Richard, 30n27
Brooks, Peter, 49, 107, 115

Brooks, Van Wyck, 43
Burgess, Anthony, 76
Butte, George, 40n2

Cain, James M., 31, 31n30
*Call It Sleep* (Roth), 27–29
Cameron, Sharon, 16–17, 40n2, 43, 45n11, 52n19
Campbell, Sarah, 30n27
*Cane* (Toomer), 140–43, 162
*Castle, The* (Kafka), 12–13, 29, 29n24
Cather, Willa, 125
Chapman, Raymond, 10, 10n2, 11n6, 13n8, 14, 105–6, 137
character narration, 4n4, 7
"character zone," 74
characterization, 10, 12, 27–29, 35, 125–26, 132, 146n28, 156
characterological sovereignty, 16–17
Chesnutt, Charles, 26
Chion, Michael, 151n33, 162, 163n1
chorality, 128–59; in *Between the Acts*, 143–52; in *Cane*, 140–43; class and, 137; defined, 130; history of, 136–43; in "Melanctha," 152–59; as mimetic, 137; as modernist, 139; politics of, 136–43; polyphony vs., 130–31; in Richardson, 131n5; in *The Waves*, 130
chorus, 129, 129n2
cinema, 14n10, 31, 31n30, 136–37, 163, 163n1, 166–68
Clements, Elicia, 151n33
Cohn, Dorrit, 118
Coleman, Dan, 9, 23n21
collective narrative, 138–39, 141
"Composition as Explanation" (Woolf), 134
compound telling, 112–17
compulsory attribution, 107–12
Conrad, Joseph, 17–18, 28–30, 33–34, 34n38, 132, 139n22, 162
consciousness, 15, 40n2. *See also* stream of consciousness

consensual speaking, 40–41, 141, 156, 162
*Conversations in Sicily* (Vittorini), 136
cooperative principle, 19, 46n13
Cowley, Malcolm, 89
Crane, Stephen, 26
Critchley, Simon, 163–64
Cuddy-Keane, Melba, 36, 129, 129n1, 130, 133, 133n11, 136n14, 139, 145n27, 150n39, 152n34
culture: phonocentric bias in Western, 25; talk as signal feature in, 32; Victorian *vs.* modernist, 17; voice in, 138

Dalziel, Pamela, 99n1
Davis, Fred, 39n1
Davis, Lennard, 20, 118–19, 121n21
Dawes, James, 56
de Man, Paul, 99, 161
de Santis, Giuseppe, 136
de Sica, Vittorio, 136
"Dead, The" (Joyce), 69–83, 74n9, 80n20, 81n21, 161
*Deceit, Desire, and the Novel* (Girard), 63
Dedalus, Stephen, 57
Derrida, Jacques, 12, 12n7
detachment, of speech from body, 17
dialects, regional, 13, 13n8
dialogue, 3, 3n2; as authorial labor, 22–24; as authorial *vs.* characterological, 6–7; empirical, 26, 29, 154; in equilibration, 132; heteroglossic, 166; homoglossic, 166; identity and, 10; James on, 46n12; lyrical, 28–29; "modernist" form of, 15; quotation of, 23; as signification of "real" talk, 20–21; "standard" form of, 14–15; as term, 7; thematic dimension of, 4; as underrepresented in literary theory, 9. *See also* voice
dialogue metamorphosis, 31n30
Dickens, Charles, 13, 33, 102
Dickinson, Renée, 119–20
diegetic sound, 166–67
differentiation, 13–14, 34, 90, 92, 100, 106, 109n9. *See also* individuation

digital humanities, 33–38
direct discourse, 3, 3n3, 5–6, 7, 24–25, 35, 38, 57, 101, 104, 107, 118–19, 132, 136, 146, 153, 160, 166
"Discourse and the Novel" (Bakhtin), 161, 166
discursive synchronies, 85, 92
distant reading, 33–38, 35n41
*Distant Reading* (Moretti), 34–35, 35n39
Dos Passos, John, 26–27
Dostoevsky, Fyodor, 14n11, 70, 109n9
*Double Indemnity* (Cain), 31
*Dubliners* (Joyce), 14
DuPlessis, Rachel Blau, 129–30, 134–35, 134n12, 139
Dydo, Ulla E., 133–34, 143

Edel, Leon, 44n8, 45n10, 49
Eliot, T. S., 32
Ellmann, Richard, 78, 78n17, 79
*Emma* (Austen), 132n10, 150–51, 150n32
empirical dialogue, 26, 29, 154
empiricism, 27, 32
endangered affinity, 43
*Everybody's Autobiography* (Stein), 134

fantasies of centrifugality, 163
*Farewell to Arms, A* (Hemingway), 57
*Far from the Madding Crowd* (Hardy), 137
Faulkner, William, 11, 13–14, 17, 29, 34, 71–72, 72n7, 73, 73n8, 83–97, 87n28. See also *Absalom, Absalom!* (Faulkner)
feminism, 5, 70n3, 133, 138n21, 140
Ferrer, Daniel, 105
Ferris, Joshua, 139n22
*Fictional Dialogue: Speech and Conversation in the Modern and Postmodern Novel* (Thomas), 9, 9n1
*Fictions of Authority* (Lanser), 130n3
*Finnegans Wake* (Joyce), 19
Fish, Stanley, 19
Flaubert, Gustave, 20, 33, 104, 106–7

Flesch, William, 120
Fludernik, Monika, 15, 21, 24–25, 138
Fogel, Aaron, 16n13, 23, 34, 34nn37–38, 36, 131n8, 132
Follansbee, Jeanne A., 99–100, 108
*Fontamara, La* (Silone), 137
formal realism, 112, 125
*Forms of Speech in the Victorian Novel* (Chapman), 10
Forster, E. M., 48n14, 132, 132n9
free indirect discourse, 3n3, 7, 24, 38, 81, 101, 104, 107, 122, 147, 150, 150n32
Free, Melissa, 74nn12–14, 75n15
Fry, Roger, 134n12
Fussell, Paul, 56n21, 63

Galdos, Benito Pérez, 131n7
Genette, Gérard, 2–3, 13, 13n9, 17, 106, 147n30, 162, 165–66
Girard, René, 63
Godard, Jean-Luc, 163, 166–68
*Golden Bowl, The* (James), 40, 44, 52n19
Goldman, Jonathan, 157n38, 158
Graham, J., 101n2, 119n17, 122–23
Green, Henry, 121
Grice, H. P., 19, 46n13
group speak, 130
*Guermontes Way, The* (Proust), 18
Gunn, Daniel, 150n32
*Guy Domville* (James), 49, 49n15

Haig, Stirling, 20, 22, 33, 104
Hale, Dorothy, 16n13
Halliday, Sam, 17, 18n16
Hamblin, Ross, 117n12
*Hamlet* (Shakespeare), 34–35, 35n39
handbooks, writing, 10–11
Hannon, Charles, 82n24
Hardy, Thomas, 137
*Heart of Darkness* (Conrad), 18, 29, 116

Helbig, Doris A., 58n24, 60n25, 62n26
Hemingway, Ernest, 14, 17, 30–31, 37, 41–42, 41n4, 42–44, 56–58, 57n23, 59–68, 71–72
Herman, David, 18n16, 19, 37, 122n23
Hild, Allison, 119n15, 120
Hite, Molly, 36, 122n22
Homer, 165
*How It Is* (Beckett), 164–65
*How Novels Think* (Armstrong), 37n44
humanities, digital, 33–38
Humphries, David, 58
Hurston, Zora Neale, 26, 28, 28n23, 140–41
Hussey, Mark, 100, 119, 119n16, 120n19
Huyssen, Andreas, 17n15

*Impersonality* (Cameron), 16, 95
indirect discourse, 3–4, 6–7, 23n20, 24–25, 32, 81, 104, 107, 122, 147, 150, 166
individuation, 4, 11–13, 17, 112, 126, 146, 159. See also differentiation
*Inexhaustible Voice, The* (Ross), 85n25, 91n30
intermental thought, 113, 113n11

*Jacob's Room* (Woolf), 122
James, Henry, 11, 11n5, 12, 30, 40n2, 41n3–41n4, 42–44, 43n5, 44–46, 46n12, 48n14, 56–57, 67–68, 71–72. See also *Ambassadors, The* (James)
Jameson, Fredric, 6, 17n15, 131, 131n7
Jewett, Sarah Orne, 26
Johnson, Samuel, 51n18
Jones, Gavin, 13n8, 44n9, 50n17
Joyce, James, 3–4, 13–14, 17–18, 20, 69–72, 72n7, 73–83
*Joyce's Voices* (Kenner), 3–4, 69n1

Kacandes, Irene, 9n1, 32n32, 131, 131n6
Kafka, Franz, 12–13, 29
Kaplan, Carla, 28n23
Kazin, Alfred, 27–28
Kelly, Cay Eileen, 163
Kenner, Hugh, 3–4, 69n1, 86, 95

Kershner, R. B., 73, 77n16, 80n20
Klein, Lauren, 35n41
Kozloff, Sarah, 25
Kreilkamp, Ivan, 17, 32
Kundera, Milan, 100
Kurnick, David, 41, 143n25–143n26

Lacan, Jacques, 12
Lamb, Robert, 42
Lambert, Mark, 33, 35, 120n19
Landy, Joshua, 163
Langford, Gerald, 111n10
Lanser, Susan, 129, 130n3, 138–39, 138n19, 139n22
"Last Novelist, The" (Kenner), 86
Lawrence, Karen, 140
Lee, Hermione, 123n24, 135
linguistic criticism, 18–21
linguistics, literary, 18–21
*Living to Tell about It* (Phelan), 4n4
Lodge, David, 23, 82n22
*Lord Jim* (Conrad), 13, 18, 29–30
Loufbourow, Lili, 145
Lukács, Georg, 37n43
lyrical dialogue, 28–29
lyricism, 32, 83

*Madame Bovary* (Flaubert), 104, 106
*Making of Americans, The* (Stein), 30n28, 42, 134, 134n12
Malcolm, Janet, 30n28, 153, 153n35
Malinowski, Bronisław, 19, 46
*Man with a Movie Camera* (film), 14n10
mannerism, 30, 32, 91n30, 111, 154
Marcus, Jane, 129n2
Matthews, John T., 85n25, 99, 103n6
McCluskey, Kathleen, 119
McHale, Brian, 20–21
"Melanctha" (Stein). See *Three Lives* (Stein)
Melville, Herman, 1–2, 12, 16–17

Mepham, John, 14–15, 15n12
Michaels, Walter Benn, 62
Middleton, Peter, 10–11, 21, 25
Mildenberg, Ariane, 119n17
Miller, J. Hillis, 19
mimesis, 3, 5, 22–23, 152, 154, 164–65
mimetic speech, 24
*Moby Dick* (Melville), 83
Moglen, Seth, 36, 43
*Molloy* (Beckett), 163–65, 167
*Moon and the Bonfire, The* (Pavese), 136
Moretti, Franco, 7n8, 34–35, 35n39, 36, 87n26, 136n15
Morrison, Toni, 157
*Moveable Feast, A* (Hemingway), 64–65
"Mr. Bennett and Mrs. Brown" (Woolf), 29n25
*Mrs. Dalloway* (Woolf), 67, 122

*Narrative Theory: Core Concepts and Critical Debates* (Phelan, James, et al), 5n5
Neff, Walter, 31
Nicholls, Peter, 36–37, 43
*Nigger of the 'Narcissus,' The* (Conrad), 139n22, 162
*Nineteen* (Dos Passos), 26–27, 29
Norris, Margot, 70nn2–3, 74n11, 77n16
North, Michael, 153

*Of Grammatology* (Derrida), 12n7
*One, The* (Woloch), 132, 132n10
*One vs. the Many, The* (Woloch), 5, 35
*Our America* (Michaels), 62
Ozick, Cynthia, 49n15

Page, Norman, 10, 10n2, 12, 14, 21–22
Palmer, Alan, 113, 113n11, 146, 146n28
paragraphing, 15
parallelism, 19, 40, 76, 92, 100, 155
Parkes, M. B., 15n12
Pasley, Malcolm, 29n24

Pavese, Cesare, 136
Pecora, Vincent P., 78n18
phatic communion, 19, 46
Phelan, James, 2, 2n1, 4n4, 5, 5nn5–6, 11, 23–24, 24n22, 30n26, 33n35, 42, 166
*Pierrot le fou* (Godard), 167
Pinker, James, 50
Pippin, Robert, 42–43
Plato, 24–25, 165
pluralism, 16, 73, 82, 128–29, 142, 158, 162
poiesis, 3, 5, 22–23
polyphony, 13, 28, 82–83, 109, 130–31
*Portrait of a Lady* (James), 68
*Portrait of the Artist as a Young Man* (Joyce), 20, 79n19, 81
postpsychological conception of speech, 66
Pratt, Mary Louise, 19
*Problems of Dostoevsky's Poetics* (Bakhtin), 104, 109n9
protagonicity, 131, 131n7
Proust, Marcel, 13, 13n9, 18, 48
pseudo-idioms, 52–53
punctuation, 10, 13–15, 120–21, 120n18

"Question of Our Speech, The" (James), 44–45, 55
quotation, 23, 104–7
quotation marks, 14–15. *See also* punctuation

Rabinowitz, Peter, 5, 5n5, 24
Rauma, Sara I., 31n30
reading, distant, 33–38, 35n41
*Reading People, Reading Plots* (Phelan), 4n4
realism, 12, 21, 22n19, 25, 27, 31–32, 58, 102, 112, 118–19, 125, 139, 154
"real" talk, 18–26, 30–31
"Recitatif" (Morrison), 157
Rée, Jonathan, 105
regional dialects, 13, 13n8
repetition, 7, 34, 41–42, 49, 100, 167
*Republic* (Plato), 24

*Requiem for a Nun* (Faulkner), 84

Rich, Adrienne, 133

Richardson, Brian, 22–23, 23n20, 131n5, 137, 138n21, 139, 139n23, 161–63

Riquelme, John Paul, 77n16

*Rise of the Novel, The* (Watt), 37n44

*Rome, Open City* (Rossellini), 136–37

*Room of One's Own, A* (Woolf), 121–22

Ross, Stephen, 11, 22, 34, 85n25, 87, 91n30, 99–100, 102n5, 108, 118n13

Rossellini, Roberto, 136–37

Roth, Henry, 26–28

*Routledge Encyclopedia of Narrative Theory*, 10, 21

Rowe, John Carlos, 41n3, 154

Sabin, Margery, 52n19

*Sacred Fount, The* (James), 45n10

Saussure, Ferdinand de, 12, 16

Shakespeare, William, 34–35, 35n39

Sherry, Vincent, 56n21

*Shoeshine* (de Sica), 136

Silone, Ignazio, 137

Singal, Daniel, 92, 94n32

Smith, William Pearsall, 51

*Social Minds in the Novel* (Palmer), 113

*Somebody Telling Somebody Else* (Phelan), 24n22

*Sonic Modernity* (Halliday), 17

Sorkin, Aaron, 31

*Sound and the Fury, The* (Faulkner), 13, 71–72, 83–97, 91n30, 108, 110, 116

sovereignty, characterological, 16–17

speech: consensual, 40–41, 141, 156, 162; Faulkner on, 109; indexical power of, 1–2; mimetic, 24; postpsychological conception of, 66; pretense of, 117–21; as term, 7; in Victorian thought, 105–6. *See also* dialogue; quotation; voice

*Speech Genres* (Bakhtin), 16

*Speech in the English Novel* (Page), 10

Spilka, Mark, 63n29

Spitzer, Leo, 136n15

Stein, Gertrude, 30, 30n28, 42, 64, 131–36

Sternberg, Meir, 21

Stone, Phil, 13

stream of consciousness, 7, 73, 86, 87n26, 89, 101, 122, 148

stylistics, 19

subjectivity, 4, 12, 17, 36–37, 71, 85, 95–96, 105–6, 119, 125–27, 130, 138n21

*Sun Also Rises, The* (Hemingway), 37, 41, 56–68, 70, 72

Svoboda, Frederic, 66n30

*S/Z* (Barthes), 106

*Talk Fiction* (Kacandes), 32n32

"Talking in James" (Yeazell), 40–41

Tanner, Tony, 132n10

telephone, 17

*Their Eyes Were Watching God* (Hurston), 28, 28n23, 140

*Then We Come to the End* (Ferris), 139n22

*Theory of the Novel* (Lukács), 37n43

therapeutic speech situation, 14

*Thinking in Henry James* (Cameron), 45n11

Thomas, Bronwen, 9, 9n1, 14, 20–22, 105

*Three Lives* (Stein), 131–35, 152–59, 161–62

*To the Lighthouse* (Woolf), 37, 122

Todorov, Tzvetan, 76

Toklas, Alice B., 131–32, 156n37

Toolan, Michael J., 18–20

Toomer, Jean, 140–43

Trabuccò, Carlo, 137, 137n17

Trodd, Zoe, 57n23

*Turn of the Screw*, 49

Twain, Mark, 13, 26

*Ulysses* (Joyce), 13, 18, 71, 74, 82, 87n26, 130, 140

"Uncle Charles Principle," 3–4, 69n1

"unitary language," 78

*Unnatural Voices* (Richardson), 161–62

*Unvanquished, The* (Faulkner), 94, 110

"verbal collaborators," 40
Verga, Giovanni, 136
Vertov, Dziga, 14n10
Verver, Maggie, 48
*Virginia Woolf Miscellany: Proceedings of the First Annual Conference on Virginia Woolf* (Dickinson), 119–20
Vittorini, Elio, 136
vocal pluralism, 128–29
voice: acousmatic, 151n33, 162–63; of author, 13, 22; choral, 128–59; dominant, 138n19; presence and, 12, 12n7; subjectivity and, 17; as term, 7. *See also* dialogue

Wagner-Martin, Linda, 37n43
Warner, Eric, 100
"Wasteland, The" (Eliot), 32
Watt, Ian, 37, 37n44, 103n7, 112, 138n20
*Waves, The* (Woolf), 12, 29, 36, 100–102, 102n4, 103–5, 117–21, 119n17, 121–27, 129–30, 147, 150, 162

*Weekend* (Godard), 166
Weinstein, Arnold, 84–85
Williams, Raymond, 43
Wilson, Sarah, 158
*Wings of the Dove, The* (James), 40, 44
Woloch, Alex, 5, 35–37, 62n27, 132, 132n10
Woodward, C. Vann, 72n7
Woolf, Leonard, 134, 146n29
Woolf, Virginia, 12, 17, 28–29, 29n25, 37, 67, 129n2, 134n12, 135, 135n13. See also *Between the Acts* (Woolf); *Waves, The* (Woolf)
Woolson, Constance Fenimore, 55
World War I, 56, 63
writing handbooks, 10–11

*Years, The* (Woolf), 129n2
Yeazell, Ruth, 40–41, 55n20

Zagarell, Sandra, 138, 138n20
Zwerdling, Alex, 129

# THEORY AND INTERPRETATION OF NARRATIVE
JAMES PHELAN, PETER J. RABINOWITZ, AND KATRA BYRAM, SERIES EDITORS

Because the series editors believe that the most significant work in narrative studies today contributes both to our knowledge of specific narratives and to our understanding of narrative in general, studies in the series typically offer interpretations of individual narratives and address significant theoretical issues underlying those interpretations. The series does not privilege one critical perspective but is open to work from any strong theoretical position.

*Making Conversation in Modernist Fiction*
  ELIZABETH ALSOP

*Narratology and Ideology: Negotiating Context, Form, and Theory in Postcolonial Narratives*
  EDITED BY DIVYA DWIVEDI, HENRIK SKOV NIELSEN, AND RICHARD WALSH

*Novelization: From Film to Novel*
  JAN BAETENS

*Reading Conrad*
  J. HILLIS MILLER, EDITED BY JOHN G. PETERS AND JAKOB LOTHE

*Narrative, Race, and Ethnicity in the United States*
  EDITED BY JAMES J. DONAHUE, JENNIFER ANN HO, AND SHAUN MORGAN

*Somebody Telling Somebody Else: A Rhetorical Poetics of Narrative*
  JAMES PHELAN

*Media of Serial Narrative*
  EDITED BY FRANK KELLETER

*Suture and Narrative: Deep Intersubjectivity in Fiction and Film*
  GEORGE BUTTE

*The Writer in the Well: On Misreading and Rewriting Literature*
  GARY WEISSMAN

*Narrating Space / Spatializing Narrative: Where Narrative Theory and Geography Meet*
  MARIE-LAURE RYAN, KENNETH FOOTE, AND MAOZ AZARYAHU

*Narrative Sequence in Contemporary Narratology*
  EDITED BY RAPHAËL BARONI AND FRANÇOISE REVAZ

*The Submerged Plot and the Mother's Pleasure from Jane Austen to Arundhati Roy*
  KELLY A. MARSH

*Narrative Theory Unbound: Queer and Feminist Interventions*
  EDITED BY ROBYN WARHOL AND SUSAN S. LANSER

*Unnatural Narrative: Theory, History, and Practice*
  BRIAN RICHARDSON

*Ethics and the Dynamic Observer Narrator: Reckoning with Past and Present in German Literature*
  KATRA A. BYRAM

*Narrative Paths: African Travel in Modern Fiction and Nonfiction*
  KAI MIKKONEN

*The Reader as Peeping Tom: Nonreciprocal Gazing in Narrative Fiction and Film*
  JEREMY HAWTHORN

*Thomas Hardy's Brains: Psychology, Neurology, and Hardy's Imagination*
  SUZANNE KEEN

*The Return of the Omniscient Narrator: Authorship and Authority in Twenty-First Century Fiction*
  PAUL DAWSON

*Feminist Narrative Ethics: Tacit Persuasion in Modernist Form*
  KATHERINE SAUNDERS NASH

*Real Mysteries: Narrative and the Unknowable*
  H. PORTER ABBOTT

*A Poetics of Unnatural Narrative*
  EDITED BY JAN ALBER, HENRIK SKOV NIELSEN, AND BRIAN RICHARDSON
*Narrative Discourse: Authors and Narrators in Literature, Film, and Art*
  PATRICK COLM HOGAN
*An Aesthetics of Narrative Performance: Transnational Theater, Literature, and Film in Contemporary Germany*
  CLAUDIA BREGER
*Literary Identification from Charlotte Brontë to Tsitsi Dangarembga*
  LAURA GREEN
*Narrative Theory: Core Concepts and Critical Debates*
  DAVID HERMAN, JAMES PHELAN AND PETER J. RABINOWITZ, BRIAN RICHARDSON, AND ROBYN WARHOL
*After Testimony: The Ethics and Aesthetics of Holocaust Narrative for the Future*
  EDITED BY JAKOB LOTHE, SUSAN RUBIN SULEIMAN, AND JAMES PHELAN
*The Vitality of Allegory: Figural Narrative in Modern and Contemporary Fiction*
  GARY JOHNSON
*Narrative Middles: Navigating the Nineteenth-Century British Novel*
  EDITED BY CAROLINE LEVINE AND MARIO ORTIZ-ROBLES
*Fact, Fiction, and Form: Selected Essays*
  RALPH W. RADER. EDITED BY JAMES PHELAN AND DAVID H. RICHTER.
*The Real, the True, and the Told: Postmodern Historical Narrative and the Ethics of Representation*
  ERIC L. BERLATSKY
*Franz Kafka: Narration, Rhetoric, and Reading*
  EDITED BY JAKOB LOTHE, BEATRICE SANDBERG, AND RONALD SPEIRS
*Social Minds in the Novel*
  ALAN PALMER
*Narrative Structures and the Language of the Self*
  MATTHEW CLARK
*Imagining Minds: The Neuro-Aesthetics of Austen, Eliot, and Hardy*
  KAY YOUNG
*Postclassical Narratology: Approaches and Analyses*
  EDITED BY JAN ALBER AND MONIKA FLUDERNIK
*Techniques for Living: Fiction and Theory in the Work of Christine Brooke-Rose*
  KAREN R. LAWRENCE
*Towards the Ethics of Form in Fiction: Narratives of Cultural Remission*
  LEONA TOKER
*Tabloid, Inc.: Crimes, Newspapers, Narratives*
  V. PENELOPE PELIZZON AND NANCY M. WEST
*Narrative Means, Lyric Ends: Temporality in the Nineteenth-Century British Long Poem*
  MONIQUE R. MORGAN
*Understanding Nationalism: On Narrative, Cognitive Science, and Identity*
  PATRICK COLM HOGAN
*Joseph Conrad: Voice, Sequence, History, Genre*
  EDITED BY JAKOB LOTHE, JEREMY HAWTHORN, JAMES PHELAN
*The Rhetoric of Fictionality: Narrative Theory and the Idea of Fiction*
  RICHARD WALSH
*Experiencing Fiction: Judgments, Progressions, and the Rhetorical Theory of Narrative*
  JAMES PHELAN
*Unnatural Voices: Extreme Narration in Modern and Contemporary Fiction*
  BRIAN RICHARDSON

*Narrative Causalities*
  EMMA KAFALENOS

*Why We Read Fiction: Theory of Mind and the Novel*
  LISA ZUNSHINE

*I Know That You Know That I Know: Narrating Subjects from* Moll Flanders *to* Marnie
  GEORGE BUTTE

*Bloodscripts: Writing the Violent Subject*
  ELANA GOMEL

*Surprised by Shame: Dostoevsky's Liars and Narrative Exposure*
  DEBORAH A. MARTINSEN

*Having a Good Cry: Effeminate Feelings and Pop-Culture Forms*
  ROBYN R. WARHOL

*Politics, Persuasion, and Pragmatism: A Rhetoric of Feminist Utopian Fiction*
  ELLEN PEEL

*Telling Tales: Gender and Narrative Form in Victorian Literature and Culture*
  ELIZABETH LANGLAND

*Narrative Dynamics: Essays on Time, Plot, Closure, and Frames*
  EDITED BY BRIAN RICHARDSON

*Breaking the Frame: Metalepsis and the Construction of the Subject*
  DEBRA MALINA

*Invisible Author: Last Essays*
  CHRISTINE BROOKE-ROSE

*Ordinary Pleasures: Couples, Conversation, and Comedy*
  KAY YOUNG

*Narratologies: New Perspectives on Narrative Analysis*
  EDITED BY DAVID HERMAN

*Before Reading: Narrative Conventions and the Politics of Interpretation*
  PETER J. RABINOWITZ

*Matters of Fact: Reading Nonfiction over the Edge*
  DANIEL W. LEHMAN

*The Progress of Romance: Literary Historiography and the Gothic Novel*
  DAVID H. RICHTER

*A Glance Beyond Doubt: Narration, Representation, Subjectivity*
  SHLOMITH RIMMON-KENAN

*Narrative as Rhetoric: Technique, Audiences, Ethics, Ideology*
  JAMES PHELAN

*Misreading* Jane Eyre: *A Postformalist Paradigm*
  JEROME BEATY

*Psychological Politics of the American Dream: The Commodification of Subjectivity in Twentieth-Century American Literature*
  LOIS TYSON

*Understanding Narrative*
  EDITED BY JAMES PHELAN AND PETER J. RABINOWITZ

*Framing Anna Karenina: Tolstoy, the Woman Question, and the Victorian Novel*
  AMY MANDELKER

*Gendered Interventions: Narrative Discourse in the Victorian Novel*
  ROBYN R. WARHOL

*Reading People, Reading Plots: Character, Progression, and the Interpretation of Narrative*
  JAMES PHELAN

www.ingramcontent.com/pod-product-compliance
Lightning Source LLC
Chambersburg PA
CBHW020947230426
43666CB00005B/216